TO:
Joseph Conway
from
Jim Blen

Confessions
of a
Gold Bug

Confessions
of a
Gold Bug

By James U. Blanchard III

ADAM
SMITH
PUBLISHING

To my son, Anthem, to his generation, and to
the renaissance of freedom in the next century

Contents

Book Three:
The Gold Bug's Handbook

Acknowledgements

First, thanks to my intellectual mentors, such as Ayn Rand, Ludwig von Mises, F.A. Hayek, Henry Hazlitt, Murray Rothbard, Milton Friedman, and a dozen other early free market thinkers.

Also, my early understanding of individualism was greatly influenced by America's own early individualists, authors like Walt Whitman, Henry David Thoreau and Ralph Waldo Emerson.

My college studies of the little-known but very important school of 19th century American individualist anarchists, such as Benjamin Tucker and Lysander Spooner, gave additional depth to my understanding of freedom and its beneficial consequences.

I give special thanks to all those early hard money investment newsletter writers, such as Vern Myers, Harry Schultz, Richard Russell and Franz Pick, as well as the many others who came later.

For miscellaneous help in researching this book, finding photographs and handling many other details, thanks to Chris Herman, Patty Jeffries, Brien Lundin, and Michael Forsythe.

The final editing and proofreading were done by Lee Berger...the best in the business!

A special appreciation and debt to my former wife, Jackie, who was instrumental in many ways from the 1960s to the mid-1980s. And of course, thanks to my best buddy and executive assistant, Lesia Hnatiw, who encouraged me to write this book and helped in the editing.

Finally, a very special thanks to my good friend Gary Alexander, who took the stacks of my writings, research, old clippings, and *dozens* of tapes dictated by me for this book and put them all together to create *Confessions of a Gold Bug*.

Introduction

There are several reasons why I decided to write this book. First, I wanted to tell the story of the exciting early days of the hard-money, pro-gold movement in the 1960s and 1970s. Another reason is that I have often been asked, "How did you get involved in all this?" or, "What is the true story of gold legalization?" or, "Is gold still a good investment and how should I invest now?"

Also, over the years I found that when you maintain a high profile in the financial services business, people want to know more about you as a person. A good example of this is the popularity and high renewal rate of Richard Russell's 26-year-old *Dow Theory Letters*. In almost every issue, in addition to his fine investment analysis, he gives away a little bit of Richard Russell, the person. He discusses his views on various non-investment issues, and shares tales of his travels, his family life, etc.

My good friend Jerry Pogue told me that the best thing he ever did was to tell his personal story in his book on penny shares (*Penny Mining Share Fortunes*). Jerry said to me, "Jim, the people who read your newsletter and your books and buy your coins or become clients of your mutual funds all want to know about you as a person and want to learn your personal views. If you make your book more personal, they will have a higher comfort level in working with you in the future, in buying your products, and in taking your advice."

Well, I thought about it and I think Jerry Pogue is right. So, included in *Confessions of a Gold Bug* is my personal story of how I got interested in gold, how I started the conferences, and how I started my coin company and my other businesses. I have included my personal views and advice on business manage-ment (in the chapter titled "Your Business Is Your Best Investment") and on enjoying life (in the chapter titled "Investing in Life"). After all, what is all the money in the world worth if you don't take time to smell the roses?

Perhaps the most important underlying theme of the book is the value of freedom and individualism, so I have included chapters on aiding the freedom movement around the world and on explaining the basic problem of collectivism.

Although the investment conclusions are important, I hope readers will not see this book as "just another hard-money investment book."

Book I

Legalize Gold!

Chapter 1

The American Dream

—Conquers a Nightmare

"Economics is a living thing—and to live implies both imperfection and change."

—Ludwig von Mises, *Human Action*

I love America. Anyone who visits my office or home will immediately see that fact. I have many historical American artifacts in my office and in two or three connected meeting rooms. Above and beyond these physical artifacts of American history, I love what the original idea of America stands for: individual freedom. Any visitor to my home is struck by the dominating presence of the Statue of Liberty; for example, a 10- by 22-foot wall mural of Lady Liberty in my living room.

Since I was 15, most of my hobbies, my investments and even my businesses have revolved around celebrating America. I have an extensive collection of autographs of great Americans, a million-dollar rare U.S. coin portfolio, Wild West antiques in my "saloon" at home, one of the largest collections of antique American guns in the nation, plus paintings, stamps and more.

Even as a teenager, I had already begun assembling piles of Civil War memorabilia, old maps, century-old newspapers, antique guns, historical artifacts and rare coins. As a result of this early interest, I majored in American history and taught the subject in secondary schools for five years.

More to the purpose of this book, it was the uniquely American spirit of rugged individualism that saved my life in those early teenage years. It was the belief that anybody can make anything out of life they want if they only capture the vision strongly enough and work hard enough toward realizing their dream, that sustained me through one of the hardest possible blows life can offer.

An Early Fascination With the American Spirit

My almost instinctive love of America is reflected in the first serious books I remember reading, at the ages of 10 to 12. They were stories of the American West; and as a result of this reading, I began to look up to the men of that era as the pinnacle of what it meant to be an American.

At first I read stories about Kit Carson, Sitting Bull, "Wild Bill" Hickock, John C. Fremont, "Buffalo" Bill Cody, and so on. Of course, those books presented a somewhat romanticized version of the ideal West, with plenty of historical inaccuracies. But the stories were not designed for the purpose of providing accurate research for historians, but to inspire young children to reach for the American ideals.

The message I got from all of these books was this: If you want to succeed, you must fight for your ideals; and if you work hard enough against your adversities, you can prevail against seemingly impossible odds. The strength of that vision kept me focused on my goals at a young age, despite life's sudden shocks—which also came early.

As silly as it may seem to many people, there was one incident that particularly focused my young mind on the romance and inspiration of American history. It was my encounter with the actor John Wayne when I was 14. But let me back up for a minute and put that event in perspective.

I was born in Greenwood, Mississippi, in 1943 while my dad, James U. Blanchard, Jr., was overseas fighting for America in Italy, France, and then across the Remagen Bridge in Germany. He fought in Patton's 3rd Army, in some of the most important battles of the late war, including the Battle of the Bulge. As soon as Dad returned home from the war, he decided to move to Houston. I was barely two years old. A decade later, in 1955, we moved to New Orleans, and I have lived in New Orleans ever since.

Dad sent me as a youngster to military school in northern Mississippi—to the region where I was born—partly because of my rambunctious nature, which admittedly needed a little discipline in those days, and partly because dad respected the military system of education. Either way, I spent a lot of my youth in uniform!

John Wayne Rides out of the Mist

In Port Gibson, Mississippi—near a major Civil War battlefield—director John Ford was shooting a Civil War action film in 1957 with his long-time friend and favorite actor, John Wayne. The movie was called *Horse Soldiers* (you may have seen it on late night or early morning television). Mr. Ford rounded up all of us military youngsters as Confederate soldier extras for the battle scenes.

At 14, in the seventh grade, I was not jaded by the phoniness of film making. In fact, since I was already reading several historical novels about the winning of the West, the Civil War, the Gold Rush, and that whole period of our greatest growth as a nation, John Wayne was a symbol of that era to me. It was difficult for me to separate fact from fantasy in the process of shooting this movie.

My role, as a Confederate student and soldier in the movie, was to charge the Union cavalry, led by John Wayne—as if anybody could beat John Wayne in a John Ford movie. I was excited about being in the film, because it was like living the Civil War all over again. Of course the South lost again, but something happened one morning that caught my youthful imagination and later helped bring me through some bad times.

One misty morning, as we prepared to shoot a battle scene, we young soldiers were all grabbing a quick doughnut and hot chocolate for breakfast when John Wayne rode up to us on his horse, from out of the early morning mist, in full stride (or so it seemed). While still on his horse, he picked up a couple of doughnuts with one hand, then a cup of coffee with the other hand. He and his horse never missed a stride.

Something about that scene struck a chord in me. History, John Wayne, and the movie blended together at that moment. The character and the actor were all one and the same. John Wayne was playing John Wayne, even before the cameras started rolling that day. I will never know if he just did that to impress us, or if he really became so caught up in his part that living it was his kind of method acting.

Years later I read articles and books about John Wayne which confirmed that my youthful impression was right. He said he would play only parts which glorified the heroic side of America. He often pulled aside his fellow actors and told them that playing any part that was less than heroic or that painted America in any kind of a negative light was not good for the children who watched their films. Other actors—Kirk Douglas was one of them—tried to argue with him: "It's just a part, Duke. It's not me!" John Wayne did not see it that way, and neither did I, at least at the time.

John Wayne was the type of fellow who personified my favorite poem, "If" by Rudyard Kipling. There is a line that reads, "If you can make one heap of all your winnings, And risk it on one turn of pitch-and-toss"—a toss of the dice—then "you'll be a Man, my son!" Wayne put up all his own money to make *The Alamo*, a movie about a time in history that meant a lot to him personally: Texans defending their freedom against Mexico.

Wayne got terrible reviews on the *The Alamo*, and it bombed at the box office, so he literally had to go back to work as an actor just to pay the bills from *The Alamo*. He eventually got an Oscar for *True Grit*, which was only marginally better than most of his other films; but I think the industry voted him this Oscar out of respect for his lifetime of work.

A lot of young kids my age liked John Wayne movies, but I think what set me apart was the fact that I did not outgrow that love of American ideals when I grew up. In time, I found more serious and academic extensions of the idea of freedom, but at gut level the ideal was still John Wayne riding out of the mist in full stride, a living symbol of American history.

Early Sources of Strength— Great American Literature and Values

In trying to piece together the elements of strength which pulled me through difficult times later on, I have realized (better late than never) that a major factor contributing to my positive outlook at a young age was the strength of my parents and their values. They taught me and showed me by example the importance of the work ethic and the personal values of honesty, courage, hard work and kindness. Because of them, I was also able to recognize those values in the heroes of the Western stories that I was reading.

Despite my parents' best training and example, however, I did not practice their values very well in my early teens. I think my grade average hovered somewhere between a C and a D until the 11th grade, in 1960. It was then, in my junior year, that one solitary teacher completely turned my thinking around. (Good teachers have that kind of power.)

I was going to Fortier High School in uptown New Orleans at the time. I was in American literature class, where I learned to love and devour the essays of Emerson and Thoreau, the poetry of Walt Whitman, and the writings of Mark Twain, among other great American writers. As a result of these wonderful works of American literature, I became "turned on" to American individualism on a higher plane than when I read heroic Western novels.

Under the influence of Mark Twain, for instance, I built my own river raft with some friends; and I dreamed of floating down the Mississippi like Tom Sawyer and Huck Finn. That dream ended when a government bureaucrat had the 32-foot riverboat destroyed because it engaged government property!

On a more intellectual level, I used Emerson, Thoreau and Whitman to develop a very individualistic philosophy. Not every detail of it was clear to me at the time—it was more of a gut feeling than an intellectual framework—but it was a half-formed combination of the heroic lives of early Americans with the intellectual ammunition of Emerson, Thoreau and Whitman.

Because of my interest in the West, I was fascinated with the entrepreneurship that went into building the great mining industries, the cattle industry, and the transcontinental railroad; and I was deeply impressed with the courage it took to be a pioneer. That was the sort of framework that strengthened me for what was to come in a few months. Even at ages 16 and 17, it gave me enough inspiration to write my own poetry and to make my own plans and dreams for college and for starting a business. I did not plan it all in a very structured way, but in an individualistic, goal-oriented way which carried me through the worst imaginable nightmares that lay ahead.

The Night of October 31, 1961—
A Halloween Nightmare

Halloween 1961 changed a lot of things. I had just started my senior year at Fortier and was out at a Halloween party, October 31, 1961. When the party was over, just after midnight, two of my friends, Jimmy Lott and Guthrie "Dockie" Pierson, and I were driving down the world-famous St. Charles Avenue in uptown New Orleans—the street where the street cars ride down the "neutral ground" between the divided lanes. Although I was unaware of it at the time, there were at least two things going against us. One was that it was just beginning to rain, and so the streets were getting slick with oil and water. The other problem was that we were riding in a Chevy Corvair, which we soon discovered was unsafe to drive in any condition!

At the time, I was in the backseat, almost falling asleep because of the late hour. I was not even aware of what was happening when the car slid out of control on the wet, oily streets and suddenly wrapped itself around a tree in the neutral ground. In a split second, the car tore in half and the two halves of the car flew in opposite directions, stopping about 100 feet apart.

We probably would have come out of the accident with only minor injuries, had the Corvair held together. But when it broke totally in half, right down the middle, I was exposed to the brunt of the impact between metal and concrete in the back seat. I remember looking up at the stars—from right on the rails of the St. Charles street car. I now can see from the front-page picture in the November 2, 1961, edition of the *New Orleans Times-Picayune*—a graphic photo which is still strange to look at—that I was lucky to live.

With a broken back and many internal injuries, I was nearly dead. It was a struggle to breathe. I remember clearly thinking at that moment, "Well, it's all over....this is it. My dreams are shattered. I'm going to die."

Then I lapsed into a coma.

"Waking Up Dead" and Struggling to Live

It was several days before I woke up in Charity Hospital, where the ambulance had taken me early on November 1. Since I was only periodically conscious, it was hard to feel anything but the raw pain. I was unconscious for several days; then came a terrible awakening.

Have you ever heard the warning, "You're liable to wake up dead"? Although it is literally impossible, that was what it felt like to me. Shortly after awakening, the terrible pain and sorrow hit me like a blow that felt worse than death.

I was in and out of intensive care for weeks. I remember having the last rites read over me several times, perhaps more than anyone in the history of the hospital. Yes, it is possible to have the last rites more than once—the people who arranged for the last rites did not necessarily talk to each other or ask if the rites had ever been read before. (Though I am not a Catholic, most of the New Orleans hospitals follow the Catholic tradition of reading last rites.)

The depression which overtook me after I woke up was natural and predictable for such an accident; but, thankfully, it did not last for very long. The pain and disappointment was a bit more tolerable for me than it would be for most 17-year-olds because of the dreams and hopes I had already developed, which were still so fresh in my mind from 11th grade American literature class.

I have forgotten my teacher's name now, but I think she would be pleased to hear that her words stuck with me and were a great source of strength for my recovery. I remembered the joy of life that emanated from Emerson's essays and Whitman's poetry. When I was reading Whitman's poetry while recovering, I came across this line, which both imparted strength and helped me realize why I could still make my dreams come true. Whitman wrote, "Enough to merely be! Enough to breathe! Joy! Joy! All over joy!" I finally knew what those words meant to their core: To breathe, simply to be alive, was more than enough; it was the unmistakable sign of life and hope. "What the hell. I can find something to do, and I love to watch NFL games!"

Since that fateful night in 1961, I have often thought about why that accident happened that night; and in a strange turn of events, I am actually thankful I went through that ultimate trial at such a young age. So few young men have a rite of passage in our modern American society. I am not recommending my own rite of passage to anyone; but the theory I have developed since that time is that when young people go through life-threatening crises, and survive them, they are much stronger for having gone through them.

Having gone through a near-death experience at such a young age, with all of that challenge and struggle, I became a far more serious youngster. I did much more self-analysis and became more philosophical; and in a crazy way, it made me a much more successful man.

Teenage Rites of Passage— A Missing Challenge to our Youth

I truly believe that youth needs a healthy rite of passage, like an Outward Bound course, or a physically challenging feat like sailing the ocean, climbing a mountain, or hiking long distances. Teamwork is important to youth, but I think it is even more important to look deep within yourself as an individual and to perform a feat "beyond yourself" while young.

For example, I later learned how one American Indian tribe gave its youth a challenging rite of passage, much like my own rite. While I was at an airport waiting for a plane sometime in the late 1970s, I was looking for a cheap Western novel to read for relaxation on the way home. The book I picked up that day was *Trask*, by Don Berry (Comstock Press, 1976), a novel based on fact and written by a historian specializing in Northwestern Indian lore.

Trask is a fictionalized account of a tribe of Indians who lived on the border between Oregon and Washington. According to the author, the Indians sent their boys, at puberty, through a trial by ordeal high up into the Cascade Mountains. What it amounted to was a life-threatening winter which, if survived, led to the full responsibilities and benefits of manhood. Many societies still have such passages, but this one is typical enough to make my point.

The Indians sent their boys up to the top of the Cascades in the dead of winter with no clothing and with orders to stay there for the entire winter. If they came back alive, by definition they were men. That may sound incredibly cruel—and it probably would be, for people raised in our society, unprepared for the trials—but the vast majority of the boys actually came back, more alive than when they left. Very few perished when faced with such a strong incentive to live—manhood. It was a trial of their spirit and their self-reliance: They had to build traps to catch game for food and for furs to clothe themselves, and they had to build fires to warm themselves.

Most boys survived the ordeal. Some died; but those who survived came back with a spirit of power and individualism, a respect for human life, and an understanding that they could rely on themselves alone. They learned to cooperate with the forces of nature, not to fight them. They also achieved, says the author, a benevolent spirit of happiness and joy, an inner spring which came from appreciating life.

Years later, the author said that scientists studying the

Indians who practiced this ritual found that they were among the happiest, most socially well-adjusted Indian populations.

Whenever I see some of our modern American youth—seemingly unmotivated and bored with life from a very young age and well into their 20s—getting into trouble as I was doing at ages 15 and 16, I wonder how much greater adults our nation could produce if we posed a similar challenge to our youth, not so life-threatening as my own example, but equally challenging.

In my own case, when I read *Trask* in the late 1970s, I made the conscious connection between those young Indians and what I had gone through myself. The same two things happened to me, as to them, after my accident in 1961: I had to learn how to survive, and I became more serious about adult life.

I also took life less seriously, as seen from a more philosophical perspective. What this means is that I was happy just to be alive; but I grew more serious about meeting my goals. Instead of goofing off at school and getting all Cs and Ds—which is what I had done until then, I studied harder (once I got back to school); and I knew precisely what I wanted from life.

At the same time, I took petty problems less seriously, because I learned to let little problems roll off my back much more easily than before. If something went wrong, I would think how small and unimportant such a problem was, as long as I still had my life and health.

The Struggle to Survive and the Will to Prevail

As a painful rite of passage, my accident truly helped me. I have no way of knowing how my life would have worked out without the automobile accident—maybe I would have ended up doing the same kinds of things with my life—but somehow I think my life would not have been as full of accomplishment.

Either way, the fact of the matter is that my mind was forced to focus on serious issues at a young and impressionable age.

I am sorry to say that there have been a number of others who have gone through this same life-threatening situation but did not fare so well. I will be the first to say that breaking your back is not the ideal rite of passage.

The adversity itself would not help you a bit. To prevail, you must beat the adversity and not just "survive" it. Like the Indian boys who went to the top of the mountain and came back down as men, you have to cheat death by sheer willpower and then make an extra effort to find joy in survival itself.

Getting so close to death and beating the odds builds up a lot of positive energy. As G. Gordon Liddy said about a similar situation—going to jail for five years—"I will not be satisfied just to survive this ordeal. I will *prevail*." That is an important difference. People have survived a life-threatening episode, but unfortunately they have not *prevailed* over it. To prevail means to beat it, to put the enemy totally behind you, and to overcome the odds.

I have found that if you are positive about your problems, you can enjoy anything life throws your way. If you want to do good things for people, even for those who cause you problems, then the blessings of life will come back to you 200 percent. Even if you get no reward right away, you will get it all back eventually—and more. A positive attitude pays great dividends, but that took me a while to figure out.

Putting the Pieces of
My Life Back Together

While I was in the hospital recuperating from various health crises, I went through numerous periods of being near death, on and off the critical list. It was a continuing rite of passage, in which I never knew whether I would live or die. I was in the hospital six months in all; then I spent four months in a rehabilitation center in Warm Springs, Georgia, the same spot where President Roosevelt often visited for his polio treatments and where he eventually died on April 12, 1945.

During that first year after the accident, I thought a lot about my life's values. At that time, I was not thinking in a political or economic context; it was more of a personal and philosophical self-examination. A year or so later, a book would land on my lap that would put all of this thinking in perspective, but I had to wander through a kind of wilderness for about a year before life came back into focus.

At times, I was pretty depressed in the hospital, because I felt like a prisoner after a while. But most of the time I spent there was positive. I took on the role of a young patient trying to cheer up people who might have been in better shape than I, but who had a negative outlook on life. I tried to entertain some nurses and fellow patients with my humor, but—as the name implies— Charity Hospital includes many charity cases, and we got some of the most down-and-out street people you can imagine in there. Sometimes they were the cases no other hospital would take.

I remember one time when an old drunken bum was dying in the same room with me. He was begging for a drink, any drink, before he died. For years, he had drunk cheap wine, so he probably had no liver left, and was clearly dying from all that drinking. I called the nurse over to my bed and said, "He's going to die. Give him one last drink. Think of it as charity—his last Communion, or something like that."

She was a wonderfully caring woman—both a nurse and a nun. She disappeared for perhaps an hour. Then in her beautiful Sisters of Charity habit, she returned with a glass of fine scotch.

I was weak, but the sight of this beautiful, elderly nurse/nun slowly comforting a dying man with his last drink was unforgettable. Some people may think it was cruel to give an alcoholic a drink, but I think the circumstance of imminent death made it the ultimate act of charity, for him. I was transfixed by her kindness.

After they had talked in low whispers, she took the glass from his mouth. There was a silence. The next day his bed was empty. Later I heard from one of the doctors that he had had one day to live. I am not a believer in organized religion, but I will never forget my beautiful Sister of Charity.

There are plenty of other hospital stories I could tell, but suffice it to say that my many months in Charity Hospital brought me in touch with the best and the worst of human and animal life, and still I managed to prevail.

By the time I left the hospital in the spring of 1962, I was already on the way to beating the enemy of depression.

Saved by Books—
One Book in Particular

One of the things that helped me through that first year after the accident was the quality of the books I had read the previous year—about determination, mental toughness, and a desire to become totally independent—and then the books I was to read during my recovery as soon as I was able to sit up and hold a book comfortably for long periods of time.

While still in the hospital, I set my mind to become self-sufficient and financially independent, and to move away from my parents if necessary. In essence, I wanted to take care of myself for the rest of my life, without round-the-clock nursing help or help from anyone else. I was very clear on wanting to learn to fend for myself in life.

The first step was physical therapy in Warm Springs, Georgia. During the summer months of 1962, I had to virtually relearn all over again how to do the simplest bodily tasks. Then when I got back to New Orleans from Warm Springs, I decided to get out of town and avoid the distraction of seeing old friends, who might get nervous around me or—worse yet—try to take care of me.

I soon made the discovery, through some friends of mine and from reading, that I could very economically stay in Mexico on my own and for a much lower amount of money than in New Orleans. This appealed to my independent spirit and my desire to prove that I could make it on my own, so I flew to Mexico City, then on to Guadalajara. I stayed there for the better part of a year, living in a small house I shared with four other fellows my age.

In Mexico I did a lot more reading and thinking, and became deeply engrossed in some of the more thoughtful and heroic science fiction (from author Robert Heinlein) as well as more of my favorite biographies of heroes of American history. Even in the science fiction reading I did that year, I gravitated toward stories of the kind of heroic figures who prevailed against superior odds through sheer determination, individualism and willpower.

After a year of this kind of reading and reflection, I figured my days of loafing around Mexico and reading books were just about over. So I returned to New Orleans and made plans to go back to school. I was beyond the usual college entrance age (almost 20 in fact), but first I had to finish my aborted senior year in high school.

As it turned out, I was so motivated to graduate from high school that I got a high school equivalency diploma in just five weeks, with all As. To accomplish that feat, I went to both day school and night school and graduated in what proved to be record time for that kind of "remedial school," where most students are not as motivated as I was.

I was two years behind my friends, and I was anxious to get to college to start catching up. But first, before entering college in early 1964, I discovered a book that turned my life around and totally dominated my approach toward college, my professors, and eventually my career.

Chapter 2

Anthem Lands on My Lap:

My Life Philosophy Takes Shape

"The government's only proper job is to protect individual rights against violence by force or fraud...to protect men from foreign invaders...to settle disputes among men according to objective laws....The greatness of the Founding Fathers was how well they understood this issue and how close some of them came to understanding it perfectly."

—Ayn Rand

In 1963, at the end of the second year after my accident, I was going through a crash course in high school studies when a medical student friend who lived across the street threw a copy of Ayn Rand's book *Anthem* onto my lap. He knew that I liked these heroic kinds of science fiction adventure books, and Rand's book was so short that I read it through in a couple of hours, the same day he threw it over to me.

Anthem struck a familiar and powerful chord within me. It is about the strength of one man's will prevailing against a fictional futuristic (or perhaps even pre-historic) state, which outlaws all individualism, even to the point of forbidding the pronouns "I" and "me." A person must call himself "we" and speak of other people as "they." In the end, a man and a woman courageously break away from this system to start a new order that is based on their revolutionary idea of individualism. The implication is that all men and women are born with natural rights, the most important of which are: the right to freedom; the right to live one's life as an end in itself, to achieve one's own happiness; and the right to hold one's property.

I quickly devoured all of Ayn Rand's fiction, numbering only three novels besides *Anthem*—but much longer than *Anthem*. From Ayn Rand's books, I learned that the worst threat to man was not the elements—storms, wind, water, and other forces of nature—but a powerful central government run by collectivists who want all individuals, especially the creative, productive, innovative individuals, stamped out.

Ayn Rand's Books Give Birth to My Philosophy

Ayn Rand's novels include *Anthem* (1946), *We the Living* (1936), *The Fountainhead* (1943) and her massive masterpiece, *Atlas Shrugged* (1957). Not content to stop after finishing her novels, I turned to her non-fiction books on Objectivist philosophy and capitalist economics. Her non-fiction books were just coming out for the first time in the early 1960s, and I particularly liked her books *Capitalism: The Unknown Ideal* and *The Virtue of Selfishness*.

These non-fiction books, though not as emotionally powerful as her novels, describe the morality of the capitalist system and the virtue of becoming self-directed, self-reliant persons. Many people criticized this "selfish" approach to life; but by defending the ego, she did not mean petty acts of self-aggrandizement, which most people call selfish. She meant to laud the virtue of people who know what they want from life and then make it happen, especially by working in harmony with other people's "selfish" goals.

Years later, after the split between Ayn Rand and Nathaniel Branden took place in 1968, Branden specialized in a field he called "The Psychology of Self-Esteem." I think this phrase sounds more palatable than "selfishness," and it is really what Ayn Rand was describing, but from a philosophical and ethical base rather than in terms of human psychology.

In the economic sphere, the only system that makes self-directed business efforts fully practical and profitable is capitalism. Ayn Rand was a tireless champion of capitalism at the very time (the 1930s through the 1960s) when it was most fashionable in the academic and intellectual world to be socialist, or even Marxist. Capitalism truly was an "unknown ideal" in the middle of the 20th century, when she wrote her major books and championed free markets in her novels.

"Capitalism is the only moral system," she would say to her followers, "because capitalism, in its pure, consistent form, is the only system based on the inviolability of individual rights." To those who brought up endless complaints of capitalist greed, she countered strongly, "If you care to do the research, you will discover that virtually every evil ascribed to laissez-faire capitalism is in fact the result not of laissez-faire capitalism but of government intervention, government controls, and the betrayal of laissez faire."

"For example," she explained, "capitalism is blamed for scarcities that are actually created by government price controls." Or, "The government, not the market, establishes a monopoly that forbids competitors to enter a particular field. Then when high prices naturally develop, capitalism is blamed once again."

Far from being your typical big-business Republican, she was not a champion of the kind of big business as practiced in our mixed (socialist and free) economy, where big business gets in bed with big government to write laws that shut out the small businessman or innovator. She often attacked big business: "Remember," she said, "capitalism means laissez faire; not government controls in favor of big business, but rather no government controls—hands off—a totally free market."

In the beginning, most of her disciples were conservative Republicans, but she was equally scathing to conservatives and liberals. "Conservatives," she said, "do not understand the nature of capitalism; they merely favor different controls than the liberals." Nobody from the left or the right, at least in the status quo, could defend themselves against her strong respect for ideas, her logic, and her relentless pursuit of truth.

Throughout the weeks and months while I was devouring her works, Rand's analysis of economics and history from the viewpoint of Objectivist philosophy rang totally true to me, as a young student of American history. Although perfect laissez faire never existed anywhere for very long, she confirmed what I had already suspected: that "the United States in the 19th century came closer to pure freedom than any other time or place in history." The spectacular result was the creation of great inventions, the rise of major industries, the expansion and development of the West—at great risk—and in the process, the birth of many 20th century fortunes.

Ayn Rand did not really change my mind; she succeeded in bringing to me a philosophy that fit the facts and feelings as I already intuitively knew them to be.

Moving From Ayn Rand to Ludwig von Mises

Having run out of new Ayn Rand books to read, I subscribed to all of her newsletters and then got into a serious study of her philosophy. I read the books which she included in the bibliography at the end of each of her newsletters; and that led me naturally into the study of laissez-faire economics—especially the works of what became known as the "Austrian school" of economics, pioneered in this century by Ludwig von Mises, Murray Rothbard and Friedrich A. Hayek.

First I read von Mises' shorter books like *Planned Chaos* and then his more difficult, longer books *Human Action* and *Socialism*. By the time I got deeply into these two latter books, I had already passed my high school equivalency in record time and was entering college in the second semester of the 1963-1964 school year, at Louisiana State's campus in New Orleans, called LSUNO then and now called UNO, the University of New Orleans.

By night I was reading the books of Ludwig von Mises, and by day my professors were telling me the diametric opposite of von Mises. Far from creating confusion in my young mind, I was pretty clear on who was telling the truth. So whenever a professor said something like, "The industrial revolution thrived on the back of labor," I would go back to von Mises or Hayek and refute the teacher's socialist interpretations.

I would speak up in class to dispute the professor's interpretations almost every day. I was known by students and teachers alike to be a real maverick, and probably a pain in the neck, if you come down to the honest facts. Whether I was talking back to a history professor, an economics professor, or a sociology professor, I would get together all my "intellectual ammunition" (as Ayn Rand called it) the night before and then try to refute their socialist theories as best I could the next day.

None of my Austrian readings at home were on the assigned reading list, but nevertheless, these books provided my real education in economics. Reading those books at the same time as I was reading their Keynesian counterparts was a great way to learn economics; and I wish more students could be presented with alternative theories like this, studied side by side, in their education.

Too often the lockstep mentality of college professors provides only limited exposure to ideas in "approved texts" on various subjects. When I was in school, there was only one approved theory in economics (Keynesian), in philosophy, in political science, and in all the subjects I took. Universities are supposed to be centers for free inquiry, so I think that this kind of lockstep thinking is a very dangerous trend. True science should not fear new ideas. Almost every great idea in history was once dismissed by those in power.

Learning About the Nature of Money
—In Theory and in Practice

Economics soon became my favorite field, but not because somebody told me it was a great way to make money. I was involved with economics more as a study of what makes the world work and what personal freedom is all about. I found from the classic economic texts of von Mises and Hayek that the government attacks a man's wealth first, because confiscation of his earnings saps his motivation for taking risks, making him a more docile citizen.

The study of economics became my passion and the key to understanding not only what had happened in the past, but what was going to happen in the future, and how I could prepare myself to prevent the government from taking what I earned.

Speaking of "what I earned," all this economics is fine in theory, but first you have to make some money in order to protect any of it. A year earlier, I had determined to live only from my own abilities and not to ask for charity; but here I was—a typical college student without much money in my pocket, wanting to practice what I preached—capitalism.

In my early college years, I started to get involved with a lot of entrepreneurial activities, including odd jobs—anything from being a butcher's helper to selling household detergents door to door. Pretty soon I started buying silver coins too, but I will save that story for the next chapter.

With a business here and a business there, I built up some seed money. As I did, I became convinced that the big threat to the American system during my lifetime (even to my small amount of money at the time) was going to be inflation.

Discovering Monetary Economics (and Gold)—My Favorite Subject

Through my studies in economics, I came to believe that the inflation of money and credit would result in the eventual, if not overnight, destruction of the dollar. I read several historical examples of government intervention in currency supply which had led to the destruction of that country's money and the fabric of its society—such as revolutionary France, Weimar Germany, Eastern Europe after World War II, the South Sea Bubble, and many Latin American inflations.

Within the field of economics, I began to concentrate on monetary economics. I soon discovered that for centuries the world market (the people, not the governments) had selected gold as their money—and for good reason: It was not easily controllable by central governments.

I learned the details of what I knew intuitively from reading about the Western miners of 1849 onward, that it takes great financial and personal risk for gold mining companies to extract one single ounce of gold from several tons of rock. In the nation where gold is most prevalent, South Africa, several thousand black miners extract a few ounces of gold per day, at high temperatures, under life-threatening conditions. The struggle to find gold has always been difficult, in every society in history. With gold, it is simply impossible to "print away" a nation's debts.

Historically, gold production has increased over the decades and centuries at an average growth rate of only 1 percent or 2 percent a year—pretty much matching the rate of population growth. By contrast, the government's volume of paper money could, and often did, grow at double-digit rates, leading to hyperinflationary rates of several hundreds or thousands of percent a year. This simply was not possible with gold, not even during the sporadic gold rush periods.

This was the way I combined my early interest in the American West (and especially the Gold Rush days) with a more philosophical study of freedom and the economic principles of the enlightened monetary theory of the Austrian school.

Going to Two Schools at Once

Throughout most of the 1960s I felt as if I were going to "two schools at once." One school was my required studies at LSUNO, and the second school was my self-directed study of free market economics. Back then, very few authors wrote about the economics of freedom. I would find a new book on freedom about once a month or so, and I would quickly buy or borrow it and then devour it. I made it a point to read every book on economic freedom I could get my hands on.

I also subscribed to various pro-free-market newsletters, like *The Freeman*, published by Leonard Reed's Foundation for Economic Education (FEE) in Irvington-on-Hudson, New York. I also visited Robert Lefebvre's Freedom School in Larkspur, Colorado, and even went up to the Big Apple to see if I could talk with Ayn Rand. At the time, her classes and philosophy were organized under the banner of the Nathaniel Branden Institute (NBI) in New York.

One day—I think it was on my summer break in 1965—I decided to fly up to New York City and walk in on the people at NBI, hoping to see Ayn Rand. Back then, at the peak of their popularity, NBI had 80 representatives or offices around the nation and an 8,000-square-foot office on the first floor of the Empire State Building.

Although I suitably impressed her staff enough that I became the NBI business manager in New Orleans, I never was able to meet Ayn Rand herself at that time. It would take another 16 years to accomplish that goal. I met all her representatives, including Branden, but I did not meet her until 1981.

From my studies in freedom I went on to even more radical libertarian studies in the American Individualist movement, including the books of the American anarchist philosophers like Benjamin Tucker and Lysander Spooner, who said that almost everything the government did was a usurpation of private interests. I was drawn to this writing as the natural outgrowth of the books that meant so much to me in the 11th grade, books like Thoreau's essay on "Civil Disobedience" and Emerson's essays on non-conformity and self-reliance.

The morality and ethics of capitalism and individualism were becoming even more unshakable in my mind, so it did not bother me that my teachers tried to lead me down a different path. I was about as hard-core as you can get—against government, against debt, and against government involvement in the money business. I guess that made me a "rebel with a cause" in a college full of more impressionable minds.

The Molding of Today's
Leaders in the 1960s

The New Orleans branch of LSU was just being formed in the early 1960s, so the university was especially dedicated to attracting top scholars who would be respected among the intellectual community. That usually meant collectivists. All my instructors, without exception, dismissed ideas such as individualism, free market economics and capitalism as intolerably old-fashioned. They claimed that the greatness of America, the unprecedented success of the American people, was accomplished "in spite of these archaic ideas, not because of them."

These noted scholars ignored the fact that early Americans enjoyed far more economic freedom than any other people in history, or they tried to show that economic liberty was the cause of endless problems and that the historical move toward stronger government and more economic intervention was necessary and desirable to correct those problems. I could see my fellow students virtually being molded by their professors' views of the world instead of thinking for themselves and challenging the professors.

Because most students let themselves be brainwashed, you can look around today and see the fruits of that teaching. The students of the 1960s are now in their 40s and early 50s and are the leaders in local, state, and federal government; investment banking; television programming; newspaper editorial departments; higher education; and big business.

You see rampant collectivism in television newscasts and anti-business themes in movies and television. You see bankers and brokers who bend over backward to do everything the federal government asks of them. A generation of Tom Haydens and Jerry Rubins can now be found in government and investment banking. Despite its being a decade of "protest," most children of the 1960s were molded by their collectivist professors into a leftist-style protest—if any—and imbued with collectivist political ideals.

If you read or listen to the news reports today—which usually make me sick to the stomach—you will hear about "greedy capitalists" who are "destroying the poor," or you will read scathing editorials against "independent small businessmen" who "ought to knuckle under to government regulations," or you will hear that "the rich are cravenly piling up profits at the expense of labor."

Each one of these ideas comes from the precise phrases which were funneled into the minds of today's leaders back in the 1960s on college campuses like mine. I recognize every one of them as something my professors said in class.

Ayn Rand was right when she said, "Ideas have consequences;" and so the collectivist ideas of the 1960s are leading us deeper and deeper into the consequences we now see around us. I put those problems right at the door of college teachers.

In those days the teaching of blatant Marxist/Leninist communism was quite popular on campus. I had one professor who was a Trotskyite, and proud of it. If not outright Marxist, the entire academic community was 90 percent collectivist in the schools of philosophy, English, economics, sociology, politics, history, and probably more. Every professor I had was anti-individual and pro-collective in his teaching.

Challenging the Professors— And Reaping the Consequences

Needless to say, I was ridiculed for my naive and outdated ideas: Professors would look down their noses at me and say, "But Mr. Blanchard, obviously you haven't read the studies of Professor So-and-so. It was long ago recognized by historians of any merit that laissez-faire capitalism was a plague to the majority of the poor and benefited only Robber Barons."

Or they would ask, "Mr. Blanchard, have you no concern for the poor? What about the undeniable fact that laissez-faire capitalism led to the destructive monopolies which stifled competition?" Or, "Surely you can't pretend to argue with the undeniable historical evidence that the many economic panics and crashes of the 19th century were caused by a laissez-faire policy."

In the face of these sometimes stern—but most often condescending—rebukes from my eminent professors, it would have been easy to join the ranks of the faithful followers in their classes. I nicknamed those students the TPs (the Tape-recorded Playbacks), because they dutifully recorded the Gospel according to Professor So-and-so in their notes and were ready, on an instant's notice, to "discuss" a historical issue by pushing their replay buttons. Obviously, this kind of rote learning made true learning more difficult.

In defense of my fellow students, they really were not given much of a choice. I was two years older, having spent much of those two years discovering the ammunition to fight this type of brainwashing. In the books of von Mises and Rand, I found a brilliant defense of individual liberty and the ideas necessary to appreciate the greatness of America's success.

I wish more teachers would allow their students access to this viewpoint, and I am glad to see that a handful of universities are admitting an Austrian economics professor or a free market philosopher to their staff these days. Better late than never.

Joining Goldwater's Campaign

Throughout 1964, in my first college year back in New Orleans after my accident, I was studying hard money economics and Ayn Rand's Objectivist philosophy while trying to work for a living. Naturally I became more and more enamored of the campaign of Senator Barry Goldwater of Arizona, who seemed to exemplify all these heroic Western ideals along with hard money economics.

As I got more and more politically involved in 1964, I became a member of Young Americans for Freedom (YAF) and was named president of the Southern Louisiana chapter of Youth for Goldwater. I was very active in the campaign, even though I missed qualifying to vote by less than a week. Having been born on November 10, 1943, I was just a few days shy of reaching age 21 by election day of 1964. (It was a shame that the enlightened youth of that day were not allowed to vote, and I am glad the voting age has since been changed to 18.)

After reading all of Ayn Rand's works and much Austrian

economic theory, I was already a hard-core, free-market-oriented libertarian at the time of Goldwater's campaign. Even though he was a conservative Republican with what I thought were a few "blind spots" in the area of libertarian philosophy, I felt that Goldwater was about as pure a laissez-faire capitalist as we would ever see running for president, and he was surprisingly close to fitting all my beliefs of the time.

Even Ayn Rand supported Goldwater for president, and she seemed genuinely amazed that such a man could even win the nomination of a major party in a collectivist society like ours. Her skeptical views were partly justified when Goldwater eventually lost by such a huge margin.

Since 1964, of course, we have seen another conservative Republican run, and win, twice. His name is Ronald Reagan. Back in 1964, I remember being very moved by Reagan's speech nominating Barry Goldwater and by Reagan's fund-raising speech for Goldwater, which raised more money than any other speech in history up to that time. (Even then, Reagan was a very articulate spokesman for free market principles, although I am unsure how much of it he deeply understood.)

In late 1964, just before the election, I put together a Youth for Goldwater conference, promoted it myself, and sold 500 tickets for a couple of dollars each. After expenses, we raised about $700 for the campaign—not a huge amount of money, but I was really excited about doing my part for the 1964 campaign. We passed out bumper stickers and campaign literature and got emotionally behind the pro-free-market movement which Goldwater was leading at the time.

In fact, I was so emotionally involved with the Goldwater campaign that I can remember crying on the night he lost the election by such a large margin. But I did not lose the dream of freedom, and neither did most of us who fought so hard to help Barry Goldwater in 1964.

Libertarians—The First Real
"Freedom Fighters" of the 1960s

A lot of us who campaigned for Goldwater were discouraged by the huge margin of his loss, but most of us did not lose the dream. Many of us went underground for a while, then gravitated toward the Libertarian Party during the 1970s (it was founded in 1971). Others tried to combine the principles of liberty with the Republican Party in the Reagan Revolution of the 1980s.

For example, Senator Goldwater's main speech writer, Karl Hess, went on to become a founding father of the Libertarian Party. On the other end of the spectrum, Ronald Reagan ran for governor of California, won twice—in 1966 and 1970—and then waited in the wings until the country caught up with the fact that Goldwater really was right after all.

These two examples dramatize the two different kinds of people who supported Goldwater. There was a heady mixture of old-line conservatives and young free market libertarians, several of whom were under the philosophical influence of Ayn Rand, Murray Rothbard, Ludwig von Mises and other great libertarian thinkers.

The Youth for Goldwater camp was a haven for several young firebrands—including the freedom fighter Jack Wheeler and Congressman Dana Rohrabacker, who was an early activist with me in the gold movement, as well as in Youth for Goldwater. We were radicalized neither by the left nor by the right, but by a whole new, highly individualistic, strongly free-market and anti-totalitarian philosophy akin to Ayn Rand's version of "minarchy" (the absolute minimum of government), with courts and police to defend individual liberty, plus a strong military defense.

The Youth for Goldwater movement was, in a sense, the first radical movement of the 1960s, founded before the leftist students started the Free Speech movement in Berkeley, burned their draft cards, and then shouted down those of us who favored free markets. In the early 1960s, we supported the truly radical idea that people ought to be left alone to make their own fortunes in America. That was the original idea behind the Declaration of Independence in 1776.

In the process of the 1964 campaign, Barry Goldwater became one of my great Western heroes—a son of immigrants who went on to become a self-made millionaire in the American West. He is a genuine pioneer, whose strong free market ideas made him the first presidential candidate in over 30 years who believed in free markets and the gold standard.

The Great Silver Robbery
Led to My First "Coin Business"

Shortly after Goldwater's defeat in November 1964, something dramatic happened to our money. The victorious Lyndon Johnson decided that he would take silver out of our money. That single act, more than any other, changed my ideas about what I would be doing for the rest of my life.

No sooner did Lyndon Johnson beat Barry Goldwater, than he proceeded to break every promise he ever made. He not only presided over a painfully long escalation of the Vietnam War and tried to pay for both guns and butter, but he also asked Congress to take the silver out of our money as Franklin Roosevelt did with our gold.

In a sense, LBJ's great silver robbery was the beginning of my lifelong career in the hard money movement and the motivating act for my first step into the coin business.

Chapter 3

The Great Silver Robbery

The Loss of U.S. Silver Coinage
Started the Hard Money Revolution

"Students now arrive at the university ignorant and cynical about our political heritage, lacking the wherewithal to be either inspired by it or seriously critical of it."

—Allan Bloom, *The Closing of the American Mind*

The mid-1960s was a painful time of transition for the United States. In retrospect it all started with the traumatic murder of John F. Kennedy on November 22, 1963, and the resulting death of his dream of a young, new "Camelot" era of leadership for America. I have often wondered what would have happened if John Kennedy with all his charisma and love of America had been a Goldwater in his ideas. Even though I disagreed with Kennedy's socio-political ideas, I greatly admired him. Just a few months after Lyndon B. Johnson became resident, in February 1964, the Beatles "invaded" America, bringing a new kind of music, haircuts and lifestyles. The Free Speech riots on the Berkeley campus of the University of California introduced us to a decade of protest on campus.

In August the Gulf of Tonkin Resolution escalated the Vietnam War into nearly full swing. Also in the summer of 1964, LBJ's Civil Rights bill was passed, and several black radicals, like Malcolm X and H. Rap Brown, deemed it "too little, too late." Racial riots unleashed a century of repressed black anger in the first of five "long, hot summers" between 1964 and 1969.

Meanwhile, in the Soviet Union, Khrushchev was judged to be too soft on capitalism (especially in regard to taking Soviet missiles out of Cuba), and he was thrown on the scrap heap of the Kremlin. A hard-liner, Leonid Brezhnev, then took over, launching nearly two decades of communist expansion under the Soviet colonial tenets of the Brezhnev Doctrine. To top it off, Red China tested the H-bomb in 1964. Times looked bleak.

All these social trends and events were pretty heavy stuff for a 20-year-old college freshman like myself, but I managed to put all of that drama on the back burner in order to concentrate on one of the most dramatic events of the 1960s—one which changed the face of the American economy for decades to come and signaled the first shot of the "Hard Money Revolution," of which I was later to become a leader.

In a sense this simple act, which went almost unnoticed in the press and on campuses, launched the age of inflation. In the long run it turned out to have at least as much impact as all the other dramatic events of 1964. What I am talking about, of course, is the loss of silver in our coinage.

What the Loss of Silver
U.S. Coins Meant to Me

The act of removing the last vestige of silver from our coinage may seem like a footnote to the history of the 20th century, but it was deeply symbolic to me at the time and it still is. In retrospect I think the move was pretty devastating to our economy. If you doubt the impact of the silver loss, consider the economic trends since then:

• Loss of silver (and previously, gold) coinage made huge deficit spending possible, as reflected in Lyndon Johnson's "guns and butter" policies of the late 1960s—the first time any administration had tried to support large increases in both military and domestic spending at the same time.

• Loss of silver in our coinage helped make fortunes for a few investors who saw the benefits in tangible assets early—and it also *lost* fortunes for millions of bondholders, dollar-savers, pensioners, and stock market speculators, who relied on various forms of paper for their total security.

• Loss of monetary discipline in our coinage was also reflected in the loss of discipline in our spending, taxing and saving habits. Loss of silver coinage launched America on an overspending spree which raised the deficit by a factor of 10— from $300 billion to almost $3 trillion—and cost us each personally in higher taxes and lower savings.

• Inflation since 1965 has quintupled the general price level, most of it coming in the peacetime years since 1974—our first major siege of inflation during peacetime in the 200-year history of the nation. Today's dollar is worth only what a silver quarter was worth in 1964—a 300 percent price rise.

• Recessions have struck the U.S. economy about every five years since 1964, each one deeper, more painful and more severe than the one before it. What is more, the recessions since 1964 have each been inflationary, not deflationary as in the past. This has given rise to a new word for our age of inflation: *stagflation*—meaning stagnation + inflation.

• Federal deficits have grown astronomically from an average $5 billion per year in the 1960s to $35 billion per year in the 1970s and to $155 billion per year in the 1980s so far. If this trend continues, we could have deficits of $500 billion per year in the 1990s. The federal debt has grown exponentially since 1964, only passing the $500 billion mark in 1975, then $1 trillion in 1981, $2 trillion in 1985 and $3 trillion by 1990.

This simple act of taking silver out of American coinage was not as serious as FDR's taking the gold out of circulation in 1933, but it was more serious in one way, because silver was the last feeble remnant of hard money in our coins. Losing all precious metals in our coinage was the first shot in the modern hard money revolution.

When Congress opted for a 40 percent "sandwich" silver coin in 1965—and later for no silver at all—it took away the last vestige of discipline from the Federal Reserve and the U.S. Treasury. Before 1965, American citizens could discipline the Treasury by cashing in their paper "silver certificates" or silver coins for a set weight of silver. By 1965, no such tools of monetary discipline were available to the public. Americans were devoid of their sovereign right to discipline the government by exchanging paper money for metal.

Since 1964 the Federal Reserve and U.S. Treasury have been free to print totally unbacked paper money to their heart's content, and that is precisely what they have done. The result is what you see on the business and economic news each night. Economics, previously considered a dry and boring subject for newspaper and television news, has leaped to the front pages and to the lead story on the Nightly News, directly as a result of the financial folly of unleashing politicians and central bankers from the discipline of gold and silver.

How I Began to Profit From the Great Silver Robbery

Starting in 1964—even before LBJ's coinage law went into effect—I began hoarding all my silver change. I bought everything I could with paper money and then kept the silver change in my pocket. I would constantly go to banks and exchange my hard-earned $10 bills for a roll of quarters, all of which were still silver.

After I turned 21 in late 1964, I would regularly go to a college hangout where I would buy a 12-ounce glass of beer for 25 cents. I always gave the bartender a paper dollar and got three quarters in change. In the early days, all three quarters were mostly 90 percent silver (pre-1965). If I had another beer, I would give him another dollar, not a quarter. It was like drinking for free and making a profit on the change. At times I may have had one too many beers, but getting the silver was almost worth pouring the beer down the sink.

By the late 1960s, I had saved enough money to buy the more expensive, older (pre-1935) Morgan and Peace silver dollars. I bought classic Morgan and Peace silver dollars for about $1.25 each. Then the price jumped up to $1.50 and I had a tough decision—whether or not to pay a 50 percent premium for silver. Everybody told me I was a fool to buy silver dollars over spot price "since they are so common," but I made a wise decision by forking over $1.50 for silver dollars now worth at least $25 and, in many cases, several hundred dollars.

I placed small ads in the local newspaper, offering $1.50 to $1.75 per silver dollar if the seller had a sufficient quantity to make it worth my while. This practice of mine offended the local coin dealers, because they did not want me bidding up the market price for "common date" silver dollars.

This turned out to be my first really lucrative business, buying silver dollars in bulk quantity for $1.50 and selling them singly for $2. Making my 50 cent profit was not designed to be a business at first, but a way to fund my growing hoard of silver coins. I would buy five or 10 silver dollars at a time, sometimes up to 100. Being a relatively poor college student, I would of course have to sell a few of my silver dollars at $2 to generate the cash flow to buy more at $1.50.

In general, I would convert every copper coin I owned into a silver coin in the 1960s, and every paper dollar I owned into as many silver quarters as the merchant would give me.

Campus Radicals Ignored the
Great Silver Robbery

Although I was personally and philosophically outraged by the loss of silver in American coinage, I felt as if I were alone in a sea of campus unrest about causes other than our coinage. As I said in the last chapter, the trendy thing was to be an extreme left-winger. Big government was supposed to be the answer to all our social problems. Big government was "naturally" the solution to the run on silver, so why fuss about such petty details, they thought. Most of my fellow students—who talked like radicals otherwise—believed that any problem in America required a governmental solution.

I could not figure out why the students who thought our government was wrong to wage war in Vietnam believed that this same government held the answer to all our social problems. Truly, the free market was an "unknown ideal."

To me, seeing the "silver window" closed at the Treasury was like seeing the government deliberately slamming the door on its own history. These coins were more to me than simply rounds of silver bullion. They were genuine pieces of American history and art, to be treasured, to bring back memories of a time when the nation was green and growing and confident, when the self-doubts of the 1960s would have seemed to belong to a different nation altogether.

When it came to the issue of silver coinage, I was still enthralled by tales of the Old West, especially those which involved gold and silver mining, such as carrying silver from the Comstock Lode over the Donner Pass in Wells Fargo wagons to the San Francisco Mint—outwitting or outfighting the outlaws,

Indians and renegade mountain men.

Because of my longstanding interest in the Old West—now combined with a new interest in hard-money economics—I became a successful investor. I hoarded hundreds of ounces of the most profitable investment coin of the last 20 years: classic 19th century U.S. silver dollars. But I probably never would have started my first coin business without the philosophical basis I got from Ayn Rand, Murray Rothbard and Ludwig von Mises. I discovered that ideas had consequences, and especially that good ideas can make you lots of money.

Gresham's Law in Action —"Bad Money Drives Out Good"

President Johnson's move to take the silver out of our coinage was signed into law on March 3, 1965, but it took a few years for most Americans to wake up to the investment opportunity of his currency debasement. I was way ahead of most people in that I had already learned the investment principle called Gresham's law, which goes back 450 years to the time of King Henry VIII's treasurer, Sir Thomas Gresham. His law states that "bad money" (like LBJ's copper and nickel-clad coins) drives "good money" (like pre-1934 gold coins and pre-1965 silver coins) out of circulation.

Put simply, why would a person give up his gold or silver coins when he can spend copper coins and get the same immediate buying power? When gold and silver temporarily have the same purchasing power as copper and nickel, a smart person will naturally spend the copper coins and hoard the gold and silver coins. Gresham's law is nothing more nor less than human nature reduced to a simple monetary formula. It is pretty obvious in retrospect, but not too many Americans saw this as any kind of "law" while it was happening.

For a few years I must have looked like a young fool, as the market value of silver dimes and quarters did not start exceeding the copper/nickel coins until about 1968. But once the public caught on to what a few of us were doing, it was too late for the average investor to profit. By 1969 it was difficult to find any silver in your change. By that time I had already stashed away several thousand silver dollars and thousands of dollars (face value) of silver change, despite being a fairly poor college student.

From this first hoard of pocket change, I was able to launch a series of profit-making companies which have, since 1971, grown gradually but steadily to more than $100 million per year in gross sales. But we are getting ahead of the story. It all started much more gradually than that.

My Introduction to Gold Investing— Attracted by the "Forbidden Fruit"

In the mid-1960s my investing was limited to a few odd silver coins, because I knew it was illegal for Americans to own gold bullion or coins. In 1967 I started considering gold. It was then that somebody gave me a wrinkled old copy of one of Vern Myers' very first financial newsletters, published right after he sold his interest in *Oil Week*.

Vern did not write from a strictly intellectual platform, as did the Austrian economists and libertarian philosophers I had read up to that point. Vern was talking more "from the gut" about practical investment issues. He was convinced, as I was, that America was going to have a rotting currency, with silver already disappearing from our coinage and gold hemorrhaging from the Treasury at record rates.

Vern published his letter from Canada at that time—a nation where gold ownership was legal. That gave me the seed of an idea for buying and owning gold, against the laws of the United

States, as an act of civil disobedience and, frankly, as an act of financial self-preservation. (I shall develop that idea in more detail in the next chapter.)

Vern Myers was one of the first newsletter writers who strongly recommended investing in gold at $35 to $40 an ounce. His newsletter crystallized my thinking and got me excited all over again to reread every economics book I had already read, but this time I looked at them from the viewpoint of investing, not economics.

I found that the number of good books on hard-money investing was limited but that the best and most timely information came from a select few hard-money newsletters. Although I could not afford it at the time, I scraped up enough money to subscribe to three of the best pro-gold letters of the 1960s: Richard Russell's *Dow Theory Letter*, *The Harry Schultz Letter* and *Myers' Finance and Energy*.

I became convinced from this reading that the death of the dollar was inevitable. In fact William F. Rickenbacker, the son of the great World War I ace Eddie Rickenbacker, wrote a book in 1968 titled *Death of the Dollar*. After reading it I met with him, and subsequently I met with all the other hard-money authors of the late 1960s, including Jerome Smith, Franz Pick, Harry Schultz, and many others. I sought out each author, first by developing a long and detailed correspondence, and then by meeting most of them personally.

An Open Letter to Milton Friedman
—Published by Harry Schultz

At the time, I was very impressed with Milton Friedman's free-market comments in his triweekly *Newsweek* column and his early books on capitalism and freedom. So I wrote him a long and detailed letter about the benefits of the gold standard, asking how he could be so consistently against government control of everything else, but not be against the government's monopoly of printing money and hoarding gold. It was a kind of "open letter" to Milton Friedman, copies of which I sent to several other authors.

Dr. Friedman sent me a letter in return, disagreeing with me, so I sent a copy of both letters to Harry Schultz. He was impressed enough with my letter to reproduce all of it in his newsletter. Almost the entire edition was made up of my long letter. Harry thought it was great that a college student could write such a cogent letter about the dollar and gold back in the days when college students were rarely knowledgeable in free market economics and only seemed outraged about Vietnam, the draft, long hair, and the other left-wing issues of the day.

The essence of my argument went something like this: Government intervention in monetary policy results in total destruction of currencies, which usually happens in just a few decades, not centuries. This trend began conceptually in the 1930s with Franklin Delano Roosevelt and John Maynard Keynes, but in actuality the destruction of the currency began in earnest in the late 1960s. I went on to say that the populace would reach a saturation point in taxes, so governments would need to use inflation of the money supply and credit to feed their spending programs.

Economists were saying that money could be made up entirely of unbacked fiat paper. Gold was a useless, even comical, old relic, they said, as a currency. After all, it was dug out of the ground in South Africa, poured into bars, shipped to the United States, and buried under the ground again, either in Fort Knox, Kentucky, or 85 feet underneath the Federal Reserve Bank of New York. How barbaric, even pagan, that such practices should continue in the 20th century. Or so it seemed to most "enlightened" economists.

On the face of it, hoarding gold seemed like a foolish waste of energy, a mythical kind of pseudo-religious monetary fetish. But what they failed to realize was that they were giving the same mythic power to government paper—made from pulp that came from trees in the Canadian woods—and that they wanted that paper to be worshiped, along with the politicians who printed it, as omnipotent sacraments of "the money temple." I argued that gold is the only practical substance for use as money because it never corrodes, it is hard to extract from the earth, and it is impossible to mass produce.

Vern Myers Sends Me
His "Road Map" to Wealth

Through correspondence with Vern Myers, I was able to put together the ideas that helped me and many other investors to make a lot of new money and protect what we already had. Once I wrote Vern one of my many long letters to ask him how he would advise a young college student with a limited amount of money to invest: What can I do with only a few dollars (outside my silver coins) to invest?

He replied, saying in effect, "You're in a very enviable position, young man...You have the time and money to protect yourself for life." He then spelled out a detailed road map of exactly what investments I should buy in order to protect my small savings. He recommended South African gold shares, silver coins, and North American gold stocks; and he told me to get hold of some gold if I could do so discreetly. He also said, "Have patience, look to the long term."

When I called a Merrill Lynch broker to ask him to buy South African gold stocks for me, he did not even know what I was talking about. After all, the stocks had these names that were terribly hard to spell or pronounce—like Hartebeestfontein, Buffelsfontein, Kloof, and West Witwatersrand. My broker literally could not find them on his quote sheet, so I had to teach him how to buy the stocks for me through American Depository Receipts (ADRs) traded in New York.

At first I made no money on these stocks. In fact I lost more than half of my little nest egg. Like so many new investors, I started investing blindly at what proved to be near the top of a cyclical peak in gold and silver. I bought Hartebeestfontein, a South African gold stock, at $7.88 and Western Deep Levels at $20 to $22—which turned out to be their cyclical highs! Western Deep Levels lost two-thirds, down to $7.50, and Hartebeestfontein went down to something like 50 cents. In bullion, I did not do much better. I caught maybe the last 20 percent of the rise in silver prices, from $1.29 to $2.56 in 1967-1968. Then prices fell to $1.29 again.

Unlike most investors, I did not lose my faith in gold and silver stocks when they went down, because I was solidly grounded in my free-market principles. Even though the gold stocks went down right after I bought them, they eventually doubled and tripled several times over. Even when these stocks were in the basement at several low points in the cycle, they always paid good dividends. With my dividends, I would always buy more shares at lower prices.

Whenever I could save up another hundred dollars or so, I would buy more stocks or more silver coins, even though silver was never a great investment in those early years. But by slow accumulation of these investments, I was able to build the foundation for the good-sized fortune I have earned since then.

If you have ever bought an investment you thought was right for the long term, and it went down, I would urge you to learn to do what I did: Use fundamental socio-economic analysis to make a long-term decision *before* you ever invest. If you do not do that, you will need to rely on luck.

But if you put your money where your *mind* is, you can make a fortune in the long run. Do not worry about the short term. If you check your premises first, the short-term market fluctuations will not get to you. If you do not feel confident, you will get whipsawed out of the market; because you will change your mind, lose faith and get discouraged by short-term losses.

Meeting All of the
Original Gold Bugs

I communicated with all the major "gold bugs" of the 1960s—Harry Schultz, Vern Myers, Jerome Smith, Bill Rickenbacker, and Richard Russell among them. Eventually that proved to be a catalyst for inviting these gentlemen to our investment conferences in the 1970s. By the time of my first conference in 1974, I had logged several years of serious correspondence on various investment topics with these gentlemen. I really enjoyed meeting them, even hosting these great thinkers in my own home, as well as visiting them in their homes.

Why was it so easy for me to meet these men? I think it is because there were not too many young people in the 1960s, especially college students, who cared much about free-market issues; so when I wrote one of these men a letter, he was genuinely impressed enough to respond to me and be willing to meet me. They probably received a letter like mine no more than once or twice a year.

These men also had a dedication to their cause and were willing to go out of their way, for no direct monetary reward, to encourage their ideas in somebody younger than themselves. Later, as a teacher of American history and economics in secondary schools in the early 1970s, I told these men that their ideas were directly affecting the lives of several hundred young people; so whenever they shared their knowledge with me, it was going to hundreds of children too. This also contributed to their willingness to share ideas with me.

By then I was also sharing their views with my mailing list in *Gold Newsletter*. But in earlier years, they shared freely with just me alone, and that says a lot about their dedication to the cause of financial freedom.

Even though I am not by any means a "grand old man" of the gold movement (yet), or an "original gold bug," I am already in my mid-40s; and it still seems to be a tragic commentary on our educational system that I seldom get a letter from a young person interested in these ideas about hard money or the free market. The vast majority of our clients are older people, many of whom lived through the Great Depression and several bear markets in both stocks and precious metals since then. They have experienced the ravages of both inflation and depression. Perhaps young people are too jaded by prosperity to consider the economic truths which I learned so early. But there are encouraging signs: There are more younger people at our annual New Orleans Conference, and the pro-free-market movement is dominated by young men and women.

The Result May Be Clear, but the Timing Is Anybody's Guess

In correspondence with another original gold bug, Colonel E.C. Harwood, I learned early that the "short term is anybody's guess." Just because the long-term trends are virtually certain does not mean we can predict the short-term swings. The mistake that many of us make is that when we know our theory is right, we expect it to happen right away. By now I realize it will always take longer than I think to happen.

Colonel Harwood brought me the wisdom of his experience, not just in markets, but in life. I now see the truth of his statement almost every day: I expect a job will take an hour to do, but it ends up taking all day. I built my dream house in the mountains of north Georgia; but instead of taking nine months, it took two years to build. Everything seems to take longer than we think, especially when we are young. That was also true of the gold and silver markets from 1964 all the way to 1979.

Despite my early problem of timing the gold markets, I can honestly say that I fully anticipated most of the economic cataclysms of 1979-1980 a decade before they happened—the surge to $850 gold and $50 silver, 21 percent prime rates along with 20 percent inflation, soaring debts, failing banks, and so forth. I always thought it would happen a lot sooner than it did, but it eventually happened. The same principles are true today. You may have to hold on to your investments longer than you think, but one thing is certain: In the long run gold beats paper every time, and gold will have it's day again.

I Finally Graduate From College—After Six and a Half Years of Intellectual Combat

Since I was getting two college educations at once—one for credit and the other for real life—you might imagine I had little time for anything else. That was not really the case. I always took plenty of time off to enjoy life, traveling for a month at a time, usually out west; skipping a semester here and there; taking a lighter class load some years; taking time off for business ventures to raise money to buy coins; or visiting the Freedom School, NBI and other philosophical training grounds which were more in tune with my reading than college turned out to be.

It took me six and a half years to graduate from college, after acing high school in five weeks! I started college in early 1964 and graduated in June 1970 with a degree in American history. On the National History Examinations, which I took upon graduation, I scored in the top 1 percent of all history graduates.

Although I majored in American history, monetary economics was my favorite subject. The monetary issue was the key issue to me: The implications and examples of government-controlled money, a vicious cycle of debt and inflation, and the eventual runaway inflation resulting from government control of money. These studies also became the basis of my political action on behalf of gold, which began in 1971, just one year after I graduated.

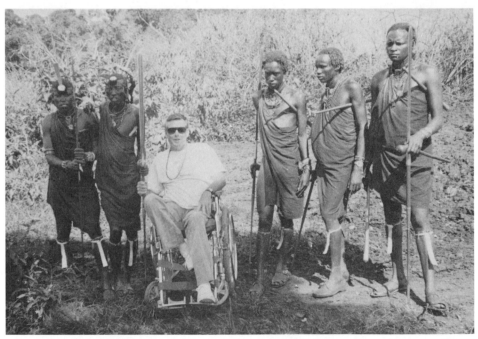

Top: Photo of me at the 1985 New Orleans Conference with (left to right), Prince Buthelezi, chief of the seven-million-member Zulu nation in South Africa; Alfonso Robelo, a Contra leader; and Congressman Siljnder at a press conference. Bottom: With Masai warriors on lion hunt in 1987, Masai Mara, Kenya.

Top: Commander in Chief of the RENAMO armed forces and president of RENAMO, Afonso Dhlakama (left), being presented with an American flag by my good friend Tom Schaaf, of the Mozambique Research Foundation, 1989. Bottom: Sailing with my good friend Mohammed, the dhow captain, off the ancient island of Lamu, Kenya, 1988.

Top: Having a lot of fun on the northern polar ice cap, but keeping a close eye out for polar bears. Bottom: Quail hunting with friends in eastern Texas, 1987.

Top left: Feeding a lion cub at Sun City, South Africa, February 1984. Top right: On a rest from my favorite recreation, Honda Odyssey racing. Bottom: My son, Anthem Blanchard, age 8, makes history by being the youngest person ever to visit the North Pole, April 1988.

Top: Almost one year before the Tienanmen Square massacre in China, I tried to have my picture taken with a Chinese soldier, but he was reluctant. He did agree to lend his uniform to our student guide. Bottom: President Afonso Dhlakama of RENAMO in Mozambique, August 1989.

Overlooking the house site in North Georgia mountains...Oops!

Top: A Masai village that tourists never see, (left to right), Anthem Hayek Blanchard, Adrianna Hnatiw, myself, my friend James, our Masai guide, with his wife and baby daughter, and Veronica Bubniw. Bottom: My good friend David Galland, who now does the marketing for the Blanchard Group of Funds, takes a break after our "James Bond" car chase, Malawi, 1986. (Notice the African baobab tree in the background.)

Top: Lesia takes a beer break and a drive through one of the emerging free markets in Beijing, China. We brought in several loads of free-market literature and distributed it to students. Our student driver (right), once he began to trust us, was very critical of government policies and was anxious for rapid change. This was almost twelve months before the protest and massacre in Tienanmen Square. Bottom: Lesia helps me finish the manuscript for Confessions of a Gold Bug *at our tent camp in Kenya, August 1989.*

Chapter 4

Legalize Gold!

"The gold standard did not fail. The governments were eager to destroy it....No government is, however, powerful enough to abolish the gold standard."

—Ludwig von Mises, *Human Action*

After graduating from LSU's New Orleans campus in 1970, I moved directly into a teaching job in a local junior high school, spending my working days talking about a subject close to my heart—American history—and spending my nights reading more about hard-money economics and political action.

By the summer of 1971 I had become totally convinced that the price of gold was going to head dramatically higher in the years just ahead of us. I was so convinced that I spent as much of my meager $4,500 per year teacher's salary as I could on several of the legal gold-oriented investments—especially the South African gold mining shares. But that did not satisfy my desire for owning gold. I wanted to hold the real thing in my hands. But that was illegal.

The U.S. government's total prohibition against owning gold bullion bars or coins in 1934 began to really bother me as a young investor in 1971, earning my first regular salary. The more I thought about it, the more ridiculous it seemed to me that free Americans were not free to buy or own gold. Most gold-oriented investors I met at the time were older people, and so they seemed to be more used to it. They just sighed and said, "Well, that's the way things are. They've been that way since I was a kid, so I might as well keep a low profile and invest only in what's legal."

Maybe it was my radical nature, my iconoclastic beliefs about free-market economics, my belief in civil disobedience I learned from the early influence of Thoreau, or just the foolhardy nature of a young man who had already cheated death, but whatever my motivation, I was not willing to accept the answer that we ought to just obey our government on the gold question. I kept looking at pictures of gold bars in books and asking myself, "How could holding this cold slab of gold metal conceivably be a crime against the state, worth up to 10 years in prison? I don't get it."

Nixon Closes the Gold Window and Makes Up My Mind—August 15, 1971

With thoughts of civil disobedience floating in the back of my brain, I was driving out west that summer of 1971, along with my wife, Jackie. Out of the blue, we heard on the radio that President Nixon had closed the gold window that night, suspending all payments of gold in foreign exchange.

Jackie and I had often talked about the possibility of this happening someday, but here it was coming through on the radio as we were driving out west. We looked at each other in amazement and commented, "This is it. It's the beginning of the end of the dollar. Gold is going to soar...and we don't own any."

Although Nixon's actions were inevitable, it got my goat that he and the other politicians could not admit that the cause of their problem was their own bad management of the currency, which made the dollar so weak and gold so strong. Instead they blamed gold as "the messenger of the bad news." By removing gold from circulation, they once again were showing the inevitability of Gresham's law: bad money driving good money out of circulation.

In effect, Nixon and the other politicians were saying out of one side of their mouths that gold was a "barbarous relic" and out of the other side that it was too "dangerous" a metal to leave in the hands of the "unsophisticated public." Since 1934 they had not trusted the American public to own gold bullion in any form, and now in effect they were forbidding foreign governments to do the same thing.

After thinking about the implications of this move for a few minutes, I made up my mind about gold and said, "Jackie, we've got to buy some gold. I don't care if it's legal or not. We've got to protect ourselves. The dollar is going down the tubes. Inflation is going to wipe out the value of whatever we own. The gold mining shares will be great for us, as far as they go, but it's not like holding a gold bar in your hand. We need to own some physical gold."

We Broke the Law, in Public, and Told the World About It

Within three weeks of Nixon's announcement, we formed an organization called the National Committee to Legalize Gold (NCLG) and held public demonstrations on behalf of legalized gold ownership. On September 5, 1971—three weeks after Nixon's announcement—we held our first demonstration, in Houston, Texas. We challenged the 1934 Gold Reserve Act by holding a privately owned gold bar in public. We had alerted the U.S. Treasury office in Houston, but they failed to show up.

We got extensive radio, television and newspaper coverage; and our Free Gold campaign was off to the races. The way I got the gold to Houston was really illegal. A friend in college on the

East Coast volunteered to cross the border into Canada, buy a 2-ounce gold bullion bar, and then smuggle it back across the border. (I still have that 2-ounce bar as a memento. It cost only $85 at the time, and was worth $1,700 by 1980 and about $750 today, but to me it is still priceless.)

It was a simple crime. Any American could have done it. The difference was that I wanted to announce it to the public.

Whenever we were about ready to make a demonstration, we not only sent announcements to the local press, we also sent registered copies to the U.S. Treasury, the Federal Reserve, the president, our congressmen, etc.; and then we would dare the Feds, the sheriffs, the dogcatcher, or anybody, to arrest us.

To help publicize these events, I contributed my last available $50 (a lot of money for a teacher in those days) toward the printing of a newsletter, *Gold Newsletter*. At the time, we thought it might only be a one-time flyer, or maybe a quarterly. In fact, the first *Gold Newsletter* was not even dated, but it was published—I can tell from the context of the articles—in November 1971. This "one-time-only flyer" quickly turned into a very popular crusade and a permanent newsletter, now in its 19th year.

Our campaign to legalize gold was surprisingly popular from the beginning. Even though public opinion polls revealed that Americans approved of Nixon's devaluation of the dollar and removal of gold backing by a 3-to-1 margin, we found that the 25 percent who disapproved were a very dedicated core of people.

Among the dissenters from Nixon's dollar devaluation were the founders of the Libertarian Party, who decided that very night (August 15, 1971) in Colorado that since Nixon so callously broke his campaign promises—never to devalue the dollar, never to close the gold window and never to institute wage and price controls—that they would form a new political party dedicated to liberty. (It's enough to make you thankful for political incompetence. The worse it gets, the stronger the counter-reaction it causes!)

Our message continued to be well received. In October 1971 we attended Harry Schultz's International Monetary Seminar in Bermuda and distributed our literature packet on gold from the NCLG. All the mavericks there loved it, wished us well, and contributed enough to pay for our trip and circulate the first couple of issues of *Gold Newsletter*. I also learned a lot about running conferences from Harry, to whom I will always be indebted as one of my great mentors.

Building a Mailing List—
From 50 Names to Millions

Once we made the decision to go ahead with *Gold Newsletter,* we faced the challenge of building the mailing list up to respectable numbers and getting our message heard. Today our company controls over a million names and addresses of people interested in gold investing, but we did not start at anywhere near those levels.

Our inventory of names started with only 50, a result of that time when Harry Schultz printed my open letter to Milton Friedman in the late 1960s (see the previous chapter for details on that). Even though my address was not listed in Harry's publication, he did mention that I was a student at LSU in New Orleans; so I kept getting letters addressed simply to Jim Blanchard at LSUNO. (Who knows how many other letters were not delivered, due to insufficient address?)

Of the 50 people who wrote to me at the time that article came out, most of them said, "If there's anything I can do to help you spread the word about legalizing gold ownership, let me know." That was the beginning of our mailing list. We kept those 50 names on 3x5 cards at first; then—in late 1971, after Bermuda—when we reached 2,000 names, we typed up the names on paste-on labels (33 to a sheet), which we fed through a copying machine to generate our mailing labels.

I sent the first *Gold Newsletter* to these first 50 people who had requested information, plus the few hundred other names I had accumulated by then, and I told them that I was starting the National Committee to Legalize Gold and that I was soliciting their contributions. I put in the first $50 myself to buy stamps and stationery and to pay for the printing of the first issue. From that first mailing, I was shocked that we got back a total of $800, including a whopping check (for those days) of $500 from my old hard-money friend Ed Durrell. I poured this back into setting up a one-room office with a phone and soliciting a larger mailing list.

It took time, but I picked up 100 names here, 50 names there, and finally hit a gold mine when John McFalls, an investment adviser in Seattle, let us use his list of 2,000 names. By the time we reached 5,000 names, we started using a local mailing house in New Orleans. These 5,000 names were committed people who were strongly motivated about gold—the kind who wrote their congressmen about gold and were actively involved in politics.

Even so, I would not want to make it sound as if we were the only people working on gold legalization in the early 1970s. In Washington, D.C., we had the help of congressmen like Phil Crane and Senator Jim McClure. Later we had help from Howard Segermark, an aide to Senator Jesse Helms at the time and now head of the Industry Council on Tangible Assets, as well as from Senator Steve Symms and many others.

There were other grass roots movements specializing more in the dissemination of the "intellectual ammunition" on gold legalization. There was the venerable Colonel Harwood of the American Institute for Economic Research (AIER) in Great Barrington, Massachusetts. There was Elizabeth Currier of the Committee for Monetary Research and Education (CMRE).

In our own organization (NCLG), I give great credit to my co-workers at the time, people such as Evan Soulé, Charles Curley, Ed Durrell, and my hard-working wife Jackie, who was the major force behind organizing the details of our efforts from the very beginning and on through our greatest years of growth into the mid-1980s. What NCLG contributed to the cause of gold ownership was nothing new in the area of intellectual ammunition, but we added a new element of civil disobedience by specializing in public demonstrations in favor of gold ownership, which continued from 1971 through 1974.

More Public Demonstrations on Behalf of Gold in 1972

In 1972 we at NCLG held at least three press conferences, including one in Los Angeles on October 24 and another on October 28 in New York City. They were well attended by the press and public, but once again the federal authorities were invited to arrest us and did not show up.

It was easy to understand why the authorities did not show up. They simply thought we would go away. "Why give those crazy kids credibility and more publicity?" They were obligated to arrest us, according to the law. Anyone convicted of illegally owning gold under President Roosevelt's Executive Order 6260 (dated August 28, 1933) was subject to a maximum penalty of 10 years imprisonment and/or a fine of $10,000. The civil penalty was forfeiture of the gold and a "fine equal to twice the value of such gold." Even forgetting the possibility of jail, the civil penalty alone would have been a stiff one to pay—twice the value of the gold—and I literally could not afford a fine of $10,000.

In the course of 1972, NCLG distributed over 200,000 pieces of literature, including bumper stickers saying, "Stop Inflation—Demand Gold." (I later found out that Ludwig von Mises put one of those bumper stickers on his car at age 90! That makes me feel good.) We also circulated a postal sticker, which said, "Why Are Americans Prohibited From Owning Gold?" and we kept publishing *Gold Newsletter*.

Our message appealed to everyone we met. After all, why should Americans suffer all that harassment over a little bar of gold? It seemed ridiculous to me, and it must have seemed ridiculous to the Treasury agents too, or they would have arrested me.

January 20, 1973
—Buzzing Nixon's Inaugural

On President Nixon's second inaugural, we hired a World-War-I-style biplane to carry a 50-foot sign: "LEGALIZE GOLD!" It cost us $600 to finance the stunt, although it took a long time to find a pilot daring enough to buzz the Capitol. As it turned out—and we suspected as much—there was a strictly supervised air corridor around the Capitol that day, which kept us out of the direct area.

The plane came near the site of the inauguration anyway, and that fact caused the Secret Service to scramble a military plane to tail our pilot and warn him off course. We were later contacted by the Secret Service and the Treasury for this trespass, but they chose not to prosecute us.

All three national network television news programs commented on the banner that night. It caused a lot of talk around Washington; and the story was picked up by all the wire services, with the following lead paragraph: "Air force and police helicopters hovered protectively in the sky when a biplane flew toward the Capitol, where President Nixon was sworn in."

Our stunt was also covered in the overseas military newspaper *Pacific Stars & Stripes*, headlined humorously as "Gold Writers In the Sky." The leading coin press also covered it thoroughly. We got a newspaper photograph of the grounded plane, and it was printed in several newspapers across the land. The publicity was certainly worth the $600 we spent.

Besides the gold bar demonstrations and the banner, we staged another kind of demonstration, called the "Gold Tea Party," in which we carried banners around in favor of legalizing gold and dumped some worthless paper money (like old Brazilian cruzados) into a river or an ocean, or even burned them in a small bonfire, depending on the location.

Political demonstrations were common all over America in the early 1970s—often to protest Watergate or the Vietnam War—so we did not look too much out of place except for the fact that we wore suits and ties. Back then, as today, the news media loved to cover such events. In most cases, they would take close-up photographs of me holding the gold bar. We would pass out literature at the press conference. It was pure media hype— "bread and circuses"—but it worked: It got the point across to the broad public.

At the time, the novelist Saul Bellow said of such public demonstrations, "Public virtue is a kind of ghost town into which anyone could move in and declare himself sheriff." I liked that Western analogy and began to think of myself as some modern-day Western hero riding into town, bringing the "monetary law of the land" to the paper money outlaws!

Almost Everybody Wanted Legal
Gold (Except the Fed)

In rallying people to our cause, we could appeal to different issues, depending on the person. Conservatives were interested in legalizing gold because they tended to understand the economic fundamentals of freedom. Liberals were concerned because it seemed to be an infringement of a person's civil rights— although they did not care about gold.

Before long we developed a coalition of conservatives, moderates and liberals. That was how we were able to sell the idea to Congress. Who can be against an idea when liberals, conservatives and moderates all favor it? The only concerted anti-gold lobby was in the Treasury and the Fed, in academia and among mainstream economists—but not in Congress or among the voting public at large.

The Treasury opposition was strong and powerful, however; and so by early 1973, the anti-gold crowd in Washington was beginning to ridicule us. The Treasury secretary at the time, George Shultz, derisively said of us, "The American people are more interested in the price of hamburgers than the price of gold."

Of course the American people were more interested in the price of meat than gold; but what he did not say was that the reason they were so interested in the price of hamburgers was that the prices of bread and meat were constantly going up, due to the debasement of the dollar in terms of gold.

Our forces were strengthening in early 1973. In February I wrote in *Gold Newsletter*: "Almost daily, NCLG hears of another congressman or senator who has either introduced his own bill legalizing the ownership of gold or has announced his backing for one of the many bills already submitted."

In that issue I listed the pro-gold leaders in the Senate. The Republicans were James McClure (Idaho), Peter Dominick (Colorado), Barry Goldwater (Arizona), Carl Curtis (Nebraska), and Ted Stevens (Alaska). The Democrat pro-gold Senators were led by Mike Mansfield (Montana), Alan Bible (Nevada), Alan Cranston (California), Frank Moss (Utah), and the prime mover, Jesse Helms (North Carolina). In the House, Phil Crane (R, Illinois) took the lead, along with Steve Symms (R, Idaho) and many others.

You can see from this partial list that it was a consortium of conservatives and liberals who were pro-gold. Despite this bipartisan support, the influence of the anti-gold lobby in the Treasury caused the first pro-gold bill to fall one vote short. On May 29, 1973, the House voted a dramatic tie, 162-162, on Congressman Phil Crane's gold legalization rider. Just one more vote for gold, and gold legalization could have arrived in 1973, about a year and a half earlier than it eventually did.

Many congressmen were supporting gold legalization for the wrong reasons. As I wrote in the February 1973 issue of *Gold Newsletter*, "Some liberals see gold legalization as a prerequisite in their plans to demonetize gold. Perhaps it's a useless exercise to point out to these gentlemen that in today's world, gold demonetization is not a matter of political control." As our fine friend and advisory board member Percy L. Greaves said in a letter to me then, "The demonetization of gold will be accomplished the same day King Canute stops the tides."

"This is not to say the government will not attempt the impossible," I continued in the February 1973 issue of *GN*. "It is a certainty the government will in the near future do a lot of talking about gold demonetization. Some of the talk will be publicized when the Congress debates the gold legalization issue. Be prepared for anti-gold propaganda and don't let it frighten you out of your long-term gold investments. If you know the facts, such propaganda can be rather amusing."

In the following issue I added, "Gold demonetization will remain an elusive dream of ivory tower economists, government money managers and inflationists of all persuasions....Ultimately, the market decides what is money."

In the early 1973 issues of *GN* we predicted $90 gold by the end of 1973 and $150 gold in 1974, and added Jim Dines' prediction that he "would not be shocked by $200 gold" by the end of 1974. (Sure enough, those prices were reached by year's end 1973 and 1974, even coming within a couple of dollars of $200.)

Despite the anti-gold frenzy in Washington, the trend toward legalized gold ownership was just warming up. I sensed that it now could not be stopped. In August 1973, Japan freed gold ownership for its citizens. There was a lot of buying there at first, but then gold sales slowed down. We used that as an example to show the politicians they had nothing to fear by legalizing gold (a little white lie?).

Then in January 1974 ownership of pre-1960 gold coins (numismatic coins) was legalized for Americans, but the post-1960 gold coins (Krugerrands, for example) were still illegal. The barriers were slowly being broken down before our eyes.

In the February 20, 1974, edition of *Business Week*, I was quoted at length about the effects of gold ownership, saying it "will definitely come in 1974." (Gold made it, without a day to spare, on December 31, 1974.) The price of gold at the time of legalization, I predicted, would be "at least $180 to $200 an ounce." (It peaked at $197.50.)

Gold Ownership Finally Legalized

On May 31, 1974, the Senate voted to allow gold ownership. So it was only a matter of time before the House gave in and the president signed gold ownership into law. But President Nixon and Congress had bigger things on their minds that summer as the last stages of the Watergate scandal were finally played out and Nixon resigned August 9.

In the middle of all that turmoil, I was interviewed by a number of newspapers and magazines about the gold legalization question. In July our local paper, the *New Orleans Times-Picayune*, interviewed me at length. I was accurately quoted in a feature article as saying, "The worst time to buy gold bullion will be right after it's legalized, because of all the publicity."

That same month (July 1974) I was asked by the finance editors at McGraw-Hill to give a speech at their Business Week conference on gold legalization in America. The speech was reviewed the next day on the front page of the July 26 edition of the national *Journal of Commerce*.

The text of my speech follows...

The Impact of Gold Legalization

When I first became seriously interested in economics, I read a small book by the great dean of free market economics, Ludwig von Mises. Entitled *Planned Chaos*, the book explained that government intervention in the economy—well-intentioned or not—will ultimately lead to complete economic disaster. By far the most dangerous power the government has is the power to create and control the money supply.

As von Mises so aptly phrased it, "Government is the only agency that can take a useful commodity like paper, slap some ink on it, and make it totally worthless."

Some years ago, Dr. von Mises told a story about the Austrian hyperinflation of the 1920s. He had already written his classic *Theory of Money and Credit*, so he was called upon by the Austrian government officials to give them his remedy for the ever-worsening Austrian inflation. He agreed to meet with the gentlemen under one condition—that they meet him at midnight on a certain street corner in Vienna.

They were baffled by his request, but they were desperate, so they agreed. At the appointed time and place, the government officials met von Mises. It was quiet in most parts of Vienna; but where they met, a constant din of machinery threatened to overwhelm their conversation.

The officials, still quite baffled, asked him, "Well, Professor, what can we do to solve our economic problems?" Von Mises simply pointed to the building and said, "First and foremost, you must stop that noise." The building was the government printing plant. The sound they heard was the printing of currency 24 hours a day.

Alas, the Austrian government did not take his advice. Inflation continued, laying the groundwork for Adolf Hitler to seize on this popular issue of inflation and ride its coattails to the first wave of National Socialism (Nazi) violence, in the so-called Munich Beer Hall Putsch of 1923.

Watch What the Government Says —Then Do the Opposite

I believe it is a good investment rule—whether or not you are an advocate of monetary gold—to watch government statements about the economy and then do the exact opposite of what their statements imply. Three years ago, Undersecretary of state Paul Volcker said there was no chance gold would be legalized. I was told by a U.S. congressman not to waste any time on something that was so politically impossible, so I promptly did the exact opposite. I started the National Committee to Legalize Gold.

Now I am happy to say that we Americans will soon be allowed to own gold and the undersecretary of State went under. I wish Mr. Volcker a long and happy life in the private sector! Even though Volcker—the head gold-hater of the United States—is gone, I am afraid it is an empty victory for those of us who favor a monetary role for gold. The Treasury is still firmly in the hands of the anti-gold forces. The philosophy of the U.S. monetary bureaucracy is still one of planned inflation. That is the main reason a private gold market is of such fundamental importance to the

American economy and to the American people.

Planned inflation, regardless of government statements to the contrary, will ultimately lead to economic chaos; and those Americans wise enough to place their trust in gold will own the money on which this country will ultimately be rebuilt. As the editor in chief of the London *Times*, William Rees-Mogg, put it in a recent editorial, "When the paper system collapses, the survivors will dig in the rubble and they will find gold."

We already have a modern example of the private gold standard at work. For the entirety of the 20th century, France has suffered through many devaluations of the franc, along with two wars and two postwar inflations, on top of their seemingly endless currency mismanagement.

This string of problems could easily have led France into a chronic inflation problem, like a Third World nation; but the French people have always been, and still are, the largest private owners of gold coins and bullion of any Western nation. They have learned to protect themselves from inflation and devaluation by placing a large degree of their savings in gold. No matter what happens to the nation of France, the middle class will survive as long as they have the liberty to trade and own gold.

Short-Term Effects of Gold Legalization

Now let me move on to my short-term predictions for a free gold market in America:

First of all, those who maintain that a free gold market will have only a minor effect on the economy of the United States are absolutely right, but for the wrong reasons. If we are talking about the short term as being from three to six months, I predict that gold will go down, initially. Why?

There will be a period of gold buying by those who really don't understand the long-term importance of the yellow metal. There will be a few weeks of national and international major media publicity. This publicity will cause "fad buying," not smart, long-term accumulation.

The first sign of weakness in the gold market will scare the newcomers (especially those who are using the futures market instead of physical possession of the metal). They will sell their gold, causing further weakness.

For a few weeks, U.S. commodity traders— who may know a lot about wheat or soybeans, but who are no match for seasoned international bullion dealers and buyers—will probably convince their clients to heavily sell short. This will cause a correction, perhaps to levels not seen since before Americans could own gold.

I can just see the headlines in the U.S. press (written via the U.S. Treasury's point of view): "Gold Loses Luster"—"U.S. Speculators Hurt By Heavy Gold Sales," etc.

At some point after the first correction in U.S. gold futures, the real professionals—international gold investors and those few Americans who understand the long-term picture for gold—will become heavy buyers in U.S. gold futures and catch the U.S. commodity dealers and their clients short, and there should be a sizable bullish move in gold.

Will the U.S. Treasury sell gold in an attempt to dampen its price rise? If they do, it will only be for the short-term effect, a public relations smoke screen, designed to make gold appear weak and the U.S. dollar strong; but there will be no large U.S. sales from United States official gold reserves. If the U.S. were willing to trade gold for fiat currencies, why did Nixon stop gold convertibility of the dollar?

Why does the U.S. Treasury steadfastly refuse to make the U.S. dollar convertible into gold, even at a price close to the free market? The answer is that they know that if the U.S. dollar were declared convertible at the free market price, the gold would soon disappear, and the only real U.S. monetary asset would soon be lost, in a futile gesture.

So don't be afraid of the empty threat that the United States will sell all the official gold. They will not!

Long-Term Effects of Gold Legalization

There will be a whole new demand factor of 200 million Americans in the gold market. If only one out of every 10 Americans buys just one ounce of gold per year, this would amount to half the free market's annual gold production. I am not saying that one in 10 will buy gold, but it is an example of the high potential of a free American gold market.

A member of the Chicago Board of Trade told me he thought that after six months there would need to be about 100 metric tons in the commodity warehouses to meet delivery demands. That conservative figure equals 8 percent of the annual free-world gold production.

I feel that Americans may well take delivery on a lot more gold than exchange officials expect. As all of us here know, the seasoned hard-money investors tend to be long-term holders, not traders. In fact, there are some gold "nuts" in this audience—including me—who bought U.S. Double Eagles at $45 each, BU silver dollars at $1.40 each and Durban Deep at $2 per share; and we have no intention of selling them, even after making three, four and five times our money back.

Another very important source of new demand will be the private mints. Already there are at least 25 private mints in the United States. They produce commemorative coins, medals and small collector ingots. It is commonly known that private mints have become an important factor in the silver market. It is estimated by the U.S. Silver Users Association that such private mintage used 11.5 million ounces of silver in 1972 and 23 million ounces in 1973.

Using a conservative figure of 35 million ounces for 1975 and taking the historic price ratio of 35-to-1 between gold and silver, one can estimate that private mints in the United States will consume one million troy ounces of gold next year, when it becomes legal. Even if we cut this figure in half, we still have an explosive new demand factor. This gold will not return to the melting pot, because of the high premiums over bullion value and the collector interest in these new designs.

The last, and most promising, source of new U.S. demand is the outright purchase of small bullion bars of between one-fourth ounce and 10 ounces. Internationally, this has been the predominant way to save gold. When Japan legalized gold in 1973, these small bars were responsible for most of the new demand; and they continue to be an important factor in Japan's gold market. I have seen estimates ranging from 20 to 40 metric tons of annual Japanese demand for small bars. I would think Americans could at least match that figure.

These four sources of U.S. gold demand will certainly have a long-term positive effect on the world gold price. I don't see how the addition of 200 million Americans—with one of the highest per capita incomes in the world—can do anything but put upward pressure on world gold markets. More importantly, Americans now will be able to choose between a continually depreciating fiat dollar and the world's oldest and safest form of money—gold.

For the first time since 1933, Americans will have regained one of the most important liberties—to choose to depend on the wisdom and honesty of politicians, or to trust the only money not subject to arbitrary devaluation by politicians. It has been said many times that gold is for people who do not trust their governments. After Watergate and continuing inflation, I think Americans in surprising numbers will vote for gold.

That ended my Business Week speech of July 25, 1974. Just 20 days later—and five days after Nixon resigned—President Gerald Ford signed gold ownership into law on August 14, 1974. It was one of his first and best moves as president.

Gold reached a cyclical peak the day before it was legalized; and a long, dull period for gold began on the very day it was legalized.

Chapter 5

Gold vs. the Treasury
G-Day Arrives—And the
U.S. Treasury Fights Back

"If the American people ever allow private banks to control the issue of their currency, the banks and the corporations that will grow up around them will deprive the people of all their property, first by inflation and then by deflation, until their children wake up homeless on the continent their fathers conquered."

—Thomas Jefferson

When President Gerald Ford signed gold ownership into law on August 14, 1974, inflation rates were announced that same week as reaching 44 percent (annualized rate) on the Wholesale Price Index for the month of July 1974. The nation was rapidly approaching the verge of a runaway, triple-digit, Latin American style of inflation as the inevitable result of going off the gold standard and raising the money supply while instituting wage and price controls. On top of that, OPEC oil price increases made the inflation uncontrollable.

The widespread sense of the failure of U.S. leadership during and after Watergate made the problem seem worse. How well I remember that soon after gaining office, President Ford circulated his little "WIN" buttons (standing for "Whip Inflation Now"). Despite those cute little buttons, you cannot stop inflation with a cute slogan any more than you can stop drug traffic with "Just Say NO" buttons.

As a case in point, while millions of people wore WIN buttons, the Fed was stepping on the gas and fueling even more inflation. After more than 60 years as the central bank for the world's most powerful nation, the Fed still could not figure out how to manage our money responsibly.

Naturally, all this was good for the price of gold.

The Only Gold Profits
Were in the Black Market

At the time gold was legalized, my good friend Charles Stahl (who died in the mid-1980s) hit the nail on the head when he said, "Most Americans who want to buy gold have already bought it, illegally." That was a tragic commentary on the stupidity of the gold ban, but it was true.

When the American government took our gold away back in 1933, it was priced at $20.67 an ounce; and when they finished taking all the gold, they priced it up at $35. Over 40 years later, gold peaked at $197.50 the day before legalization. What a cruel hoax! Gold's biggest percentage gain (855 percent) only benefited the government and foreign investors. Any American who wanted to make money on gold from 1933 to 1974 was forced into being a criminal.

Months before gold legalization took effect, gold fever was already raging, due to the black market for Krugerrand gold coins. The premium for Krugerrands was growing—from 8 percent to 10 percent to 12 percent—because the demand was so high the government of South Africa could not mint them fast enough. Obviously, some people were buying gold illegally before December 31, 1974.

In the fall of 1974, I could see the handwriting on the wall in the Treasury. They were going to crucify American gold owners again by pummeling down the price of gold once it became legal to own it. I went on record in the November 1974 *Gold Newsletter* as saying, "It is my feeling that gold will attempt the $200 mark before this year is out but will not accomplish that lofty level."

In the last *Gold Newsletter* issue of 1974 I predicted, "In the short term (first quarter 1975), we may well see some weakness in gold as heavy profit-taking develops by long-term gold holders who will be perfectly willing to unload a portion of their holdings to American newcomers." True to form, gold fizzled out at $197.50 on December 30, but the market took a lot longer than the first quarter of 1975 to recover from the worldwide unloading of gold in early 1975.

All through the fall of 1974 the Treasury threatened to sell gold just as it was legalized—or to try to postpone the date of legal gold ownership. (The gold-haters were still in charge of the Treasury.) Between Christmas and New Year's, the government issued several warnings cautioning gold investors against getting involved with the "speculative" metal. (Does the government ever warn people against pork bellies or plywood or other commodities? No, just against gold.)

On G-Day—December 31, 1974—the Treasury Slaughtered the U.S. Public

The week gold was legalized turned into quite a circus of conflicting forces, broken promises, and bald deception by the U.S. Treasury. Here is my day-by-day rundown of events, based on my own marginal notes on the yellowed *Wall Street Journal* clippings I saved from the first week of 1975.

• On Monday, December 30, 1974, the gold price rose to a record high London a.m. setting of $197.50. (The p.m. setting was $195.25.) Gold did not reach those levels again for almost four years! It was so high that day because traders around the world pushed up the price of gold in order to sell to Americans on the opening bell on Tuesday. The U.S. Treasury also sold gold in order to discredit it in the public eye. It was all part of an anti-gold government campaign; the Treasury was afraid the mystique of gold would spell the end of their funny-money game.

• Tuesday, December 31, was the first day of legal gold trading in America. The price opened lower, at $189.50, then crept up to $190.50, and slid down to close at $182.50, down $15 in just 36 hours. The tone of anti-gold trading was set on the first day it was legal to buy gold. And a bloody series of trading nightmares awaited Americans during the next few days after the midweek holiday, New Year's Day, 1975.

• On Thursday, January 2, 1975, gold fell another $11.50, to $175 an ounce. The rout was on.

• On Friday, January 3, the U.S. Treasury announced that on Monday it would auction off 2 million ounces of gold from its hoard of 276 million ounces. This announcement depressed the price of gold even further. (They must have been chortling down at the Treasury as they stuck it to the average American investor.)

• On Monday, January 6—in addition to selling 2 million ounces of gold as promised—the Treasury also brought in 10 million ounces of gold from Europe to glut the market even further. Our Treasury—which is sworn to uphold the Constitution and to act in the best public interest—actually sold gold for as little as $153 an ounce in order to glut the market and give gold a black eye. I guess they figured "the public interest" meant keeping paper money strong.

As it turned out, the Dresdner Bank bought 402,800 ounces of the gold the Treasury sold on Monday at an average price of $166.34 per ounce. That was undoubtedly the shrewd work of my good friend Dr. Kurt Richebacher, who was director of the Dresdner Bank at the time.

• On Tuesday, January 7, gold settled in around $170 an ounce and closed at $169.50, so it looked like the government had done all the damage it could do at least for a while.

• On January 8 gold leaped $10.50 in London, back up to $180. At the time, I wrote, "The strong rise in gold is a slap in the face for the stupid U.S. government, which sold gold for as little as $153 on Monday, when two days later it would be worth $180. I predict that by 1978, gold will be $300 to $350....but only a very few people will have the guts to buy gold, gold shares, and strong currencies in the face of a bum press and a fanatic anti-gold government."

Bankers and Brokers
Also Anti-Gold

The private sector establishment was almost as anti-gold as the government. The week gold became legal, a Chase Manhattan banking executive warned that gold would be a "threat to the standard savings accounts of Middle America." (A professional politician could not have milked the votes any better than that.)

At the same time, the president of the National Association of Securities Dealers (NASD), Gordon S. Macklin, called for imminent SEC regulations to warn investors of the heavy markup in gold, saying that "the market price of gold purchased may have to rise as much as 25 percent to 35 percent for the investor to recapture his cost." He warned about the high cost of transfer charges, storage, insurance, assaying, reprocessing and resale. Of course he was all wet. The spread on gold bullion was just about 3 percent to 5 percent.

As a result of the legalization of gold and the widespread prejudice against it, *Gold Newsletter* started to evolve from a political-action flyer into an investment publication in early 1975. The reason was clear. The preponderance of financial information in America was anti-gold. We would provide an alternate voice.

Whether you looked at brokerage houses, government bureaus, Wall Street investment firms, or any other major financial firms, gold was serious competition. It was the enemy of their high commissions on stocks and their interest-rate spreads in savings accounts. *Gold Newsletter* gave the public a new way of looking at their investments.

We also decided to change the name of the NCLG to the National Committee for Monetary Reform (NCMR), with more of an investment angle rather than political action.

All through the early 1970s Jackie and I were still teaching school, but gold legalization happened during our year's sabbatical, 1974-1975. Things were getting so exciting, we decided to officially quit our teaching jobs and take a chance on this gold business. Exciting things were beginning to happen, and we had big plans for the future.

Little did we know that the first Dark Ages for gold prices were about to begin and that we would fall on some hard times before gold finally reached its old highs in 1978.

1975-1978—The Disappointing Dark Ages for Gold

People who talk about today's disappointing gold markets often look back to the "glorious 1970s" and especially the "late 1970s" as the Golden Age of great price rises. But it was not like that at all. I still believe that the most disappointing time for buying gold in the last 15 years was between 1975 and 1978. If you think about it, gold has gone up dramatically only twice in the last 15 years, for only a few months each time—from late

1979 to early 1980 and from late 1982 to early 1983. At all other times, gold showed very slow gains, precipitous drops, or a long, sideways motion.

Back in the so-called "golden era" of the late 1970s, it took three years and eight months for gold just to reach the level at which it traded in London the day BEFORE gold legalization took effect! The period of the late 1970s obviously was a time that separated the men from the boys. After living through the "golden age," I have found that the ups and downs of the 1980s have been much easier to understand and accept. In both decades, however, I was holding gold for the long term and advising others to do so. If I were holding gold only for the short term, I would not have stayed in business so long.

By February 1976 gold broke below $130, then to $120, then $110. Gold finally bottomed out at $102 in August 1976, but it never really took off very fast after that, nor did it reach $200 until more than two years after it bottomed. If there ever was a disappointing time for gold, it was 1976.

In a late 1976 *Gold Newsletter* article, Houston gold expert Doug Johnston showed our readers how gold had been purposefully pushed down to $102. His article, "The Great Gold Smash: IMF Gold Auctions and U.S. Dollar Imperialism," showed among other things that the Russians sold gold in the West in trade for our grain, and they were aided in this by many central banks in Europe, acting through the BIS and our very own Treasury (surprised?).

In conclusion Doug said, "Gold has taken about everything that can be thrown against it—broken promises, auctions, you name it—but now, gold is going to come into its own." By November 1976 *Gold Newsletter* was saying, "The August lows have all the earmarks of a major bottom." And indeed it did "come into its own"—to $850 within three and a half years.

As late as April 1977, I wrote in *Gold Newsletter*, "I have not felt better about gold since 1974, but I don't believe we shall see the old gold high ($197.50) surpassed until some time in the first quarter of 1978." In January 1978 I added, "A further 20 percent depreciation of the U.S. dollar against the major hard currencies would mean a gold price of $210 in 1978." In fact, it was the second half of 1978 when gold finally surpassed $200, then $210 and then slightly higher in early 1979, before gaining $500 in just about four months.

A big factor in gold's rise was the terrible leadership of the smiling peanut farmer from Georgia. Gold bottomed out at precisely the time he was nominated for president; and it began rising steadily throughout his term, accelerating to its peak when several embarrassing events happened to him in quick succession in late 1979—the 52 Americans taken hostage in Iran, then Russia invading Afghanistan, combined with 20 percent inflation and 20 percent interest rates, while he seemed hopeless at preventing any of those problems.

People who kept the faith in gold through those dark years of 1975 to 1978 eventually made five to 20 times their money in the following three or four years simply by investing in bullion and, particularly, in South African gold shares in the late 1970s and then holding them until 1980.

The simple key, as I have said before, is to identify the long-term, undeniable trend and then to keep the faith through the short-term corrections. These corrections will wash out most investors, particularly those who had not built the proper philosophical base before investing.

NCMR "Fights City Hall"

Despite our move in the direction of investing instead of so much political action, NCMR was still involved in lobbying for sound money policies at the national level. After gold was legalized, we corresponded several times with Secretary of the Treasury William E. Simon, imploring him to reduce the amount of Treasury gold being sold on the open market at ridiculously low prices.

His actions—intended to help "balance the budget"—were lowering the price of gold and defeating his own purpose as well as ours. I still have a copy of a letter our Washington attorneys wrote to Mr. Simon on June 27, 1975, regarding the proposed June 30 sale of gold. In the end, we did slow down the hemorrhage of Treasury gold, which has stayed level at 262 million ounces for several years now.

Let me give you a little background about Treasury gold. Before 1971 the Treasury sold gold for $35 per ounce, then at $42.22 after Nixon's devaluation of 1971. By the time of Mr. Simon's term as Treasury secretary (under Gerald Ford, 1974-1976), he was selling gold for as little as $100 after gold had traded on the free market at $197.50.

The point which I made to Secretary Simon in mid-1976, as gold approached the $100 level, going down, was that he was not only depressing the price of gold for all of us who had invested in it, but he was also needlessly and artificially lowering the value of the remaining huge hoard of Treasury gold reserves. Selling gold at $100 was like Jacob's brother Esau selling his half of the birthright for a bowl of soup.

I told him that I thought, in the future, when governments will be forced back to at least a partial gold standard, the wealthiest nations of the world will be those who own the most gold. Our nation will need our Treasury's gold as an emergency savings, as an alternative currency system when the dollar is finally destroyed. Our "family jewels"—in both a personal and a national sense—should not be sold for a pittance, but held as a core position until such time as gold returns to its historical role as a medium of exchange and a unit of account as well as a store of value.

NCMR co-sponsored a demonstration in front of the Treasury building on September 19, 1976, with placards reading, "Save the gold to save the dying dollar," "Without gold, a dollar is only a piece of paper," "Stop Treasury gold sales," "Money should be as good as gold," and "Gold back the greenback." Along with me, the demonstrators included newsletter editor James Dines. We were joined by U.S. Representative George Hanson (R-Idaho), who commented for the record: "Selling U.S. gold stocks is like bleeding a patient with pneumonia. Our gold reserves are still our most important monetary asset, and the Treasury Department is piddling it away."

Rep. Hanson made good political points by adding that "90 percent of the U.S. gold sold is going to foreign interests, and much of it to oil-rich Arabs. Gold has served in the past as a warning when government corrupts the money supply. The Treasury wants to break the thermometer that tells how bad the fever is." Larry Patterson, editor of the *Patterson Investment Newsletter*, then arranged to have pickets present at each monthly gold auction in the future. (They were held each third Tuesday of the month.)

These demonstrations went on month after month, year after year. In May 1978 I was again at the Treasury steps with more placards, "We demand honest inventory before any gold sales" and "Selling U.S. gold causes inflation." Joining us were several other pro-gold groups. While the news stories covered the Treasury auction, the pictures appearing in most newspapers were of me and the other picketers. I do not have all the clippings by any means, but I have those pictures which appeared in the *Miami Herald*, the *Dallas Morning News*, the *Cincinnati Enquirer*, the New Orleans *Times-Picayune* and more.

Whether or not all our efforts were part of the solution, the Treasury's gold hemorrhage stopped. Years later, when the American Gold Eagle was scheduled to use Treasury gold for the minting, I worked through the Industry Council for Tangible Assets (ICTA) and my own personal representatives in Washington, D.C., to stop this use of Treasury gold. I am proud to report that only a very small amount of Treasury gold was used in this new bullion coin effort. The bulk of it came from newly mined gold in America and from some of America's GATT (General Agreement on Tariffs and Trade) trading partners.

Discovering the Hidden
Secrets of Fort Knox

One of the other projects NCMR got involved with was to ask for an auditing of the Fort Knox gold. There was great resistance at first, but finally the Treasury listed the actual number of gold bars, their size and purity. Until then the Treasury had been claiming that we had 264 million ounces of gold in reserve, and that it was made up mostly of .995 to .999 pure bars. What we found was that it was almost entirely made up of melted gold coins from the 1930s, at .917 (22-karat) purity.

During the 1950s and 1960s, when America was selling a lot of gold to keep the dollar strong, we were selling all of our best .995 to .999 bars to the foreign nations who would not accept alloyed gold. That meant that most of what was left was the .917 alloy melted down after FDR's confiscation of 22-karat gold coins, like the Saint-Gaudens $20 gold pieces and the Liberty and Indian series.

Ed Durrell, an associate of ours at NCLG, was one of the first people to publicize this fact. After his death, the Durrell Foundation continued his work. The bottom line from his investigations was that we had a lot less pure gold than the government had previously reported. It reminded me of a quotation from Frederic Bastiat, that government "no longer holds a balance in its august hands, but false weights."

Durrell's research confirmed to us that a lot more gold coins were melted down for bars than most people assumed, making the surviving coins more valuable. This caused a premium to be tacked on to the common-date $20 gold pieces of the Liberty and Saint-Gaudens variety. A premium over the gold value exists because of the relative rarity of the old U.S. gold coins compared with bullion coins like the Krugerrand, Maple Leaf and U.S. Gold Eagle. I believe this premium will grow dramatically as we enter the 1990s. We will see a doubling and eventually a tripling of the premium over the gold content. In the meantime gold will head much higher. So interests in the old Liberty and Saint-Gaudens Double Eagles will enjoy a classic double play, thanks partly to Franklin Roosevelt's great gold meltdown.

Do I Support a Gold Standard?
Yes and No

Even though I often speak out strongly in favor of gold as an investment and a protection against government paper, I knew in the early years of NCMR—and I know it more so today—that a gold standard would be impractical, at least until people change their basic ideas about big government and debt. I believe my position represents the consensus of those who think seriously about the gold standard. Instituting it by fiat today would be catastrophic, but there are some practical and gradual steps we can take toward a gold standard.

Alan Greenspan, the chairman of the Federal Reserve, was also an early student of Ayn Rand and even wrote Rand's Objectivist platform on the gold standard. In fact I remember reading Greenspan's more radical work from the 1960s and noting that it almost perfectly paralleled my own thinking at the time. In one famous passage he wrote, "An almost hysterical antagonism toward the gold standard is one issue which unites statists of all persuasions. They seem to sense that gold and economic freedom are inseparable."

Although Greenspan argued in 1966 that gold was the only disciplined standard for preventing inflation, he also noted that it was too impractical to impose upon a nation that is not first committed to some reduction of overspending.

William Rees-Mogg, the former editor of the London *Times*, who became a close friend and confidant of mine in the 1970s, wrote a book called *The Reigning Error*, in which he says that although all the problems of our modern economy can be traced to the lack of a gold standard, it will not be used again until all other systems have been tried and have failed. In the last sentence of his book, he writes (and I paraphrase), "In the end, our descendants will dig through the rubble of Western civilization and discover gold." But before that happens—before all other systems have been exhausted—Lord Rees-Mogg argues, a return to the gold standard would be premature.

How do we get to a gold standard from here? I think that privately owned gold is the first major step back to the gold standard. When citizens own a sufficient hoard of gold coins, then we practically have an unofficial gold standard. People can trade paper for gold anytime they want. Before governments officially call their currency worth a certain weight of gold, however, the next step is to reduce the debt and to drastically reduce the size of the federal government.

Misconceptions About Gold Bugs

One of the reasons I used the term *Gold Bug* in the title of this book is that a lot of people put a negative twist on those words. I want to present the philosophical and positive side of the words. While some people in the press paint the gold bug movement as egotistical, greedy, one-track-minded, stubborn, dull, ideological, boring, etc., I have found that when you really take a careful look at the industry over the decades, this is a very interesting and caring group of people who have consistently been far ahead of the crowd.

For a long time I have had a theory that one of the reasons why the best newsletters are successful is their human quality: their chattiness, their candor, and their clear writing style.

Economics was considered the dullest of dull subjects in the 1960s, but it was our economic newsletter industry that changed all that. We have some exceptionally clear and knowledgeable writers in this industry—people like Mark Skousen, James McKeever, Richard Russell, Jack Pugsley, Richard Band, Douglas Casey, Howard Ruff, Vern Myers, Harry Schultz, Robert Prechter, Harry Browne, the Aden sisters, Jim Dines, Adrian Day and Richard Young.

I think those who have criticized the hard-money movement have not looked closely enough at their product. Taken as a whole, there may be a few egotists and cranks in our camp, but you can still get a far better economic education and investment advice from any one of several dozen hard-money newsletters than you can from the mainstream press or the institutional investment newsletters from Wall Street brokerage firms or stock market gurus.

While some of these hard-money newsletter editors might not make a good stock pick, gold call, or other recommendation more than once every six months, when you think about it, that often is enough. What you really get from these writers is their winning philosophy and the knowledge of what makes them see an opportunity. If they deliver education and entertainment along the way, two or three good picks a year is all you need.

Even the mistakes gold bugs make are not likely to have very serious consequences, because the independent thinkers who subscribe to our various newsletters are successful and profitable investors, who have enough independence to think for themselves. They are not the kind of people to just follow our advice blindly. I have found that if you do not back up your case well, the subscribers write you a letter and let you know where your logic did not hold water.

Even after a decade of flat gold prices trading between $300 and $500, the gold bug group is a powerful philosophical movement in America. Still, it is a small group. If you put all the subscription lists for all the hard-money newsletters together, it would probably total a number far smaller than the number of people who subscribe to just one of the major investment journals such as *Barron's*, *Business Week*, *Forbes*, or *Fortune* and very much smaller than the mailing list of the giant of the industry, *The Wall Street Journal*.

The alternative investment newsletters will always be fairly low in circulation, because only the contrarians win. If we got too large, I would be concerned. It is always more comfortable for me to invest while I am a lonely individual acting against the masses than when I am joining the newest bandwagon. I have always found it is more profitable to take a step back and look at the bigger picture through an examination of the fundamentals than to follow the latest fad.

The criticism that the hard-core gold bugs are never bearish simply is not true. In covering our 1980 conference, in fact, the leading Wall Street weekly, *Barron's*, headlined the event by saying, "Some Speakers See Softness in Silver & Gold." Among those speakers, several predicted lower-priced gold, including farsighted old eagles like Vern Myers, Jim Sinclair, Harry Browne and Harry Schultz, among others.

I remember Harry Browne speaking on a panel with me and saying, "For me, the bull market in gold ended in March...or February...or...." He shot me a glance and said, "When did the bull market end?" Actually it was January, but I said, "I don't think it ended yet." Yes, I readily admit that I still predicted $1,000 gold and $50 silver in late 1980, even after they had already peaked in 1980, and that was a mistake. As fate would have it, my predictions made worldwide headlines, as did the Aden sisters' a year later. Maybe members of the the press love the wildest high numbers they can find and ignore the more restrained, often more accurate, predictions.

Nevertheless, I can also learn from that mistake. I think that if we ever see another huge peak in gold, as we did in 1980, more of us will be careful to take some profits but also to keep a core position for the tough times that will continue afterward.

Now that I finally have reached 1980 in terms of the history of gold prices in the 1970s, I would like to backtrack to 1974 and the first NCLG conference. That way I hope to introduce you to some of these gold bugs in a more personal manner.

Chapter 6

A Gathering of Eagles

The Birth and Growth of the NCMR Conferences

"The gold standard was the world standard in the age of capitalism, increasing welfare, liberty, and democracy, both political and economic... everywhere destroying the fetters of age-old prejudices and superstitions, sowing the seeds of new life and new well-being, freeing minds and souls and creating riches unheard of before."

—Ludwig von Mises, *Human Action*

About a year before gold was legalized, I came up with the idea of holding a small, intimate conference of *Gold Newsletter* subscribers. The experience of attending Harry Schultz's Bermuda conference two years earlier made me yearn to meet the same quality of people here in the United States. Since we were still teaching school in New Orleans, I wanted to hold the meeting in my own hometown, to make preparations easier.

Now that gold was well on its way toward legalization, I wanted to give the people on our mailing list a chance to hear some of the top hard-money investment experts who wrote for us each month in *Gold Newsletter*. I felt these speakers could help our subscribers decide how best to invest in gold once it was legalized. On top of the gold legalization problem, there was also a sense of economic crisis in the air in October 1973. It all had started with the Yom Kippur war, which quickly resulted in the Arab oil embargo and increasing oil prices under the influence of the new oil cartel, OPEC. As a result of this oil crisis, inflation began rising toward double digits for the first time since the Civil War.

For this and other reasons, gold on the free market (outside the United States) began to soar in late 1973, just as we were promoting our first investment conference. In the many years since then, I have hoped for a good rise in the price of gold while my conference mailings are going out, because that more than anything else brings in a good response. I think that was one major reason for the success of our first conference.

By the time we met in New Orleans, gold was in the process of setting a new record at $130; and the 30-page cover story of the January 1974 issue of *National Geographic* was all about "GOLD!" As we gathered in New Orleans, we all had a sense of excitement about the years that lay ahead of us.

Every conference since then has had a sense of electricity as we enter the reception hall for the first night's festivities, but none more so than that first Friday night in 1974. People who had been harboring free market ideas for years, maybe decades, were finally able to join other like-minded people who shared their views.

Famous Faces in the First Conference

In that first conference we featured over a dozen speakers — such as Franz Pick, the grand old man of gold investing; John Hospers, a philosophy professor from USC, who ran for president on the first Libertarian Party ticket in 1972; central banker

John Exter and economist Hans F. Sennholz; investment advisers Tom Holt and Bill Tehan and many others.

As it happened, however, some of the most interesting people in that conference were in the audience, including the billionaire silver investor Bunker Hunt, son of Howard Hunt, and at least a dozen investment analysts who would later build national reputations. At the time of the conference, silver was approaching $6 per ounce; and one of my great early mentors, Vern Myers, was predicting silver prices of $10 and $20 per ounce—ironically because of Bunker Hunt's early attempts to corner the market. (It was six years later that this Hunt fiasco finally hit the front pages.)

Here is what I wrote February 11, 1974, in *Gold Newsletter* after the January conference: "Vern (Myers) sees the possibility of a silver corner in 1974 which would send prices to such fantastic levels as $10 to $20 per ounce. Even I find this hard to believe, but remember how we were all shocked at the explosion in the price of gold. Not so long ago, $50 gold seemed fantastic, and now $100 gold seems conservative and downright boring! In 1968 there were headlines all over the world when gold 'leaped' 10 cents to 20 cents per day. Now a movement of $2 or $3 per day barely draws a mention.

"Vern may turn out to be right about a silver corner in 1974. Bunker Hunt (who attended NCLG's 1974 monetary symposium) has been very active in the silver market. Mr. Hunt has taken delivery of 20 million ounces of silver and there is a strong rumor that he has an additional 27 million ounces in futures contracts." In February 1974, silver first topped $6 an ounce and averaged $6.05 for the last week of February. I still believe that first surge was a result of the first foray by the Hunt brothers toward cornering the silver market.

Besides Bunker Hunt, several future conference speakers, entrepreneurs and good friends of mine were there at our first conference in 1974, hiding out in the audience—people such as future mining share analyst Jerry Pogue (who was then executive vice president of a major publishing company and had not yet heard of a "penny stock"). Joe Bradley was also there; he now edits *Investor's Hotline* and has been one of my very best friends of the last 15 years. He tapes all the speeches and workshops at each NCMR conference.

The audience at the first conference, to the best of my recollection, also included such entrepreneurs as Larry Abraham (who also conducted a workshop on silver) and Gary North. Jim McKeever, editor of *The Inflation Survival Letter*, also was there. (That letter eventually became one of the biggest and finest newsletters in the hard-money movement, *Personal Finance*). Jim McKeever has long since started a new letter, the *McKeever Strategy Letter* which was ranked No. 1 by the *Hulbert Financial Digest* in three out of four years.

All these people were part of what I call "the core group," taken from my original 5,000 names. Because this little list of mine was so small, we prepared for a small, intimate conference of maybe 250 to 300 people; and even that seemed optimistic. We ended up with 750 people, which meant we had to frantically change hotels and banquet halls at the last minute. Even then, we could not fit everyone in the same room at the same time and had to use closed-circuit video monitors in various adjoining rooms.

Imagine getting 750 responses for a $300 price tag, from a mailing list of only 5,000 today. On top of the $300 fee, each person also had to spend several hundreds of dollars on air fare and lodging. That shows how dedicated our small core group of people was back then.

Partly because I was still teaching, the first NCLG conference began on a Friday night, January 18, 1974, and ended Sunday at noon. We met at the beautiful Fairmont Hotel (formerly the Roosevelt Hotel) off Canal Street in downtown New Orleans. We conducted the entire seminar over the weekend so that the people who had full-time jobs would not need to take any time off from work to attend the conference. In fact, we delayed the start until 9 p.m. Friday so that everybody could catch an afternoon plane and still make it to New Orleans in time to hear all the speeches.

Since we were all so excited about these new and thrilling economic issues we were learning about, we talked late into Friday night and then started again early Saturday morning for a full 12-hour day. The speakers made their main presentations during the all-day session, and on Saturday evening we had a big banquet.

The program was capped by special workshops Sunday morning from 9 a.m. to noon, when we adjourned. We called this first conference "Investing Toward Freedom," and we covered the gamut of the investment prospects for building personal prosperity in America in an era of legalized gold.

The press was enamored of us gold bugs in New Orleans. We were covered by The Associated Press, the *Washington Post*, the *Journal of Commerce*, the New Orleans papers and several more publications, even though we had not really courted the press and did not send out any press releases.

How We Weathered the Gold
Collapse of 1975 and 1976

We have already covered the dismal gold markets of the late 1970s. In that context, I think our people weathered the problems in gold very well. Most of the people who attended our early conferences were pretty sophisticated investors. They already had bought gold in the form of gold mining shares or coins, plus a lot of silver. Some of them also had bought illegal gold Krugerrands or bars, as I had done.

The big topic for discussion in 1974 was how high gold would go once it was legalized. One of the benefits of getting everyone together and sharing ideas was that we finally came around to a pretty accurate way of looking at the prospects for gold after its legalization. By the end of the 1974 conference, there was a pretty widespread consensus that gold would probably go up to $200 around the time of legalization, then plummet back toward $150 once gold was legalized.

Because of this consensus, our people were well prepared for the bear market in advance; and some of them were able to still be in a profitable position when gold eventually fell to $103 per ounce, because they had bought some gold illegally. Whether or not they broke the law, our people were so well schooled in their basics that they realized gold at $100 in 1976 was the best buying opportunity of their lifetime; and most of them took full advantage of it.

After the legalization of gold at year-end 1974, the Second Annual NCLG Conference—held March 13-16, 1975, in New Orleans—became the first annual meeting of the National Committee for Monetary Reform (NCMR). About 1,000 people attended, a new record. At that second conference, we were all very excited by the implications of legalized gold.

Among our 26 speakers in 1975 were Julian G.A. Baring, Anthony S. Boeckh, Nicholas Deak, John Exter, Donald Hoppe, Dr. Gary North, Dr. Alexander Paris, Lord William Rees-Mogg, Harry Schultz, James Sinclair, Jerome Smith and Julian Snyder. Gold was still over $150 at the time, so we were fairly hopeful this price would prove to be the post-legalization bottom. Alas, we were wrong.

By the time of our third conference, the first to be held in the second half of the year (September 16-19, 1976), we were suffering through a very bleak time for the metals. Because of the drop to $102.20 gold on August 30, 1976, our NCMR conference attendance went down to 700 people (our lowest ever). Nevertheless, most of our 34 speakers and 700 attendees were hardcore gold bugs, and they still saw $120 gold as a great buying opportunity.

Economic Insights—A Decade
Ahead of the Financial Press

New speakers at the 1976 conference included Dr. Antony Sutton, Timothy Green, Dr. Art Laffer, Harry Schultz, Dr. James McKeever (now graduating from audience to speaker's platform), Alexander Paris, Dr. Murray Rothbard, Jim Sinclair, Montague Guild and the noted French Finance Minister Jacques Rueff, who had stopped French inflation in its tracks back in 1958 by instituting gold backing for the French franc under Charles de Gaulle's new regime.

Along with our old favorites, these gentlemen were the cream of the world crop of economic and financial thinkers. Because of the growing quality of our speakers, the NCMR conferences of the 1970s had been far ahead of the financial press and the investment crowd. Some of the fairly "new" crises that you see in today's magazines and investment television programs—such as the savings and loan crisis, bank failures, inflationary recessions (stagflation), the Fed's money monopoly, penny stocks, money market funds and more—were often introduced in the 1970s at our NCMR conferences.

As early as 1974, for instance, I spoke on "the harsh beginnings of economic stagnation and raging inflation." Later on, that phenomenon was called *stagflation*. In September 1976, a panel on "Inflation vs. Deflation: Possible Effects on Precious Metals" included predictions of several events that did not dominate the news until years later. The panel predicted new limits on the amount of cash you can take abroad, explosive effects of new loans to developing countries, more monetary inflation and credit expansion, and the sale of IMF gold (which happened in 1978).

At one point, former Federal Reserve official John Exter said, "We're going to have some major defaults, and there's nothing the Fed can do to prevent it." Back in the 1970s you simply could not find these kinds of insights in the mainstream financial press. Only a handful of newsletters and conferences were talking about these problems, which have become commonplace in the 1980s.

Among our first-time speakers in November 1977 were Nobel laureate F.A. Hayek; Colonel E.C. Harwood, and my old idol, the 1964 presidential candidate Senator Barry Goldwater, who thrilled us all with his hard-core backing for the gold standard. He probably put the case for gold more powerfully than any other presidential nominee of this century.

I will profile some of these special speakers in the next chapter, but now I want to show you how our conferences evolved during and after the dramatic gold price spike of 1979-1980.

Anticipating the Dramatic Gold and Silver Spike of 1979-1980

When we met for our fifth New Orleans conference November 2-5, 1978, gold had just set a new record above $200 per ounce; and our conference drew a record 2,500 people from all 50 states and 26 foreign countries. At long last, we had arrived at a level of attendance which, on average, we have been able to maintain ever since. Among our speakers were some of the establishment elite, including Alan Greenspan, now chairman of the Federal Reserve.

In a dramatic speech that year, Colonel E.C. Harwood (one of the original gold bugs), predicted, "Gold will double in purchasing power [in just a few years and] the 1978 price of $200 will be the bargain of the decade in the long term." How true. Gold never came close to $200 again, and probably never will.

For my own part, I delivered a speech titled "You Will Be Tested," which was based on my years of anticipating higher prices in gold, only to be disappointed time and time again. In that speech and in the December 1978 *Gold Newsletter*, I still had the moxie to predict that gold would reach "$800 by 1982." Such a high figure was pretty much laughed at, even in 1978, since gold was then only slightly over $200; but gold hit $850 within just 13 months, earlier and higher than even I expected.

Our conferences were in full flower by 1979, with a Hong Kong conference on April 26-28, followed by a very successful Acapulco conference June 28-July 1 and our regular annual New Orleans conference in the fall. On April 2, 1979, Citibank began offering gold certificates for sale to the general public. It was like seeing a white flag go up on Wall Street. Gold was now "acceptable" to the nation's biggest banks. Gold was rising strongly throughout 1979, and every prediction we had made for 10 years was coming true.

My Contrarian View of the
Reagan Years

In our November 1980 New Orleans conference, we reached our peak attendance—4,732 attendees. Reagan had just been elected president; and our mostly conservative audience finally felt vindicated by the messages they had heard from us throughout the 1970s: Gold had hit $850, we had 18 percent inflation and a 20 percent prime rate, and the dollar had sunk to record lows. That was the bad news, but the good news was that gold had soared on that news and Reagan had been voted into office to solve those problems and make a better world for our children. However, I was concerned about the likelihood that his solutions would open up new problems that would be based on debt.

In my keynote address to the 1980 conference, I predicted that Ronald Reagan would go down in history as our nation's biggest debtor and biggest spender and that ultimately he would be an ineffective champion of smaller government. Talk about belching in church, I had really done it this time. The audience was silent at first, then skeptical. After my speech, a lot of people told me I was all wet. They were respectful enough not to demand their money back, but I got the distinct feeling I was going a little too far with my contrarian theories on this subject.

My prediction was so shocking, even to the reporters, that it made the biggest headlines, nationwide, of any of our speeches at that convention or any since then. However, it proved to be true. Our national debt tripled during Reagan's eight years in office. The deficit was $900 billion when he was elected, and today it has tripled to $2.8 trillion.

I also was convinced that since the major brokerage firms were finally introducing gold to their product lines, we had better start to change our focus to include other new investment opportunities. It was not that my investment focus changed, but the markets had caught up with us. We had talked mostly about gold in the 1970s—partly because it was the most undervalued investment then; but when gold had traded at around $660 (in our 1980 conference), other investments seemed to make more sense for the short term.

So starting in 1980, we turned our attention more toward other, more undervalued investments. Still, because I tend to be a maverick, they were investments which were considered a little too far out for the traditional investor or broker—things like commodities, collectibles, strategic minerals, mining stocks, undervalued land, foreign currencies, rare coins, stamps, gem-stones, and other slightly off-beat investments.

Why Isn't the Top Investment Conference Part of a Wall Street Brokerage Firm?

Why were we so far ahead of our time? I have often wondered why the world's largest annual gathering of investors was started by a schoolteacher from New Orleans rather than one of the mega-billion-dollar, traditional brokerage houses on Wall Street.

I believe that the answer to that question is that Wall Street in the 1970s had a very limited outlook and a limited number of investments—primarily just stocks and bonds. Wall Street had a prejudice against gold, and so our support of "forbidden fruit" carried some special appeal to investors who were tired of the long bear market in stocks that lasted from 1967 to 1982.

It is no secret that there would be no demand at all for an alternative investment conference if the nation had no inflation and no debt, or did have a gold standard. We thrive on chaos; and the more economic unrest we see in the nation, the more attendees we will have. When gold is high, our conference attendance is high. Press coverage is also high when our attendance is high. At the 1980's conference, when we had over 4,700 in attendance, we had literally dozens of reports in the press, including long articles in intellectual journals like *The Atlantic*, *Barron's*, *Harper's*, and *Reason*.

One of the mainstream money managers who visited our early conferences explained it far better than I could. André Sharon, then vice president in charge of international research for Drexel Burnham Lambert in New York, visited our 1978 conference and wrote a startling research abstract for his own company to send to thousands of their institutional clients, employees, and worldwide offices. I feel André's essay captures far more eloquently the spirit of what we offered to investors than anything I could write. Here is an excerpt:

> "I attended the Fifth Annual Conference of the National Committee for Monetary Reform in New Orleans, November 2-5. NCMR is by far the leading 'hard money' coalition, and its conventions represent the largest gathering of gold advocates in the country. Here are my impressions and conclusions:
>
> "To the investment establishment (both buy and sell sides) accustomed to thinking in terms

of traditional analysis, the views and approaches encompassed by speakers and attendees alike appear little short of sacrilegious. Virtually every conventional assumption is challenged, and the disorienting trip through unfamiliar territory produces culture shock. It is like a confrontation with an alien tribe that does not automatically accept the conventional value system and, by daring to raise some rude and uncomfortable issues most investment managers refuse to discuss, forces some startling conclusions.

"Four days of meetings reveal no uniformity of views—quite the contrary. A number of speakers explained the inevitability of massive deflation, others the impossibility of avoiding hyperinflation. I heard why the stock market would soar and why it would collapse.... Indeed, about the only commonly held beliefs were the veneration of the same patron saints (von Mises, Hayek) and abhorrence of the same demons (Keynes, Samuelson). The credo was: Paper money is barbaric.

"The key to the entire conference was that each individual investor must assume personal responsibility for his or her decisions, and that the important ingredient was that they not go in over their head. The stress on the individual rather than the institutional investor, and the emphasis on real—repeat real—capital preservation were the overriding themes. I departed with a strong conviction that, however strongly one may disagree with this or that particular speaker, the overall concerns they addressed themselves to, and the emphasis on practical 'how to' approaches, were more than just proper and correct. Collectively, I believe they repre-

sented the only meaningful concern of investment strategy: the preservation of capital in real,
after-tax purchasing power....These questions
have nothing to do with esoteric macroeconom-
ics mumbo-jumbo and everything to do with the
price of muffins and the cost of sending kids to
school.

"2,400 concerned individual investors had
gathered to signal institutional money managers
that they would not passively tolerate the relentless expropriation, via taxation and inflation, of
the purchasing power of their savings...the attendees were years ahead of the rest of the
'sophisticated' community of investors in aware-
ness, and hence in their rejection of conventional approaches. They knew about the subter-
ranean economy at least a decade before ivory
tower financial analysts discovered the real world
and began to write about it. So now, in a belated
acknowledgement, far from being the lunatic
fringe gold bugs depicted by the media, they
were actually ahead of their time. The mountain
has come to Mohammed."

Eleven years ago, when André wrote these words, gold was
the laughingstock of lower Manhattan! As a foreign-born investment banker, he was one of the few who understood the yellow
metal; but his compatriots almost daily called gold investing
"The European Disease" and wished it would go away. Now, by
1990, the mountain of Wall Street has indeed come to the
Mohammed of gold, for every major brokerage house now has
a gold department and also trades in commodities, currencies,
and other alternative investments (including rare coins!) which
we were among the first to promote and explain.

Besides being advocates of gold, another thing that sets us
apart from a Wall Street kind of conference is our consistent and

coherent economic, political and investment philosophy. As Ayn Rand told our audience in 1981, successful investing emerges only from right thinking. The right philosophy leads to good long-term thinking, which will not let you go astray following every little short-term trend. That is why we add geopolitical speakers to our gumbo of investment advisers every year—placing investments within a context of free enterprise economic and political principles.

We also differ from Wall Street in our outlook toward the federal government. We are skeptical that Big Brother has our best interests at heart. We believe that nobody acts in his or her own best interest better than the person whose money is on the line. This is why we teach self-directed investing, through our conferences and publications. As André Sharon wrote so eloquently to his Drexel partners, each person is responsible for protecting and preserving his or her own wealth. The way to do that is to learn all you can from the best teachers—the kind we bring to New Orleans each fall.

Behind the Scenes at NCMR

In the first five years of sponsoring these conferences, Jackie and I ran almost everything by ourselves, from our home. From 1975 on, Bob Meier helped me plan the program; but I wrote the direct mail promotion myself, while Jackie supervised the mailing process and took care of the details of the accommodations, and so forth.

In 1979 I hired professional convention managers David Galland and Mat Kelemen, who organized the conference details for me. David brought in the idea of a big screen so that all the thousands of people in the hall could see the speaker's face in detail. David also designed the program, got to know all the speakers, and handled the marketing. Mat streamlined the exhibit area, luring some of the major brokerage firms to our conference so that we could move away from being strictly a gold bug program. David and Mat also streamlined the program to a "show business" pace.

What is the big deal about running a conference? For starters, a gala reception for 3,000 people at one conference involved ordering 3,000 pounds of shrimp—just to be on the safe side. People were piling their shrimp three or four inches deep and coming back for seconds, and we still had plenty left over. That is the New Orleans style, and we never want to compromise on either quality or quantity.

Backstage planning resembles the kind of energy you would see backstage at a Broadway revue. A couple of speakers will be rehearsing in the corner, getting "into costume," so to speak; a couple of others will be kibitzing with me or other old friends while my conference staff frantically tries to get them on stage in plenty of time.

Conferences Are Like Show Business

Early on, I discovered the convention business is a lot like shooting a movie. The stars are the speakers, not me or my staff. Many of our speakers are world-famous in many areas, and some of the investment advisers have well-developed egos. In a sense, we are putting on a "show" based on the drawing power of our top-name talent. If you look at it this way, you have to take the view that the stars are entitled to their little eccentricities; so you learn to take with a grain of salt some of the inevitable ego trips of your stars.

If you look upon a conference as a movie, then the staff's role is best done when it is invisible, except in the final credits. You do not see the faces of the film editors, assistant producers and camera grips on the screen, but you do see the influence of their work by the act of "not noticing" it. Likewise, people come to our conference not to see us, but to see the stars. Most speakers must be invited from eight to 12 months in advance in order to secure a place on their busy schedules. Then we have to lay out a balanced program, with a combination of what the speaker wants to say and what subject we asked the speaker to cover.

There are endless physical details, about 10,000 of them in all. Who will sit at the head table? When? How many microphones? How many props—projectors, blackboards, overhead slides, remote microphones? How many water pitchers are needed? How many people are likely to be in each of eight competing seminars? What will the signs say in front of each seminar, and how do we make sure any handicapped person will find his or her way wherever they wish to go?

Over 1,000 tables and 3,000 chairs are set up for each general session. Speakers often have handouts, sometimes only at the last minute, which must be passed out to each attendee. Speakers may come with a boxful of slides without telling us about it in advance. Others change their subject and talk about science fiction. Some sit in the audience until they are frantically paged by our staff. Others have a plane to catch 20 minutes after their speech is over, and we hire a VIP police motorcade to get them to the plane on time.

A few years ago, Harry Browne made this same point in his fine newsletter. "You may not be aware that many of the speakers at these seminars are as concerned about their images and billing as any Hollywood actor," he said. "One speaker stipulates in his contract that he be billed as the 'keynote speaker'—even if his speech comes at the end of the conference. Others make demands regarding the type size in which their name appears in the sales brochures."

Harry made my point better than I could by saying, "I'm surprised that we speakers haven't hired Hollywood agents to negotiate these things for us. And, in order to sort out all the conflicting demands, I'm surprised that the seminar promoters haven't used the Hollywood system of introducing the 'stars' of their productions. In fact, when I close my eyes, I can picture the credits rolling for the big spectacle...

"James U. Blanchard III

in association with
the Rivergate Conference Center
presents
A David Galland extravaganza

NEW ORLEANS '82

Starring (in alphabetical order)..."

Then follow the names—dozens of them. A typical New Orleans conference has over 70 speakers. If I invited only those speakers with whom we have never had a minor conflict over the amenities or fees or some business venture or the other, I doubt we would sign up even 10 of those 70 speakers. One of the big secrets of our success is that we let the stars be stars.

Although some of the speakers have gone so far as to publicly criticize me or my coin business at the conference or elsewhere, I am willing to overlook that and invite them back. They are the stars. They are entitled to have it their way on stage and backstage; for without their names, we would not have a conference.

Predictions of the 1980s—
Right on the Money

By 1981 gold was back down to around $430 during our fall conference, but the consensus among our speakers was that gold would go much further down before it hit a bottom of around $300 in the spring of 1982. For instance, Jim Sinclair foresaw "$280 to $320 gold by March." The Aden sisters said "$300 to $320 by June," which was right on the money. Here were the leading gold bugs and they were predicting much lower gold. (It is not true that we are always bullish on gold!)

Gold was no longer our main focus in the 1980s. By then we

had as a regular feature a series of "Wall $treet Week" panels, hosted by Louis Rukeyser, which probed the minds of several stock market experts. In 1981, for instance, the three stock market analysts on Lou's panel picked a 1982 low in the Dow Jones industrial average of 700, 750 and 840, for an average of 763, just 2 percent off the exact bottom figure, 777.

The following year, they did just as well. The Dow had taken off from 777 in August but stalled out at 1000 at the time of our conference. One thousand was the traditional "barrier" for the Dow, left over from several past bull markets. The unanimous prediction of the Rukeyser panel in 1982 was that this bull market was a special bull, and that it would keep going up. All of them picked highs of from 1200 to 1500 the next year—all-time records—and sure enough, the market hit record ground in the middle of that range of numbers.

Specifically, one panelist, Montague Guild, picked Chrysler as his best stock. It was unpopular due to the federal bailout of the firm, and so it had dropped down to $3 a share earlier in the year. It was $8.50 when he recommended it. By all traditional standards, it was too late to take profits; but in the next year, Chrysler moved up to over $30—a tenfold increase overall. Even at the late entry point of $8.50, a $10,000 investment mush-roomed to $35,294 in a year. Several other top picks from panelists doubled in value that year, though the market rose by much less.

Precious Metals Profits of 1982-1983

In our conference of late 1982, Peter Cavelti made a good case for a little-known metal (at the time) called palladium. It was trading at $65 an ounce as he spoke. Within two or three months, this virtually unknown metal had nearly tripled in price, to $185! As a result of this single tip, one Texas oil man told me he made $480,000 in the palladium futures market in four months after hearing Peter.

Other investors have made equally good killings based on information picked up in New Orleans. A California business-man, for instance, told me he saved $2.3 million in taxes with a strategy he learned here in 1982. An Australian has made the long trek to New Orleans for many years because he always gets at least two gems that more than pay for the high cost of his trip.

Our predictions have never been limited to just gold or the stock market. In fact, they have never been limited to just investing. In 1987 climatologist Dr. Iben Browning predicted a drought in the grain states in 1988, which would in turn provide a great investment opportunity in leveraging the grain commodi-ties complex. Obviously, that prediction came to pass in 1988, with corn and soybean prices shooting to the sky when the rains failed to come. In 1989 Dr. Browning once again hit the mark when he predicted that a major earthquake would shake North America on or around October 18, 1989.

Conclusion—Why a
Gathering of Eagles?

A gathering of eagles is important not only for the profits they can bring to our attendees, but for promoting the future of freedom in our times and beyond. In retrospect, an annual gath-ering of eagles was one of my best ideas ever. Not only are these conferences financially profitable for the company—we have never lost money on a conference yet—but they offer a long list of other important benefits.

Once a year the world's best advocates of individual liberty and free markets gather to help spread the word about freedom, the underlying fact that makes their wealth possible. Investors from all over the world are not only learning how to protect their savings and make big profits, but even more importantly, they are learning that freedom is their most important asset, and it must be treasured. Without it, they will become the richest men in a concentration camp.

I believe that many of the geopolitical, philosophic and economic speeches at these conferences have had a fundamental and important impact on economic and public policy issues in the 1980s and that they will continue to have this impact in the years to come. The annual New Orleans conference is a way for me to meet great minds that have shaped my life. In the process of making money, we also make new friends and build business associations with old friends.

Most of all, I am proud of the New Orleans conference for helping to spread the idea of freedom. That is why I have reserved a whole chapter for the conference appearances of just a few of my favorite advocates of freedom, headed by Ayn Rand in 1981.

Book II

Ideas Have Consequences

Chapter 7

The NCMR Hall of Fame—
Headed by Ayn Rand

Great Minds and Great Speakers
Who Have Graced Our Conferences

"Ideas have consequences."

—Ayn Rand

Some of the greatest minds in economics and philosophy have spoken at our conferences, including presidents and princes, Nobel Prize winners and great authors, making for a wide variety of the great and near-great celebrities and speakers of the last half of the 20th century.

For instance, we have had President Gerald Ford speak at our conference, as well as presidential candidates like Barry Goldwater, Pat Robertson and Jack Kemp. We have had princes too, such as Prince Gatsha Buthelezi, leader of the Zulu nation of South Africa. We have featured some of the more outspoken political commentators of our time, such as Jeane Kirkpatrick, James Watt, Arnaud de Borchgrave, G. Gordon Liddy, J. Peter Grace, John Kenneth Galbraith, Alan Greenspan and William F. Buckley, Jr.

Our guests have included best-selling authors Robert Ringer, Douglas Casey and Harry Browne; former Soviet Ambassador to the United Nations Arkady Shevchenko; and Karl Hess, Barry Goldwater's favorite speech writer and a man who had a great influence on me in the late 1960s, helping me get away from strict Randian Objectivism and more into the political and economic radicalism of our Founding Fathers.

Of course, we have made virtually all of the top investment advisers and top free market economists the center of our program. Louis Rukeyser has spoken at every NCMR Investment Conference from 1978 to 1988, with three 40-minute investment panels based on the *Wall $treet Week* format.

There are very few people I wish could have spoken for us but did not. Some of them are currently in political office and so are not able to come to speak for us—people like Margaret Thatcher, who has turned Britain around with her drive toward privatization and away from socialism. My favorite living ex-presidents, Reagan and Nixon, are always too busy to come, although I still invite both of them every year.

In one sense I almost hate to mix politicians in the same chapter with Ayn Rand and Friedrich Hayek, because philosophy and economics seem to me to represent the highest level of understanding of the real world, while politics reflects the dark side of man's nature. But I realize that some of these few politicians I have invited to speak have truly helped the cause of freedom—especially for gold investors—despite their unfortunate choice of profession.

In the remainder of this chapter, though, I want to focus entirely on my own super-heroes: Ludwig von Mises, Ayn Rand, Milton Friedman, Barry Goldwater and Friedrich Hayek. I think each one of them will go down in history as among the most influential minds of the 20th century.

My Greatest Regret

I guess my greatest regret is that my most influential economic mentor, Ludwig von Mises, died in 1973, before I could get out my invitation to him to speak at our first conference in New Orleans. Even if he had still been alive at the age of 92, I am certain he would not have been able to come to speak at our conference; but I would dearly have loved to meet him personally or to invite him to speak, even if he had to refuse the offer.

I corresponded with Dr. von Mises several times between the mid-1960s and his death. It was not until after he died that I found out that I had some small effect on his life. Shortly before his death, von Mises attended a picnic with Percy Greaves, who noticed our NCLG bumper sticker saying "Stop Inflation—Demand Gold" on von Mises's car. It was one of our NCLG publicity stunts that year—a bumper sticker made to look like the infamous Nixon inaugural banner we had staged earlier in the year. It was printed in January of 1973 and von Mises died just a few months later, so it had to be some time that year that he had our sticker put on his car.

I knew von Mises had strong feelings on legalizing gold, and so I was proud that we could help him express those feelings on the bumper of his car, at least for a short time!

My Long Courtship With Ayn Rand
Finally Paid Off in 1981

The most influential person in my life was Ayn Rand; and the crowning achievement of my life was being able to lure her to New Orleans to speak for us, just three months before her death. By doing so, I know I was instrumental in adding a measure of joy to her final months.

Inviting Ayn Rand to speak at our conferences became a kind of annual ritual for me from 1973 on. On the surface it was frustrating, because she never answered a single one of my letters until 1981. But I took that as a challenge to write a better letter the following year. I used all of my best sales copy techniques when I wrote her that annual letter.

I tried to reach her in new ways each time—ways that would appeal to her ego, telling her that our people revered her and would give her the longest standing ovation she would ever receive. Another time, I told her that everyone in the audience would be society's super-achievers, the kind of people she wrote about in her novels. But none of these techniques worked.

As it turned out, I was literally talking to a brick wall all those years. I later learned that she got so much mail, and could not afford to hire a secretary to sort it out and answer all her fan mail, that she never even opened most of her correspondence. So that is why she never replied to my letters. Someone else mentioned that she got a good measure of hate mail, so naturally she would not wish to open such mail and subject herself to such abuse.

In the end, I found the way to get her to New Orleans, and none too soon. By 1981 I had a young son, Anthem Hayek Blanchard, who was barely one year old when I wrote Ayn Rand the letter that finally brought her to New Orleans. Before I talk about the letter, I think my son's name needs a little explanation. When Jackie and I were planning a family, Ayn Rand and Friedrich Hayek were the living people who most influenced our intellectual life, so Jackie selected the name Anthem Hayek for our son. At first I thought that was a little radical for a child's name. I thought children should not be saddled with an intellectual-sounding name. It could cause them some teasing in their peer group.

Jackie was adamant about the name, so I gave up arguing with her by using what I thought was a foolproof ploy. "Listen, Jackie, if you want to name the child Anthem Hayek, I'll sell you my 50 percent rights to the naming of the child for a bag of uncirculated Morgan silver dollars, or I'll pay you a bag of Morgan silver dollars to buy your 50 percent rights to naming the child. Whoever buys out the other person first, names the child." She agreed to that offer, and I forgot about the whole thing for a while. But she did not forget.

Jackie scrupulously saved her money, a dollar here and a dollar there, for a couple of years. She eventually saved up enough to buy a bag of silver dollars, which cost her about $3,000 to $4,000 during the years she accumulated them. (The same bag would go for about $40,000 to $50,000 today.) One day she dropped this bag of silver dollars on my desk and had already drawn up a contract for me to sign, agreeing that I would waive all rights and privileges of naming our child. Of course, I signed it. What else could I do? It was my idea to buy the rights to naming the child. So our new son, born in October 1979, was named Anthem Hayek Blanchard.

By the way, I really like the name Anthem by now, and Anthem has not had any serious teasing about his name either. More parents have started selecting unusual names for their children in recent years, so his name is not so unusual when compared with others.

The name Anthem is what opened the door for me to reach into Ayn Rand's reclusive life. I wrote her a two-page letter telling her that she had influenced our lives so much that we named our first child Anthem. I told her that she was the one person most responsible for putting my life together following my crippling automobile accident and that her books helped me develop the philosophy that empowered me to overcome any handicaps to gaining the success in business that I have reached since then.

Because I did not know how much longer Ayn Rand would live (she was 76 then), I decided to pull out all the stops in this 1981 letter. In the meantime, I had come in contact with a friend who told me about the problem of mail delivery and processing, and she said she would be able to hand deliver my letter to Ayn Rand. Knowing this, I put all of the benefits from all of my past letters into a tightly organized, single-spaced, two-page letter, along with the name Anthem going for me, and one more special new hook.

In the P.S. portion of the letter, I put my best offer to her. (In the direct mail business, we know that most people read the P.S., even if they skip the rest of the letter.) My P.S. was based on her love of private trains, which was evident in her greatest work, *Atlas Shrugged*. I knew she hated to fly, but she loved trains. So I offered her a choice of first-class air fare for her and her friends or a ride in a private rail car, knowing she would prefer the rail car.

That did it. Almost immediately I got a phone call from Ayn Rand herself—what a treat that proved to be—and then an immediate follow-up letter of acceptance. She had been moved by my son's name, but even then, was still on the fence until she read the private rail car offer at the end. The only problem was, I did not know how to find one.

Finding a Private Rail Car

Now I had to go about finding a private rail car! Although I made the offer in good faith, I had no idea how to rent one or even whether they existed anymore! After a couple of weeks and after searching up several blind alleys, I heard about a fellow named Roy Thorpe, a young entrepreneur in Florida, who was president of the Private Rail Car Owners Association of America. (Only in America could such a unique organization exist!) He was in semi-retirement at the time, living most of the year in a private resort hotel he owned in the Bahamas.

I contacted Roy at his hotel, and it turned out—much to my surprise—that he was also a dedicated disciple of Ayn Rand. In fact, he was so excited about taking part in providing a private rail car for her that he offered his services free. It turned out that he had become interested in rail cars as a hobby business through reading *Atlas Shrugged*. As a result, he not only donated his own services and his private rail car, but he offered us the services of his private chef for the trip.

The whole process was more difficult than it seemed on the surface. Roy had to take his own private rail car up to New York, then escort Ayn Rand and her entourage down to New Orleans, and also make all the arrangements with Amtrak. His chef had to find out Miss Rand's favorite meals and those of her friends. As it turned out, being an immigrant, Ayn Rand most loved the typically American Thanksgiving fare—turkey and dressing, mashed potatoes, gravy and peas.

The trip down to New Orleans came off without a flaw. (The trip back, as we shall see, was a different story.) When we met at the New Orleans train depot, she told me she was very thrilled with the whole experience. She had not been outside of New York, except for her annual Boston speech, in years. She was in failing health from a lung operation and told me that this conference could be the final crescendo of her life and she would make the most of it, which she did.

Ayn Rand's Final Speech—
In November 1981

Ayn Rand's speech at the 1981 NCMR conference was the most dramatic moment of my life. We have had former presidents, freedom fighters, and the world's greatest Nobel Prize-winning economists, but her speech was by far the most dramatic in the history of our conferences.

Her speech was titled "The Sanction of the Victim," and it was a stirring call to the entrepreneurs in our audience—and by extension, to her intellectual heirs—that they should not fall victim to those who would disparage the true builders, creators and pioneers of the American Dream—the businessmen, the industrialists, the entrepreneurs.

At first, she appeared hesitant, asking the photographers not to take pictures of her. I am sure she felt self-conscious about her obvious aging. But she jettisoned all her age and health concerns within a couple of minutes and was extremely animated throughout her speech, which was followed, as I had predicted to her it would be, by the longest standing ovation in the history of our conferences, and by a question-and-answer session which was even a greater highlight than her speech. Though in failing health, her wit was razor sharp as she met every question head on, with several interruptions by cheering and a few more standing ovations.

In the course of answering questions, Ayn Rand made some statements that earned headlines locally and all throughout the nation, saying the Soviets were a phony superpower and in actuality were "the weakest, most impotent country on earth. They are like bullies. If the U.S. fought with them, you'd be surprised at what a cowardly performance they would put up. They are to be dealt with very, very strongly or not at all."

When asked whether the media's leftward bias was a conspiracy, she said not, but added, "They are practicing the only kind of morality they have been taught. They are the conditioned robots of their college professors."

She said a few more controversial things: "The Moral Majority is struggling—with Reagan's approval—to take us back to the Middle Ages by the unconstitutional union of religion and politics." Of the feminist revolution, she was skeptical, being a champion of the heroic male in her novels. Knowing this was unpopular, she joked with the audience, "I guess you can call me a male chauvinist pig."

In President Reagan's first year, she predicted (as I had the year before) that he would be an ineffective champion of free enterprise. "President Reagan is not an advocate of freedom," she said. "He is an advocate of the mixed economy theory, which will fail."

She was genuinely surprised when she received a standing ovation over and over again. It would have been a sad thing for her to have died not knowing how loved and admired she was by so many. I am very thankful I was able to show her the depth of her influence on so many people.

After her speech, which took place early on a Saturday afternoon, we went to a late lunch with her and toasted the historic occasion which brought us together. I toasted the fact that her ideas would revolutionize the world in the 21st century, long after she was gone, and that the intellectual revolution she started in this century would live forever.

In a moving moment for me, she returned the toast, saying that I was the living embodiment of how her ideas work best, how right thinking leads to right investment decisions and wealth, and that I would become one of her "intellectual heirs" who would carry her ideas into the 21st century. It was a very special, very emotional moment for me, and for her.

My wife, Jackie, asked her to autograph my original, frayed edition of *Anthem*, the same one which was thrown on my lap back in 1963. It also had been the first of Miss Rand's works that Jackie had read. We asked her to dedicate this copy to our son, Anthem, as a keepsake for him to read when he grows up, as a book to help him realize how important her ideas are to the next generation and how important his name is.

She signed it, "To Anthem Hayek Blanchard, from your namesake Ayn Rand." Then, in a highly emotional moment, she boarded her private rail car, waved goodbye and sped back to New York.

I called her several times over the next three months, regarding the fund-raising for the *Atlas Shrugged* manuscript and planned television mini-series; but in early March of 1982, just about three and a half months after her speech, she was dead.

The rumor has been circulating for years since her death that she "caught a cold in New Orleans, from which she never recovered." That simply is not true. She had no cold when she left us, and word came back to us later that she caught the cold on the train back to New York when someone left the window of her bedroom open and others kept up a din all night long which kept her from sleeping.

Whether or not the train ride back contributed to her health problems, she was already in failing health due to her major operation. But even if she caught the cold as a result of visiting New Orleans, the fact that she left life on such a high note gives me a great sense of contribution to her final years. Since she had become such a recluse, she did not realize just how many young entrepreneurs had been affected by her works and how many successful people felt they owed so much of their success to her influence. Our 1981 conference brought her, albeit belatedly, in touch with her own power.

Hosting My Two Favorite
Nobel Prize-Winning Economists

Next to Ayn Rand, my two favorite conference speakers have been the two Nobel Prize-winning economists Milton Friedman and Friedrich Hayek. Each of them has spoken twice for us.

Ever since I first wrote Dr. Friedman my long "open letter" about the gold standard, I had kept corresponding; and he was very kind to send me his thoughtful answers to my various questions. When his book and television series *Free To Choose* came out in 1979, I was very impressed by the hard-core free-market aspects of the program. At one point, he emulated a trick Ludwig von Mises pulled on the Austrian government back in the time of runaway inflation (see my 1974 speech on the subject, in Chapter 4). Dr. Friedman actually went to the government printing presses and yelled over the din, "Do you know what we need to do to lick inflation?" Then he turned off the switch on the printing press and said in a much quieter voice, "Turn off the printing presses."

I thought *Free To Choose* was an eloquent and entertaining way to present freedom to average Americans. Dr. Friedman was firm in all his writings, however, that a gold/dollar convertibility standard would be disastrous. In a 1981 letter to me, he wrote, "A gold standard makes no sense for a single country; it makes a good deal of sense if it is international. Hence the problem is not U.S. dollar/gold convertibility, but world dollar/gold convertibility. The possibility of that is negligible. It is not desirable that it occur in the present state of government manipulation of markets around the world." He went on for over a thousand words of a personally typed letter to explain his position at length.

As I have written elsewhere in this book, I basically came to agree with Dr. Friedman that a gold standard would be impractical in the world as it is today. But I think Dr. Friedman also was drawn a bit more to my view over the years, that such a goal is eventually desirable if it is accompanied by greater government restraint worldwide. Yes, of course, this is impractical; but as an end-goal, a gold standard is the end of a long road of other more practical moves, such as balancing budgets and reducing governmental size.

In his 1981 letter, he added, "The only possibility I see for the emergence of anything like a real gold standard is on a private level," referring to the new, privately minted bullion bars and coins available from the Gold Standard Corporation in Missouri. Since then, various governments have also minted one-ounce gold coins for wide distribution, providing the framework for individual choice in gold vs. paper money.

Dr. Friedman spoke twice at NCMR, first in Montreal in 1980, where I made what we both agree now was "a foolish bet" that gold would top $1,000 by 1985. I lost. So the next time he came to our conference, in New Orleans in 1985, I paid him the bet agreed upon, a half ounce of gold. He ribbed me about missing my guess; but he was good enough to give our editors an hour-long interview for *Wealth* magazine free of charge, which frankly was worth far more to me than the price of a half ounce of gold.

He seemed to enjoy our gloom-and-doom conferences, meeting many of the people and genuinely liking them. He wrote me, "People who attend your conferences are not a bunch of crazies. I know and have met many of them. Indeed, two of our neighbors here at Sea Ranch, whom we have gotten to know somewhat, were at the Montreal conference. Of course they are basically in the same court as you and I are."

It is a credit to his true desire to spread freedom in the world that, when I asked permission to translate *Free To Choose* into Polish and produce 5,000 copies (to be printed by the anti-government, pro-freedom underground), he agreed to give his permission without charging royalties. He does not generally give his "intellectual ammunition" away free of charge; but when there are people who cannot otherwise afford the knowledge, and who hunger for it, he is the first to give away the philosophy of freedom, freely.

Professor Hayek Toasts an Amazing Coincidence

I first met Professor Hayek in one of our early overseas investment conferences, held in Lausanne, Switzerland, in 1976. It proved to be his first speech for a business-oriented seminar, and he chose the subject of the privatization of money. He was a thorough speaker and a disciplined writer, so the study he made in preparation for that speech resulted in a book he later wrote on the subject.

In a sense, I would like to believe that he was motivated enough by the spirit of our conferences, and by our work toward legalizing gold, that he chose to delve into a subject which had not commanded his attention up to that time.

After his 1976 speech, we took Professor Hayek to a dining room in a private chalet in the mountains. Together with Harry Schultz and a few others, Dr. Hayek and I discussed the history of several important economic ideas. Toward the end of the evening, when we were all directing various toasts to each other, Dr. Hayek stood up to propose his toast, in honor of the fact that, as he put it, "On this exact date and in this same room, the world's best economists joined me to found the Mount Pelerin Society. May tonight's gathering prove of equal historical importance."

My jaw dropped. It was an amazing coincidence—one I had not dreamed could happen, since Professor Hayek did not even know where we would be holding the dinner that night, and I had no idea that this was the place where the Mount Pelerin Society had been formed. (The Mount Pelerin Society has been one of the most influential worldwide pro-freedom organizations over the last four decades.)

At that memorable evening dinner in the Swiss chalet, I was able to give him a special toast as well. I got a chance to explain to Professor Hayek that his ideas had already been having a great effect on many investors, economists and philosophers in the United States, and he was genuinely surprised by this news, just as Ayn Rand had been.

Thankfully, Professor Hayek has lived a long and full life since then and has grown in this realization that his ideas have greatly influenced American students, like myself, since his landmark book of 1940, *The Road To Serfdom*. He had a large following in America even before he was awarded the Nobel Prize.

Like Ayn Rand, Professor Hayek also sent a signed copy of one of his books, along with a photograph, to my son, so that my son would know what his middle name, Hayek, meant in later years. We may never again have speakers of the quality of Hayek and Rand, but my intellectual life is quite complete just having met each of them. By helping to spread their word to the rest of America, I have done my part to plant the seed of freedom to flower in the next century.

Hosting My Political Hero, Senator Barry Goldwater

In one way, I dislike mixing a politician in with great philosophers like Hayek, Rand and Friedman; but this is one politician who would probably agree with me. In his salty language, he would probably agree that his line of work has fallen prey to some pretty chicken-livered, blow-dried media dandies in recent decades.

Senator Barry Goldwater spoke for us twice in New Orleans, first in 1977 and then in 1986, upon his retirement from 30 years in the Senate. Both of these meetings were very emotional moments for me, finally being able to meet the man whom I had championed to the point of tears back in 1964.

He told our audience in 1977, "I am convinced the gold standard is absolutely essential for free enterprise, which requires dependable money." He blamed most of our current economic problems on President Roosevelt's decision to go off the gold standard in 1933, to devalue the dollar from $20.67 to $35 in gold—a price picked, said Goldwater, by the flip of a coin—and to confiscate American gold holdings. He called the gold theft the "modern, sophisticated version of the ancient, reprehensible practice of coin clipping and one of the greatest tragedies of American finance."

He explained why gold was the people's form of political discipline. "When the dollar was redeemable in gold," he said, citizens were able to express their displeasure over government extravagance by redeeming their paper dollars in gold, thereby diminishing the size of the gold reserve upon which the credit structure of the nation rested.

"One serious consequence of the imprisonment of gold," he continued, "is that we Americans have lost the power of the purse. We are virtually helpless in trying to control government expenditure and in trying to achieve a balanced budget." The result has been "a devastating inflation and monumental indebtedness." The government, he said, thinks it can balance the books by creating more reserves, at will, "but the penalty is all around us. It is continuous inflation and possibly an ultimate crash."

With all that bad news as a backdrop, he then told our audience he was very encouraged by the outcome of America's renewed right to own gold. He also cited the legislation passed that year to re-establish the right to make contracts payable in gold or foreign currencies. Another sign was the futile attempt by our government to demonetize gold. Like von Mises, Goldwater said such efforts were "singularly futile." "Gresham's law, that bad money drives out good, is beyond the power of governments to control. Imprisonment and the threat of the guillotine did not assist France with its historic fiat money experience."

"International commerce requires money of the highest quality, and gold is still number one," he concluded. "The world will never be crucified on a cross of gold, as William Jennings Bryan once warned, but it could easily drown in a flood of unsound paper currency."

Would it not be great to hear one of our next presidential candidates from the two major parties talk like that?

In his 1986 visit Senator Goldwater gave a moving farewell to his service in government, in one of his last speeches before stepping down from the Senate in late 1986. This valedictory address was much more political than economic in nature. Like an Old Testament prophet with his eyes going dim, his frame slightly bent, but with incredible fire in his eyes, he warned the "youngsters" in Congress to start looking out for the national good instead of their own parochial interests. As did Ayn Rand before him, he sparkled in an impromptu question-and-answer session that was often interrupted by applause and he received a standing ovation at the end. Just before his speech and after, Goldwater and I had time alone to talk about ideas, the past and the future. With strong conviction in his voice and steady, clear eyes he said, "Times will get worse first, but I believe freedom and the American spirit will prevail!"

Ayn Rand, Friedrich Hayek, Milton Friedman and Barry Goldwater. We have had presidents and princes, but I would not trade any of them for these great, action-oriented thinkers who have literally shaped the best ideas of our century.

Chapter 8

Building a Coin Company

—From Bottom to Top in Ten Years

"The road to the performance of great things must always lead through the performance of partial tasks. A cathedral is something other than a heap of stones joined together. But the only procedure for constructing a cathedral is to lay one stone upon another. For the architect the whole project is the main thing. For the mason it is the single wall, and for the bricklayer the single stones."

—Ludwig von Mises, *Human Action*

I had been trading coins on an informal basis since 1967, but by the late 1970s I had become much more active in this end of the business. It started as a natural outgrowth of the conferences and the publication of *Gold Newsletter*. In a couple of our 1976 issues of *Gold Newsletter*, for instance, I advertised coin sales in bulk quantities for our subscribers.

In the conferences and in *Gold Newsletter*, I was telling people how to profit in gold and silver coins; but I was not showing them specifically how to do it, or from what company to buy, until I hit on the idea of turning my own informal buying and selling operation into those small ads and announcements

121

telling people where they could buy bullion and rare coins.

Several people at the conferences in the late 1970s had asked me where they could get some coins, and I had asked them what they needed. As often as not, I would have some of those coins in my safe, and I would sell them to the customer as a simple one-on-one exchange. Those who wrote to me through the mail asked the same thing and wondered why I did not start selling them coins through the mail instead of just at the conferences.

By 1978 I had published several pieces of literature promoting silver dollar sales with my home trading company. The business was organized out of my home as a sole proprietorship, with only a secretary and some part-time help. Finally, in early 1979, we were so backed up with orders that we organized my sole proprietorship as a closely held company, under the name of James U. Blanchard & Company, Inc.

The name was not intended as some kind of an ego trip. I just wanted our customers to know that I personally stood behind every sale and that they could rely on my company with the same faith they had previously shown in me, personally, through the conferences and in *Gold Newsletter*.

Starting a Formal Business During the
Metals Peak in 1979-1980

In late 1979 the prices of silver and gold were beginning to climb dramatically, so we had a full-service coin company ready at just the right time to serve all of our early clients with the best ways to profit from the big moves that year. In that first full year as a company, 1979, we grossed $2 million in sales; not bad for a fairly informal operation.

In 1980 it seemed that all of our predictions were coming true at one time: higher inflation (eventually peaking at 18 percent to 20 percent), higher interest rates (peaking at a prime rate of 21.5 percent), explosive debt formation, a crippling recession (that could have escalated into a Great Depression), and outbreaks of international conflicts in several nations at once—Russia invading Afghanistan, the Sandinista revolution in Nicaragua, the kidnapping of our 52 American hostages in Iran, and so forth.

The investors on our mailing list were by now probably more sophisticated than any other group of investors in the nation, so they were getting suspicious of the spiky nature of the silver and gold markets. In late 1980 at our annual NCMR conference, several of these investors pulled me aside to say something like this: "Jim, the bullion markets are so volatile they're beginning to scare me. I like big profits as much as the next guy, but frankly I want something that hasn't moved that high yet—something with all the advantages of gold and silver bullion, but without the wide price swings. I want some protection along with my profits."

Many of our people were at or near retirement age, and I could see why they should not have to gamble with their nest egg on bullion alone. The problem that faced me at the time was that I could not just send them to any number of coin shops and bullion dealers without making a full-time study of who was reputable and who was not. That was when I decided that I would help people profit the same way I had profited over the last 12 years or so, by diversifying into several different types of coins, not just silver dollars.

Our company got off to an impressive start in October 1980, when we entered a joint venture with Texas Millionaire Gordon McClendon to purchase a Sigismund III 100-ducat 1621 Polish gold coin for $120,000, which was a world-record high price for a "modern" gold coin (as opposed to ancient Roman or Greek coins). We got front-page coverage in all the coin papers, with this odd typographical error: "Gold Expert Julian Blanchard Pays Record $120,000 For Poland 100 Ducat Gold Piece..." (*World Coin News*, October 7, 1980). The main article and picture caption got my name right as "James," but the headline gave me a more distinguished first name.

Even before the big spike in silver and gold—to $50 and $850 per ounce, respectively—in January 1980, I put several of our early customers into the kind of coins that were bullion-based but had not yet been discovered by the collector or investment community widely enough to bid their premiums up to astronomical levels. This would give them profit potential with the bullion component and downside protection with the rarity premium. It was a new kind of "double play" in coins.

Semi-Numismatic Coins

What should I call this new category of coins we were trying to promote? The rare coins were called numismatics, and the junk coins traded strictly near their bullion price. But these new coins were seemingly caught in the middle, so I reasoned they were *semi-numismatic* coins—that is, although they were not yet rare enough to be rated as having numismatic quality, there was a strong likelihood that they would be sold at higher numismatic premiums in the future.

I was among the first, if not the first, to promote this kind of semi-numismatic coins. At first, they were composed mostly of $20 Saint-Gaudens gold coins and common-date MS-60 silver dollars. Throughout 1979 and into the early part of 1980, when gold peaked, we were selling these coins at large volumes, yielding a great profit to those who got into the market early. As it turned out, the coins we sold in 1979 and 1980 at the peak of the market were the best way to invest in gold and silver at the peak. They went down only a small fraction compared with the collapse of silver bullion.

If you had invested $50 in an ounce of silver in 1980, you would have watched it lose 90 percent of its value in the next few years, down to $5 an ounce. But if you had used that same $50 to buy a brilliant uncirculated Morgan silver dollar in 1980, you would have seen it drop to only $35 in 1982's market bottom; then you would have seen that same silver dollar recover to be worth well over $50 in 1986 and then much more, considering the likelihood that the MS-60 coin of 1980 could be an MS-63 or even MS-65 by today's standards, due to the refinements made in the grading of coins since then.

In the decade since gold and silver peaked, we have grown to become one of the biggest rare coin dealers in America and one of the biggest hard-money brokerage firms in the world. Due to our versatility in many areas, we can literally claim to be the largest full-service rare coin and metals dealer in America; but I certainly did not start out with that kind of growth in mind. I never invested in big buildings or plush furnishings, nor did I build up a huge inventory of coins. It was strictly pay-as-you-go financing, and I operated out of my own home for as long as I possibly could.

In the first year of operation, I handled all the coin marketing and sales myself, until the orders started overwhelming me in January 1980. That was when I contacted some of my oldest and most trusted friends to help me order, store, handle and market these coins. For several years, they were my key employees at Blanchard & Company.

Our Offices Grow—Like Topsy

At first we operated out of my house on Hillary Street in uptown New Orleans. It had four bedrooms upstairs and four downstairs, so we had put $8,000 of renovations into it and turned some of the downstairs bedrooms into offices. When we outgrew that space, we moved into a "shotgun house" on Oak Street, so named because of its narrow front with all the rooms lined up in a row, resembling a shotgun barrel. In 1979 and well into 1980, that shotgun house held the entire coin company—the vault, the mailing operation, the sales area.

As I look back on it, we were pretty lucky, despite operating out of several old homes in uptown New Orleans, without much security and in a fairly high crime area. I would often work 15-hour days in 1979 and 1980, leaving the office late at night, many times after midnight. One night I drove home after midnight with 500 Krugerrands in my briefcase. I was so tired that I forgot all about the briefcase—leaving about $300,000 worth of gold coins in the front seat of an unlocked car in an unsafe neighborhood—but the coins were all still there in the morning.

Finally, we had to use both of our buildings at once—the Hillary Street home and the Oak Street office—putting the shipping operation into Oak Street and the sales staff on Hillary. Then a third building came into play, on Magazine Street in New Orleans. All three of these buildings were within a few blocks of each other in uptown New Orleans, but it was getting ridiculous running from one building to the other when you wanted to visit another department. We needed to consolidate all these operations in one location, and to do that we needed to move to the suburbs of New Orleans, to Metairie.

In Metairie in late 1980, we found a 20,000-square-foot tin shed which was available for the unheard-of low price of $3 a square foot per year! (Remember that this was the peak of the real estate boom in the Sun Belt.) We grabbed up this rundown old bargain and moved everything up to the top floor, with room to spare. We spent the next six years remodeling it step by step until we finally filled up every square inch of it—including the carport, which I used to store my large motor home until that area, too, became offices.

We were bursting at every seam of the old tin shed by the end of 1986, when we moved to our current office in the Whitney Bank building at 2400 Jefferson Highway in Jefferson, Louisiana, where we operate on five of the six floors.

Throughout all of these moves, I have always felt that renting or leasing property is a better investment than buying it. As it turned out, the real estate market in the Sun Belt peaked around 1980, so it proved to be a good decision. New Orleans property, in particular, has been going down in price ever since the oil price decline of 1985-1986, even while the rest of the nation's real estate market has been recovering; so I have felt good about leasing instead of owning property. With the office glut in the Sun Belt, it is really a renter's market now; and we have been able to make attractive deals, both in Metairie and in our new spacious offices overlooking the mighty Mississippi River in the Whitney Bank building on Jefferson Highway.

Weathering the Bear Markets

The metals tended to whipsaw the newer investors around during the early 1980s, trending downward the entire decade. After opening with a bang at $850, gold trended down and will likely close the decade at around half its peak price level. But the bear markets of the 1980s did not bother me as much as other investors and newsletter editors, because I had already lived through the terrible drop to $103 in 1976 and knew my fundamentals were right. That is why I looked at every $300 bottom as a new buying opportunity for those who had not made their initial purchase of gold yet.

The public's timing and patience was not as good as my own personal timing, because I had a long head start on the public at large. Typically, the great masses move into an investment after it is popular instead of in the down days when you cannot seem to generate buyers. Once gold had moved from $300 in early 1979 to $850 in early 1980, the public's head was turned to the profit potential of gold; and so we were seeing all kinds of new clients pouring calls into our switchboard, buying metals at the very top of the market.

Despite the drop in metals prices from their 1980 peaks, I still felt the safest and soundest way to protect yourself from government control, confiscation, taxation and spending is with the metals. So I continued investing in gold shares in the early 1980s and studied the role of gold coins versus bullion. I found that some of our semi-numismatic coins and rare U.S. coins had performed far better than bullion, for the reasons I mentioned over and over again in our literature at the time—these coins had beautiful designs, they were in uncirculated condition, and they had built-in rarity plus silver or gold content.

In the bear market of the early 1980s, there was one major difference from the down market of 1975-1976: Gold was now a part of the mainstream at long last. The price of gold was quoted on the evening news, all the major brokerage firms had gold trading departments, and everybody was interested in making a million dollars in gold and silver (after the markets had peaked).

My challenge was to help these people make money despite the inevitable short-term falling price of gold and silver bullion. To make that possible, we began to market proof "modern-issue" gold and silver coins from the world's leading mints—issues such as the Chinese Panda, beginning in 1982; the British Royal Mint series; and many others. These coins usually carried a considerable premium over their metal content, which aroused some questions and criticism.

Why Pay Any Premium at All?

Today the common question—even among many investment advisers who otherwise like gold and silver as investments—is "Why buy coins at any premium at all when you can buy bullion coins at just a few percentage points over spot?"

This is a familiar argument, often coming from the same people who kidded me in the 1960s for buying U.S. silver dollars at $1.25 and $1.50 when I could have gotten silver quarters and dimes at face value.

I figured at that time, and still do, that when I can get a classic American coin that is more than 100 years old—like the 1881 to 1885 Morgan silver dollars—that coin has a lot more value than just the silver in it. (Where else can you get a genuine piece of American history for less than $50?) Today I can apply the same reasoning to century-old British sovereigns and other European gold coins minted from the 1880s to the 1920s.

The argument against paying any premium for rarity was best expressed by my banker uncle. When I was paying up to $2 for silver dollars back in 1970, I visited my uncle, who owned a couple of banks in Mississippi and was president of the American Small Bankers Association. I went on the pretense of asking his advice about silver dollars, but mostly I wanted to ask him where I could get some silver dollars and whether he had any to sell. He gave me a long lecture about why silver dollars are a terrible investment.

"Jimmy," he said in his best avuncular tone, "don't you know? Silver dollars earn no interest. They're a wasting asset. There were entirely too many of them minted. You should see how many tons of these bags passed through my bank over the years, at not a penny over face value. Besides, the greenback is strong; it's as good as gold, and inflation is low. Why would you want to waste $2 on a $1 coin?"

You get the idea. He went on and on about how stupid my investment in silver dollars seemed to be, to him. What was worse, he had no more silver dollars to sell me. I did not mind it if he thought I was naive, but I was hoping he had some of those "tons of bags" to sell me at under $2 a coin.

Obviously my uncle and I disagreed. But my uncle was not alone in thinking I was crazy. All the leading lights of the numismatic world seemed to agree pretty much with my uncle. They thought that only a few rare-date old silver dollars would ever be worth much more than double their face value. The collector would buy a common-date silver dollar to fill a slot in a collection, but an investor would not think of buying up whole rolls (20 coins) or bags (1,000 coins) of silver dollar coins as a way to make any money.

The Same Arguments Prevail Today

My uncle's arguments back in 1970 are identical with the criticisms of today's market in modern issues and common $20 U.S. gold coins and silver dollars of the 1880s-1920s. The same people in the numismatic and banking world are now criticizing me for buying and selling modern gold and silver issues for premiums ranging from a low of 15 percent for brilliant uncirculated foreign silver coins up to 75 percent or so for a classic Saint-Gaudens $20 Double Eagle coin from the days of Teddy Roosevelt's presidency. I think that 10 to 20 years from now these coins will be selling at premiums of 100 percent to several hundred percent, just as the Morgan silver dollars are selling today; but you still hear that people think I am crazy for dealing in anything but "modern junk bullion" coins or common Double Eagles and U.S. Morgan dollars.

Once a coin gets to a certain stage of rarity, experience has shown me that it really soars completely out of the gravitational field of the metal's underlying bullion content. That is what happened with rare MS-65 silver dollars in 1989, some of which sell for $500 to $1,500, with just $5 worth of silver in them at current prices. The bullion component in rare coins is insignificant. Blanchard & Company, Inc. and The American Rare Coin Fund (Kidder Peabody) proved this in July 1989 when, as a fifty-fifty partnership, we (The American Rare Coin Fund and I, personally, through Blanchard & Company) paid nearly $1 million for one silver dollar (the 1804 Dexter dollar). Someday, I feel the limited-issue gold and silver coins of the 1980s will be considered rarities and will command prices only faintly related to their underlying bullion value.

In 1988 we moved more strongly into U.S. rarities, but I will save that story for a later chapter. Now, with U.S. rarities, modern issues, bullion and more, we are a fully diversified precious-metals dealer, servicing client needs from A to Z— from small bullion bars to common-date silver dollar rolls, to the most exotic single rare coins costing $50,000 to $65,000 and more. Quite literally, we have an investment for every stage of the cycle, an investment for all markets from bull to bear and in between.

But the bread and butter of my business and my personal investment decisions will continue to be gold and silver coins. I feel it is a matter of only a very few years until we see prices like $1,500 to $2,000 gold, $2,500 to $3,000 platinum, $500 palladium and $50 to $100 silver. However, I am not saying those are sane and sensible prices. I think those are blow-off peaks, and you should sell out at least a portion of your portfolio before reaching those peaks. The top of any market mania would not be supported for very long.

Staying Ahead of the Markets

The fact that I started *Gold Newsletter* so early and at such a young age has helped me get a jump on the markets in a number of other business ventures as well. Being first has several distinct advantages, not the least of which is the fact that it gives you a platform from which to jump into other new markets before your competitors see the opportunity arise. For instance, we have been able to pioneer these moves:

• We were the first to put on large investment conferences every year, continuously, since 1974.

• We were the first company to adapt modern direct-mail mass marketing techniques to the sale of gold and silver coins.

• We were the first to branch off into several new and profitable investment vehicles, such as modern proof issues, foreign silver dollar-sized coins, and semi-numismatic coins.

• We were the first hard money investment firm to spin off a broadly based mutual fund, the Blanchard Strategic Growth Fund, and other funds now in the same family of funds. (Note: The Blanchard Group of Funds is a personal investment, not a part of Blanchard & Company, Inc.)

One of the things that still bothers me is that people say I am some kind of "eternal gold bug" who always says "buy" and never says "sell." The truth is, I have often warned people of peaking prices and said low prices were a great buying opportunity. I follow my own advice and have gotten rich doing so! People can talk all they want about my being an eternal gold bug (Yes, I am the first to admit I have made some mistakes!), but the fact is, our group of companies has put people into the *safest* kinds of hard-money investments at just the right time in the markets:

• In the 1970s I constantly recommended straight gold and silver bullion, junk silver coins and South African mining shares. Those are precisely the investments that grew by the greatest percentage in the 1970s.

• When bullion and blue chip gold stocks peaked in 1980, our major editorial emphasis shifted from *Gold Newsletter* (bullion-based) to *Market Alert* (coin-based), moving most of our people into a safer type of hard-money investment: semi-numismatic coins like U.S. silver dollars and Saints.

•When silver peaked at $50 and gold at $850, I recommended Morgan silver dollars and classic U.S. gold coins instead of bullion. Just about every issue of *Market Alert* from 1980 to 1985 contained recommendations for classic U.S. gold and silver dollars, which fared much better than bullion.

For instance, when gold declined from $875 to $509 (-42 percent) in the four months from January 21 to May 23, 1980, the value of the 12-coin U.S. gold type set, which we promoted heavily during those months, was actually up 47 percent. When gold further dropped to $480 by early 1981 (-45 percent overall), the 12-piece type set of gold coins was up fully 50 percent in price.

• In 1982 I published a book called *15 Ways to Make Money in a Gold Bear Market*, and it delivered precisely what the title promised—15 ways to make money on the downside of gold. So we have helped our clients make money in the gold portion of their portfolios in all types of markets.

• Also in 1982 we published two major buy signals on U.S. silver dollars. As it turned out, 1982 was the bottom of the market; and those dollars soared in value through 1986, despite the drop in silver bullion from $15 to $5 between 1983 and 1985.

• In 1985, when the Supreme Court ruled that non-SEC-registered newsletters could mention stocks, we moved our subscribers into a selected mix of penny mining shares and blue chip gold and silver mining stocks. Since then our top 20 stocks—printed in a book, which we sent to over 10,000 new *Gold Newsletter* subscribers—went up over 300 percent on the average and over 1,000 percent in several cases, before declining some 50 percent on average after the stock market crash of 1987.

• Also, since 1985 we have moved our clients into the "modern classics," such as the phenomenally successful Panda series of gold coins, the large commemorative silver coins like the Kon-Tiki or the Falkland Islands coin, and the first sets of platinum and palladium coins—in order to profit from those new, more thinly traded platinum group precious metals.

• Since July 1986, the mutual fund I started—Blanchard Strategic Growth Fund—has helped its clients make money in the stock and bond markets as well as in gold and silver. I guess that makes me a "reformed" gold bug! (The fund's management company, Sheffield Management Company, is completely separate from Blanchard & Company, Inc. I co-founded the Blanchard family of funds with longtime friend Michael Freedman in 1985.) Depending on the stage of the cycle, we can help investors make money in one of at least five different investment media: stocks, bonds, currencies, foreign securities or precious metals.

The time will come, I believe, when it will be vital and urgent to move out of stocks and back into gold; and our mutual fund is prepared to do just that. In fact, the Blanchard group of funds now has a separate Precious Metals fund, managed by Peter Cavelti, and a Blanchard Government Guarantee fund (The Paper Money Market fund).

All in all, we have tried to move our clients into the right kind of hard money investments at precisely the right time. I am not ashamed when somebody calls me an eternal gold bug; because I still believe that there is always at least one type of precious metal investment that will be making money for the savvy investors, at least protecting what they have already made and performing at a better comparative rate than most paper investments.

Protection Against Gold Confiscation

After seeing gold confiscated for more than 40 years, from 1933 to 1974, I feel that the right to own gold should be the First Amendment in any economic or investment Bill of Rights. However, with a strong central government that hates having any competition in the money business, the right to own gold is a right we must protect at all times. The price of liberty, said Edmund Burke, is eternal vigilance; and that applies to protecting our right to own gold.

As we head into a possible time of crisis in the 1990s, we need to be forewarned and forearmed against the attempted forcible taxation or confiscation of the wealth of the most successful Americans. In a future crisis, you can bet there will be a call by the leftist-trained students of the 1960s—now in powerful offices throughout the land—to get those "greedy capitalists" to give up their "hoard of wealth" in the form of privately owned gold, at gunpoint if necessary.

The possibility of gold confiscation is another compelling argument for putting a big percentage of your gold and silver investments into numismatic and semi-numismatic coins, which would be exempt from gold confiscation and which are currently exempt from dealer reporting requirements (for coins with 15 percent or more premium over their melt value). This is one more reason to consider a sizable investment in gold coins that are protected from broker reporting requirements.

In the future, the government could seize the store of privately held gold in order "to pay the national debt" or some other noble-sounding purpose. I think it is very important for you to make plans now to hold on to your gold when the time comes for the government to come knocking on your door.

Chapter 9

Your Business Is Your Best Investment

A Quick Summary of My Debt-Free Management Style

"No one should expect that any logical argument or any experience could shake the almost religious fervor of those who believe in salvation through spending and credit expansion."

—Ludwig von Mises, "Stones into Bread: The Keynesian Miracle," *Planning for Freedom*

Coming from a longtime gold bug, it might be surprising to some readers of this "confession" that I think, for most people, a private business is still your best investment. You will make more money in your own field of expertise a lot easier than you can make money in an unrelated field, such as studying investment cycles and strategies and trying to outguess the short-term market moves in stocks or metals.

In mid-1988, I sold my business to a partnership between Allegiance Capital Corporation and General Electric Capital Corporation. I received a handsome settlement, enough so that I do not need to work ever again. But as Ayn Rand pointed out, work is sometimes the essence of life. Work has always been very important to me. Sometimes it has been difficult, but mostly it has been productive and just plain fun. In business and in "leisure," I always have enjoyed the thrill of the adrenalin rush—of a big success. So you can see why I am still working as president of Blanchard & Company on a long-term management contract, because work was never a job to me. I work because that is what I enjoy doing most.

The point of this is that everything our business is now worth—including the money I received for the company in 1988—all comes from the original $50 I put up for the formation of the National Committee to Legalize Gold in 1971. That is quite a handsome return on investment over a 17-year period, and it was all accomplished with very little downside risk.

Until I sold the company, the only time we had ever borrowed money was to finance short-term inventory sales and cash flow—a very short-term loan. The problem with most business failures—and many successful businesses—is the lack of cash, often resulting from high debt loads. It is an assumption in most businesses that you must borrow heavily in the beginning in order to realize profits in the end. I do not agree with that at all. Most people can start small and pay as they go.

You can grow without debt. Or you can find partners who want to invest in the business. You just have to be patient and be willing to grow more slowly than you might like to grow at first. For small businesses in search of positive cash flow, take this lesson from what I have been able to do: Start small and grow in stages, debt free all the way.

An Example—Part-Time Publishing

If you would rather not take the big step of entering business with your whole nest egg at risk, then do it in your spare time and at low cost. I got into direct-mail publishing in my spare time while spending eight hours a day, nine months of the year, as a schoolteacher. I enjoyed doing my "hobby" business—it seemed like play to me—so I never felt trapped in the moonlighting ghetto of needing a second job to live.

Here is how a typical new project worked for me back in the early days of NCMR. In 1975 I wrote a special paperback report on how to invest in gold and silver. I bought advertising space and direct-mail lists with the plan to sell the report for $10, although I printed it at a cost of only about 50 cents each. The report was manually typed, and we reduced the pages to fit book size at PIP (Postal Instant Press). On the surface, selling a 50-cent product for $10 looks like a rip-off; but the investment advice I gave these people was so concise, so practical, and so profitable that anybody who followed my advice would have made a fortune within five years.

I had a post office box under a business name and sold the report by mail. Some days I could not even open my mail box it was so full. On a single day, I got over 500 checks of $10 each, which was more money coming in on one day than I earned in a full year as a schoolteacher. ($4,500 per year was the level of Louisiana's commitment to quality education in those days. It is not much better, in inflation-adjusted terms, today.) The return on investment (ROI) ratio was obviously phenomenal, and I was enjoying the research and writing tremendously. Every step of this business process was totally under my control, with no need to go into debt.

The people who bought the report were getting a top-quality piece of research. In those days, the hard-money investment concept was so fresh, new, crystal clear, and revolutionary that I could have charged $50 per report and still have been inundated with checks. But before you go out and try the same thing, I do not think it likely that anyone could repeat the process today at anywhere near that profitability level. Now there are "special reports" and hard-money newsletters growing on trees, so we could not expect nearly that kind of response rate on an investment report today.

The point of this episode is to demonstrate how to start a profitable business on the side. If you find something that you really love doing and you can make money on it in your spare time, then try to start a lucrative second career that is more profitable than your main job and more enjoyable. If you succeed on the side, then quit your main job and move into what you really love doing and can make money doing.

Second Careers Can Be Lifesavers

When your work is so much fun that you gladly work 30 or 40 hours a week on it in your spare time, then it is pretty certain you can make more money on this than you can make as an eight-hour-day "wage slave" with no share of the company profits. Working part time at first, you can keep your own expenses low while pouring most of the money back into the business. In good times, you will want to build up a nest egg for the bad times. The enthusiasm you have for your second business will also rub off on everyone around you.

In the course of hosting my investment conferences, I have met several professionals who studied economics and investments so much in their spare time that they became self-taught economists and newsletter writers. Two former medical doctors come to mind—the four-term Republican congressman and Libertarian presidential candidate Ron Paul and Dr. Al Owen, who is now editor of *Newsletter Digest*.

A young dentist I have recently met, Steven Funk, got so involved in opening new ventures in the Far East that he quit his dental practice and now works on several ventures linking Western entrepreneurs with new investment opportunities in the Far East.

Not only is owning your own business still the best way to make money, but it also is a great way to live. It is the American

Dream in action. That does not mean it is easy. It takes a lot of 15-hour days at first, and it also takes a special tolerance for risk. More accurately stated, it takes a special skill for avoiding risk. In my case, you will find a clear pattern of avoiding financial risk at all costs...

Tentative About Business at First

As late as 1975, even after gold was legalized, Jackie and I were still somewhat hesitant about leaving our teaching posts to tackle this gold and silver business full time. Jackie was a teacher at Booker T. Washington High School, and I was teaching at Colton Junior High School. We both taught history, and I threw in a little economics on the side. We could not bring ourselves to quit our teaching jobs "cold turkey;" so we took a leave of absence first, in the 1975-76 school year, to find out whether we should give up our teaching jobs permanently. We decided to give our best efforts to our new business for just one year and then see what happened.

In that first year of full-time work in gold and monetary conferences, *Gold Newsletter*, and special reports, we planned and organized our first offshore seminars to complement our annual New Orleans conference. The first offshore conference was in Bermuda—recalling Harry Schultz's 1971 conference there—in 1975, and the second was in Lausanne, Switzerland, in 1976. Jackie did all the office work and hired temporary help when necessary. We operated out of our home, with my office in the den and Jackie working in the dining room!

This was probably too frugal an arrangement for a business that was taking off in size as fast as ours was, but I have always had what I call a "peasant mentality" about debt: Why should I spend money on overhead or arrange for massive long-term loans for buying office buildings when I can avoid the hassle and the cost by working out of my home?

I often went to an extreme with that kind of debt-free management style. At one time, as late as 1980, the entire coin company was housed upstairs at our place on Hillary Street, even though it was not zoned for business. We pulled off that trick by asking the people to park a block away and not look too "businesslike." That worked for two years before we moved into some properly zoned office space.

Debt-Free Management Style in Action

I preach a lot about the evils of debt, so it would be inconsistent of me to build a company based on debt. From our beginnings in 1971 until I sold the company in 1988, we bought everything in our personal and business life with cash. In fact, my home in Metairie was covered in the local newspapers as the most expensive house ever purchased in Metairie for cash. We moved into the house to celebrate our own kind of American independence, on July 4, 1981.

On the business side of the ledger, the growth of Blanchard & Company came about entirely free of debt—an unheard-of strategy in this age of go-go bank financing. I would simply sell coins at a slight profit margin, buy more coins with the proceeds, and then sell them back once again to a growing customer base, yielding the necessary capital for further expansion. Except in the rare instance when we needed to finance a short-term, multimillion-dollar inventory coin purchase, all the growth has been debt free.

The coin company is not the only business venture I have financed this way. Any new venture in the Blanchard group of companies started gradually from a small portion of coin profits, and then it either grew quickly into a profit center by itself or was terminated equally quickly. When something started working, we grew gradually by reinvesting the proceeds and socking away a certain percentage of the profits for a rainy day so that we did not need to raid the treasury or run to the bank to fund new and unproven ideas. We financed several publications this way.

Instead of going to the bank for a multimillion-dollar loan, which frankly scared the heck out of me, I would dip into "the mattress" and pull out a few precious profits to start a project in as small and risk-free a manner as possible. Happiness is positive cash flow. In a business like coin sales or publishing, which is noted for being cash-poor, we usually had a good-sized hoard of paper money, as well as the real thing—silver and gold.

I also discovered that financing new projects within an established company is much more profitable with equity financing than with debt financing. In other words, if you can sell up to 30 outside people on investing in a part of your idea, you can secure $10,000 of investment capital from each of them and raise a $300,000 nest egg rather quickly. That is enough capital to start most businesses. Spread the wealth around, make it in everybody's best interest for you to succeed, and you probably will.

As a result of these and other debt-free techniques, we were able to survive several bear markets in gold during the 1980s. For instance, after more than two years of declining gold prices from January 1980 to June 1982, we managed to salt away a seven-figure cash cushion in the "Shearson Daily Dividend" money market fund by the end of the bear market. We did not need to lay off any employees in that bear market and had not a penny of long-term or short-term debt by the time gold started taking off again in the summer of 1982.

We were able to survive in bad markets as well as good because we were strictly a cash-and-carry business. We did not engage in any sort of margin activities, nor did we store coins for customers, except for special short-term requests. By avoiding highly leveraged growth, we eventually enjoyed far more growth than many of our more rapidly expanding competitors.

"Debt-Free" Hiring

Another element of our debt-free management style is the way Jackie and I were so careful about hiring new employees. Jackie liked to hire temporary help first, so that she could get to know them on a no-risk basis before hiring them permanently. I did the same thing in a slightly different way. I liked to get the optimum mileage out of a very few dedicated and talented people by offering extra incentives to them, as independent contractors, for producing extra profits. I made a point of cutting costs and unnecessary overhead wherever possible, so that I could pour some of that money into their pockets instead.

For instance, I would rather find one good artist and one good writer and then turn them loose than hire a whole editorial and art department complete with several managers in the middle and a lot of bureaucratic paperwork. Because of this, I found that visitors were amazed that we turned out so much good material each month with what amounted to a skeleton crew of highly skilled and highly motivated producers.

When looking for new employees, I do not care for the standard procedure of placing ads in the paper and wading through a bunch of high-flown resumes from people who have mostly been reading books and articles about how to market themselves through a resume. I do not much care what schools they went to. I would much prefer to hear about someone through word-of-mouth in my peer group, and then observe the person in action on the job, in a loose structure, to see what he or she can do for me now, not what they claim to have done in the past.

Mixing Business With Pleasure

I have always tried to mix business and pleasure as much as possible. That has resulted in several business ventures which never would have existed if I had tried to separate business from pleasure. A number of chance encounters have led to some lucrative and personally satisfying business relationships over the years.

For instance, in January 1980 when gold was peaking, I went down to Costa Rica partly because I had heard it was a beautiful country, but also for some very important business reasons.   I originally went to Costa Rica to see Jerome Smith, who was a strong and early influence on me. I had corresponded with Jerome over the years and came to know him well. He is a self-educated economist who quit his executive position and started publishing his studies on the silver shortage, which he said— against all odds—would cause silver to hit $50 by 1980. Sure enough, that prediction came true right in January 1980; so I went down to Costa Rica partly to congratulate him, but also to look into Costa Rica as an investment haven.

While I was there, several people, including Jerome, said I must meet the Aden sisters, who had maintained a phenomenal track record as investment advisers since 1976, accurate in both timing and price projections. I got to know both of these delightful sisters and their families on that trip and future trips and grew to know them very well over the years. In fact, I entered into a partnership with them in 1981, which continued until I sold the company in 1988 and they took their newsletter to Dan Rosenthal of *Silver & Gold Report*.

The Aden Analysis, which we co-published with the Adens from 1982 to 1989, was an exceptional newsletter with an enviable track record except for their call of $3,000 gold, the one prediction that generated the most press coverage. Except for that call, they have actually had quite a profitable record in a soft-spoken, conservative style of technical analysis, and it has been a real pleasure being in business with them.

The Blanchard Strategic Growth Fund also grew out of my habit of mixing business and pleasure. I have known Michael Freedman, the current president of the Blanchard Funds, for more than a decade, since the early years of the NCMR conference. Since then, we have had a tradition of meeting once a year in New Orleans for dinner, going out as early as 5:30 and staying until 11 p.m., bringing each other up to date on our work, our mutual friends and our business ideas.

Eventually we hit on the idea for the mutual fund. Michael was semiretired, running a few joint ventures to keep the money coming in, but he was open to the idea of co-founding the fund with me. That is what I mean about mixing business with pleasure. Without our pleasant tradition of having dinner once a year, the fund might not even exist. As of late 1989, our group of funds had over $450 million under management, so the annual dinner reunion paid off!

The Bottom-Line Payoff:
Cashing Out Your Company

All these principles were my motivating force behind building America's premier full-service rare coin and bullion company. The company literally went from almost nothing to the top in less than ten years, on the basis of the principles in this chapter. Following our incorporation in 1979, the company grew from $2 million per year—with just a handful of people—to $115 million in sales—with 145 people in 1987. That is an average growth of 66 percent per year for eight years, all on the basis of the management principles in this chapter...and let's not forget some lucky timing!

In mid-1988, when I sold my company to Allegiance Capital Partners and General Electric Capital Corporation, I was prepared for a difficult transition—because of all my reading about takeover situations—but I think I was not really prepared for how difficult it was to change from an entrepreneurial "mom and pop" business (grown large) to a more corporate-style environment in the mold of the third largest company in America, the General Electric Company.

I was excited about getting the power of GECC behind us, to help build the company to an even stronger cash position, but it did not always work out well at first. After a year of getting used to each other, however, things started looking up strongly when we started working more closely with another GECC affiliate, the Kidder Peabody brokerage firm. In particular, we were able to work out a joint venture to market the coins that were bought for the Kidder Peabody American Rare Coin Fund, which owns the largest inventory ever in U.S. rare coins...$22 million.

The first year in partnership with Allegiance/GECC was tough, but necessary. I would advise any primary owner who wants to sell his or her privately held business to find out from the prospective owners: (1) Their commitment to putting money into the business operation as well as the front-money to buy it, and (2) Their long-term commitment to your business. If you run into any kind of snag in the marketplace and have a couple of bad months, their commitment may turn on a dime. That is one of the big problems with leveraged buyouts in general.

Seeing the two styles of management side by side, I must say that I feel more comfortable as a sole owner or part of an entrepreneurial team. As I write this book, I am still young (45) and eager to put these principles to work again. When my management contract is up, I will be in my early 50s. At that point, I can either retire or start a new business. I think you can tell from my writings here that I would not be comfortable without having at least some business deals in the works and perhaps a small company built around them.

No matter what age you are now, I firmly believe that a business of your own will always be your best investment. If you are employed by others and enjoy the nature of your work, that is second best. Either way, if you can make money while having fun, so much the better; but life is too short to spend half of it on a treadmill you cannot enjoy.

Clockwise from top: The national media picked up this shot of the famous gold legalization banner just before takeoff to buzz Nixon's inauguration. Robert H. Meier helped plan the 1975 conference and has remained a good friend and business associate. My good friend Joseph Bradley recorded the 1974 conference and every conference thereafter. John Kamin, newsletter writer and coin expert, addressing attendees of the 1974 conference.

Top left: I'm pictured here receiving the Gold Legalization Award, with Robert Bleiberg (left), editor of Barron's, *and Lord Rees-Mogg, then editor of* the Times *of London. Top right: Nobel Prize-winning economist Milton Friedman has spoken at several of our conferences. Bottom: Barry Goldwater (left), and my good friend Nicholas Deak, founder of the international precious metals and currency trading company, Deak and Company, spoke at the 1977 conference.*

Still together after all these years...the heart of the hard-money movement posing for a photo at the 1989 conference. (Top row, from left to right), James Dines, Richard Band, Ian McAvity, James Dale Davidson, Ed Gunther, Doug Casey, Dr. James McKeever, Harry Browne, Walter Perschke, Adrian Day, Vern Myers, Clark Aylsworth. (Middle row), Lew Rockwell, Joe Bradley, Dr. Gary North, Larry Abraham, myself. (Bottom Row), Mark Skousen, John Pugsley, Howard Ruff.

Top: A typical shot of our conference Investors' Market exhibit. Middle: Ayn Rand, the most popular speaker we have ever had at the NCMR conference. Bottom: As the conferences grew, we began using a big screen.

Top: Richard Russell addressing a packed crowd from the big screen. Middle: My good friend Eric Watson, perennial master of ceremonies for the New Orleans conferences. Bottom: In addition to the New Orleans conference, NCMR sponsored conferences in Hong Kong, Bermuda, the Bahamas, Australia, Mexico, Canada and South Africa. Here I give the opening remarks at our 1980 conference in Johannesburg, South Africa. At right is Owen Harwood, then Finance Minister of South Africa.

Clockwise from top left: William F. Buckley, Jr. has been a frequent speaker at our conferences. Franz Pick, one of several who claim to be the "Original" gold bug, pictured at his last NCMR conference. Mark Skousen delivers his talk "The Battle for Investment Survival" as General George Patton at the 1986 NCMR banquet. Louis Rukeyser has either spoken or moderated panel discussions at a dozen NCMR conferences.

Chapter 10

The Ten Minute Manager:

My Personal Management Principles

"Work is not a curse, it is the prerogative of intelligence, the only means to manhood, and the measure of civilization."

—Calvin Coolidge

Even though I do not take time to read many books on the art and science of business and management, I have been able to develop a unique body of management beliefs over the years. At first I did not consciously think about why I did what I did; but in thinking about the subject for this book, I have been able to isolate certain principles of my management style that have been responsible for building a fairly large business over the last decade.

Here, in a short, bulleted fashion, are what I think are the top ten ideas that would be valuable to anyone operating a company, or a department, or even a small family business. Ken Blanchard (no relation) wrote a book called the *One Minute Manager*, so you can call this chapter my short course in the "Ten Minute Manager."

(1) Go the Extra Mile

"Going the extra mile" is a principle from the Bible. It also works in business, where going the extra mile is the habit of giving more effort than is minimally necessary in your job, thereby insuring customer satisfaction and high employee morale. In a sense "going the extra mile" is the psychological equivalent of "debt-free management" in the financial realm. A poorly done job is like a debt hanging over your head. By working harder, you avoid the debt of owing somebody a much better job next time.

The habit of going the extra mile also pays great financial dividends. Quite simply, it is a smart business practice. I can point to a list of as many as 40 or 50 different business associates on whom, had I not been extremely understanding and gone the extra mile to understand the person and his or her particular problems, I would have long ago given up and ended the business relationship.

Instead, I can figure up almost to the dollar how many millions of dollars in profits have been made because of nurturing these relationships through hard times. This is another example of how a philosophy can, and does, have a dramatic impact on your life, your business and your pocketbook. Ideas have consequences.

The philosophy of going the extra mile and turning the other cheek really works for me. It is disarming because so few people practice it. Sometimes you get hit on the other cheek, but by and large it works.

(2) Give People Their Freedom

I have always believed in finding good people and then giving them their freedom to work. By giving them "too much" freedom, I might have to put up with more mistakes from them than they would otherwise make, but most of the time I will get more from them than from any two employees who are closely watched and regulated in a tyrannical, military style of organization. Obviously, this is much easier to practice when you have only five or six people working for you than when you have 50 people. When over 100 people work for you, that is when you have to hire middle managers who feel the same way you do.

While you need a certain amount of structure for your business to work right, if you give your people freedom in their lifestyles and hours, they will not feel overly threatened, will feel more secure on the job and therefore will give you a lot more effort. I am familiar with several industry leaders who find it very difficult to turn a profit, and if you look at their organizations you find the most alarming problem is employee turnover. They drive good people into the ground. The people either leave (if they are good) or they go through the motions and stay there just for the paycheck. When the work environment is depressing, you just do not win either way: It is no fun and it is not very profitable either.

Traditional management is basically militaristic, assuming that people are inherently lazy and have to be watched every second. Modern management styles are more tolerant, based on the belief that people want to find their personal satisfaction by working hard in a job they enjoy. People want to self-actualize through their work, and they will use their mistakes to grow on their job.

I probably go to the extreme in practicing tolerance of human foibles. I overlook the fact that some people might be inherently lazy; or, put more accurately, their lives have become so unsatisfying that they have no real goal in life, either at work or at home, and they need help.

The militaristic management style may have made some sense back in the 19th century, when most work was repetitive and dull and when there was not much of a service economy. In our modern age of information, however, success is built more on the satisfaction and service you bring customers, which is more likely to happen in a positive work place of confident individuals than in the old time-clock world.

Of course, in giving people their freedom, what you are really doing is delegating authority. It took me a long time to learn that delegation of authority in running a larger business is one of the key factors of success.

I can remember that many years ago, when I would go home at night, I would say to Jackie, "Look, this just isn't worth it. I've worked a ten-hour day, I'm going to have to work two more hours tonight, I handled a half a dozen petty problems today and got bogged down by a lot of petty politics and personal conflicts. I feel like my blood pressure is high. Life is too short. We're going to do something else for a living."

In other words, I had reached one of those typical entrepreneurial crises in management when I suddenly realized that I was taking on too much responsibility myself. That is when I learned to delegate. It probably saved my life, and certainly made my life a lot more fun and the company a lot more profitable.

By the time I sold my business, I had learned to delegate so much that when I sat down to figure it out, I discovered that in the two years before selling my business, I had spent a total of one year out of the office (combining both pleasure and business trips). Yet the business had never been more profitable.

Delegation of authority, first and foremost, depends on finding the right people whom you can trust. That is not easy, but you can do it. I like to think I had a good feel for people and whether they were out to take advantage of me or whether they were the "go the extra mile" types. Maybe that is a natural talent. I do not know. But I am convinced that if you cannot learn to properly delegate, you can hire someone who can. I have often delegated a million dollar transaction—and even $5 million dollar transactions—to someone within the company whom I could trust.

I have done the same thing in private business transactions. I once concluded a $30 million transaction and did very little of the negotiating myself. Most of it was delegated to trusted allies, one in the financial area and one in the legal area.

So remember that delegation is your life-support system!

(3) Mix Work and Play

When 90 percent of your employees are upbeat, it is really hard for the remaining 10 percent not to catch the bug. A lot of the people in our company enjoy being with each other not only in the work situation but in their own private time as well, and I think this is healthy for the company. People go through cycles in their work and eventually will reach a time when they are not pleased with their jobs; but if you build up enough loyalty and satisfaction during the good times, it is like money in the bank to support you when you are feeling down.

If people realize no one will reprimand them if they need to get away from the job for a while, they will be the better for doing so. I will go so far as to say that I would not object if they wanted to walk around the block, blow off some steam, get some perspective on solving a problem, or even go to the beach for the afternoon. As long as people do not make a habit of running away from their daily work problems, this can be a very therapeutic way to solve them.

I would much rather own a company that had a lower profit margin and a lot of people who enjoyed their jobs than a company with great short-term profits where nobody enjoyed their job. I want my people to be able to afford their success, to share in the profits they help produce, and to have an incentive to do more. If you have a bad day and a bad problem facing you, it will take you much longer to solve that problem if you have a negative attitude than if you go into your office relishing the challenge of the day. You almost enjoy solving each problem, so you move quickly through one problem and then tackle the next one.

A big key to enjoying life is to love your work, because that is where you are likely to spend over half your waking hours for over half your life. I love my work and look forward to going to the office each day, but I also think it is very important to be able to leave it all behind at the end of the day.

It is important to mix business and pleasure as much as possible, even though the dear old Internal Revenue Service would have us divide every activity into one or the other slot. How can you separate a business dinner from a social dinner? What if a dinner starts out socially, but one ends up getting more business ideas than if it were a business lunch?

What if a "personal" pleasure trip ends up with an article in one of my publications, concerning certain business lessons I learned there? Was the trip business or pleasure? Obviously it was both, and I would have it no other way.

(4) Accept Your Mistakes—Learn From Them

I feel that most people should take a more philosophical attitude toward their job than they do. The job is not your whole life. If you do something wrong, you should not have the attitude of fear—"When my boss finds out about this, I'll lose my job," or "I'm a terrible person and I always fail." Ask the best of yourself at all times; but when problems arise, try to realize that bad days are not all your own fault. Often, the problems have nothing to do with you personally, so try to shrug them off.

In the early days of building my company, up until about 1983, I used to come home and say about once a week, "Jackie, I don't need this grief. I don't need to get in the middle of all these personal conflicts. Let's get away from it all. Travel. See the world." At times I wanted to chuck it all, go somewhere—to a desert island or a western frontier—and live off my investments.

Then something clicked in my mind. I remembered *Trask* and all the lessons I learned while recovering—how small and unimportant these daily problems really are. From then on, I would start to take personality problems in management more philosophically. If necessary, I would let the conflicts happen, throw up my hands and say, "I've done what I can. If it works out, fine. If it doesn't, it won't be the end of the world or of the company."

A problem or crisis on the job is not that big of a deal if you look at the problem in a longer-term perspective. You learn to live with a certain level of failure. You are going to miss deadlines, make mistakes, pick a losing investment, write sales copy that does not generate responses, lose a big sale, and so on. But if you know that you are not going to get your tail chewed off for making a mistake, you will keep on going.

(5) Take Some Chances

The pioneers are the ones who get the arrows in the back. If I am not getting an arrow in the back now and then, I am probably not turning up enough new ideas. I think what is wrong with most of corporate America, and especially government workers, is the unwillingness to take chances and make mistakes. Everyone is protecting his own turf, hiding in the woodwork, keeping a low profile. Productivity becomes second to protecting one's own turf, and that usually means avoiding responsibility for fear of making a glaring error.

If the work place is to be a happy environment, a manager must be willing to take a risk that people are good, that they are motivated by the same spirit as he is. This means the manager might get burned sometime; but if he goes into any new deal or business arrangement believing that most people are good, he finds he will make more money than if he distrusts the other man and protects his rear flanks at all times.

Because of my attitude of giving the other guy the benefit of the doubt, I have found that most people indeed are good, and some people are wonderful—kindhearted, trustworthy and hard-working. If you run into a bad apple now and then, you might get hurt, but you will more than make up for it with the many people who are good and can help you make more money in joint ventures. That leads me naturally into the next point.

(6) Give "Too Much" Away

In some business meetings I have attended, everybody is sitting around suspiciously taking the measure of the other guy, "knowing" that the other guy will not give up certain points. I have found that if, from the beginning, you give away the very point they think you would "never" give up, this will break the ice so completely that you will also get more than you bargained for in return.

If you rank your goals in any given venture from 1 to 10, you might subconsciously be limiting yourself. Most people would not dare to conceive of getting a "12"—some extras they had not even conceived of as possible—but if you go into a deal giving away more than the other person expects to get, even in his best-case scenario, your generosity can be so disarming that it breaks down all his defensive barriers.

This is supposed to be the opposite of good negotiating strategy—the way you read about it in the best-selling books on the subject—but it has certainly worked well for me over the years. If you get only 80 percent of what you wanted, while the other guy gets 120 percent of what he wanted—the macho mentality says it is a bad deal. But I say, "So what?" If you walk away with only 80 percent of your "half" of a $2 million deal, you have $800,000. So what if the other fellow has $1.2 million?

If I am correct in believing that most people are basically good—easy to get along with, not hard-nosed unless driven into a corner—then you can go right down the line in giving them everything they want, even if it looks on the surface as though you are getting the losing end of the deal.

If you go into a negotiation with the attitude that you like this person and want to find common ground, the tension tends to disappear. If you go into a meeting in a positive spirit instead of with a structured agenda, you will find out a lot more about what you can gain from the relationship. I mentally go into a meeting asking myself what I want and what they want, and I make up a list of items that person would never dream I would give up. Then I give up his best wish and find it is a lot easier to ask for that one item I wanted the most.

(7) Don't Cut Off the "Bad Guys"

Almost every time I have had some really negative business experience, I have found that I would only be cutting off some great future income if I cut the person off totally. If I had put him on my blacklist and moved on to some other person to take his place, I would have lost millions of dollars for the company over the years. Only by forgiving and forgetting can you get to the point where you can discover the person's good points and make money working with him. For instance, if every late delivery or inferior product I receive were to upset me enough to cut off a supplier, I would lose a lot of good business relationships.

So many people operate on a blacklist principle. Under this theory people can be "OK" for a while, but only until they make their first big mistake. As soon as that first mistake happens, you give up on them and write them off as unreliable. But if you take a step back and put yourself in the other fellow's shoes, you will see he may be affected by business problems which are not apparent to you, and the mistake might really be only a one-time foul-up.

Sometimes people go beyond good business sense in attacking others, but if you realize that they may be facing bankruptcy, having personal problems, or just trying to cut corners too fine, you can understand that at least most of their failures are not personally related to you. If you attack them back, you are wasting positive energy. There is always a way to make money or friends out of the relationship instead of spending several days plotting how you can get back at somebody you imagine has failed you or attacked you.

(8) Stay Lean and Mean

Management consultant Peter Drucker wrote that a company will keep growing as long as it has an objective. Once it reaches this objective, however, the new objective often becomes "proper management procedures" instead of new growth in new directions. I object to an overly structured organization in that mold. I have always wanted to remain loose enough so that I can respond to the new challenges of the moment.

I would not care to work in a company whose only goal is to "manage" the company better by following procedures to the letter. I like being "lean and mean" so that I can act fast, even if it is totally outside the structure of the company. Managing for the sake of managing does not interest me. I prefer the brainstorming meeting in which you try out all the angles of a new "dream project." Even if only one idea out of ten eventually works, I am satisfied.

Of course, having too many new projects can dilute the retained earnings of a company and squander its talent. But if you are rational enough to realize that the largest amount of the money you make can be channeled back into new ways of serving your clients, you will avoid getting into the kind of rut that guarantees low growth and stagnation.

I look at bear markets the same way: as a great opportunity to get lean and mean for the next phase of growth. In a way, the negative bear market of 1980-1985 was actually a positive time for us. During the bear market of the early 1980s, we built up for the bull market we knew would come. If it had not been for that bear market, we would not have trained our lean sales staff to meet future demand.

We used the bear market to troubleshoot a new mainframe computer system, and we automated our inventory process. We built a tight, skilled editorial and marketing staff, and we designed a more sophisticated vault system. We have not only self-financed this growth, but we are set for a position of tremendous growth, unlike some of those who went into debt.

(9) Keep Communications Positive and Pleasant

I think there should never be an incident in any of my companies in which people lose control of their tempers. Any disagreement should be settled behind closed doors and even then with a certain amount of emotional restraint. You just create too many long-term problems when you use abusive language or raise your voice against someone.

If you get into a screaming argument, both of you will come away with deep negative feelings against the other. You do not "work it out" by getting angry, you drive it deeper. You get badly hurt feelings when you give vent to anger and frustration. It can create a longstanding feud, that may never get resolved and it does not solve any problems.

In my more than 20 years in business, I think I have never yelled at, or used abusive language against, a person who has worked with me. There have been dozens of times I wanted to, but I just had to sit on it for a while, usually overnight. The next day I would see it in perspective and feel it was ridiculous to get overly excited about the problem. I might write a memo stating the things that should be changed, but I would not use any of the personal emotional language that would confuse the issue.

(10) Build Incentives Into the Job

In the early years of our company, when we were small, almost every skilled professional on our staff was hired as an independent contractor with incentive clauses for superior performance. This philosophy comes mostly from my basic instincts, combined with trial and error; but I find a lot of what I have practiced by instinct is now reflected in some of the new management techniques.

Even some huge corporations now use some of the same techniques I developed in our small company. They call it "Intrepreneurship," or the art of promoting "individual entrepreneurs" within a corporate environment.

Because of the incentives I built into the fee structure of certain key people, we have seen our creative people motivated to attack market problems with new ideas, knowing that some of their pay is tied to the level of sales they generate.

One Last Tip

I think I owe a certain amount of my success to luck, being in the right place at the right time with the right product. I also owe some of it to hard work. But there are plenty of people who are both lucky and hardworking, but who forget a very important third point. Call it a positive attitude with thanksgiving, appreciation, and humility. In a short phrase, "Don't let success go to your head."

One key to my own success is that I truly think I am the same person now that I was when I was making $4,500 a year as a teacher, or when I was a student at LSUNO. Because of my positive attitude toward life, I have the ability to genuinely see good points in everyone I meet. That generates trust, and trust is the basis of most entrepreneurial ventures.

The Retirement Myth

I do not believe in retirement. Under the old theories of the life/work cycle, people would work their fingers to the bone until age 65 and then have five or ten "golden years" in which to live the "real life" they have waited to enjoy. Today, though, people can enjoy their jobs and also do what they love doing. If a hard-working person retires without ever finding what he wants to do in life, he may end up spending 20 or 30 years just sleeping late, eating too much, taking it easy and getting bored or sick. There is no way I would be satisfied with that kind of life. I think it is even damaging to your health not to feel a certain drive in your daily life. Many retirees have no goals to live for.

By contrast, I have mixed retirement into my life all along. I started out as a workaholic putting in 15 or 16 hours a day, but when I took off I also took a prodigious amount of time off. I would take two weeks here, a week there, and occasionally a month at a time, working hard about nine or ten months a year and traveling the other two or three months.

I see no reason why you should work yourself into an early grave for no real reward along the way. If you have a good group of well-motivated people working for you, and if you have delegated the work to them, there is no reason at all why you should not be able to take two to three weeks off at a time.

As far as writing and creative thinking are concerned, the best work I have done has always been into a dictating machine, either on the road or at home in a relaxed environment. It all flows together in my mind when I can concentrate in a quiet corner and just dictate it. You can say what you like about writing with computers, but dictation is the only way I can talk as fast as my mind comes up with the ideas I am writing about.

In summary, life for me is fully balanced in the moment. It is not all work today and all relaxation later on. I call that kind of split between work and pleasure "the retirement myth." Since I learned early that life can end at any moment without warning, I do not put off living the full life of work and play that is most fulfilling to me this very day.

Chapter 11

Investing In Life

"We get only one crack at life. It lasts but the snap of a finger. What a waste, what a shame, to be lowered away for all eternity without once having your mortal soul purged with the emetic of High Adventure."

—Dr. Jack Wheeler

I am continually dismayed by the fact that so many successful people work so hard to achieve success but, once they achieve their goals, they do not take the time to enjoy the peak experiences life has to offer. Something inside of them drives them on to harder and harder work until they drive themselves to an early grave. Life is too short to pass up those special adventures you always dreamed about. I say: Bring your dreams into reality all through your life.

Some people divide their work life from their play life with great precision. Others seem to be "all work, no play" or the reverse. Those who work too hard end up on an operating table or dead from hypertension or a heart attack. Those who do not work, but only play, live a life of lurching from one financial crisis to the other, finding their "fun" in a series of local, low-cost recreations—completely ignoring the great, wide world around them because of their personal and financial limitations.

160

I like to work hard, play hard, and mix them up constantly. After "serving my time in the trenches" for more than a decade of 12- to 15-hour workdays building a business, I finally slowed down around 1983 when I was approaching 40 years of age. When our company finally climbed all the way to the top of the ladder in the specialized business of diversified precious metals and coin sales, I took time out to consider all the places I wanted to go in my life and all the things I wanted to do. More than most people, I know that life is a fleeting treasure and you have to plan to enjoy it here and now, not wait for some mythical "golden years" in which you will finally start living (if you are still alive).

Making My Wish List

Back in 1982 I had made a list of 20 places I wanted to see and things I wanted to experience. The other day I took out the list again in preparation for writing this chapter, and I found that I have completed well over half of the trips I put on that list seven years ago.

This list is not complete, but I have been to Australia, New Zealand, Hong Kong, and Bora Bora. I went on an adventure fishing trip in Canada and on safari in Africa six times. I sailed up the Amazon. I visited the controversial borderlands between Nicaragua and Honduras and between Mozambique and Malawi. I visited Nepal, China and Thailand (twice), flying over the "top of the world"—Mount Everest—just before visiting the magnetic North Pole and the true (geographical) North Pole.

As I write this chapter, I have just returned after spending two weeks in an Irish castle, so the list is rapidly being ticked off at the rate of two or three new adventures per year. I have no doubt I will do all of the adventures on my list, and even more, within the next few years.

I must admit I am something of an adrenaline addict. Sometimes I push things to the limit for that extra excitement of taking time out to "live on the edge," swimming among the sharks on the Great Barrier Reef in Australia, white-water rafting (including canoeing over some unexpected waterfalls) in the Rockies, and off-road ATV racing in Prescott, Arizona, and the north Georgia mountains. Don't get me wrong. To invest in an adventurous life need not be dangerous, but sometimes the unexpected happens...

Getting in Over My Head

More than once, my adventures literally took me "over my head." While snorkeling off one of the Grand Caymans, I got my feet caught in a reef with the tide rising over me. It was easy to get mesmerized by all the sea life under water so that I quickly forgot what was going on around me. As it turned out, my tennis shoes got caught in some coral. I tried to jerk my foot out of my shoe, but that only made it worse.

There was no way I could extricate myself, and nobody was there to see my problem. I tried to yell to friends on the shore, but they could neither hear nor see me. Finally I was able to pull my foot out of my shoe just before the tide was about to cover my head. I was too tired from that effort to work up the energy to swim back. My shoe finally floated loose and eventually beat me to the shore, because I was just exhaustedly floating in.

Another time, on the Great Barrier Reef, I put a chicken sandwich in my pocket, dived overboard and started feeding the little colorful fish. This caused a feeding frenzy—which is a good way to see a lot of colorful fish come to swim around you and try to bite the food out of your hand. Lured by all this turmoil, a huge shark, at least 14 feet long, approached and started circling just below me.

For some reason, I did not have a whole lot of fear at the moment I saw the shark; it was more like fascination. I yelled to my friend Joe Bradley, "Hey, there's a big shark down there.

Take a look." Joe thought I was pulling his leg and, to make matters worse, I got a case of the giggles, which confirmed to Joe that I was joking.

Finally Joe looked down and his face got white. The shark was twirling around underneath us, getting closer to us with each circle. My legs were dangling down like nice morsels for the shark, but by then my flimsy little chicken sandwich was totally dispersed and so were the fish, so the shark swam away after the other fish.

As if this were not enough, a little later I saw about five moray eels guarding my only exit from a shallow reef. Their bodies were all wrapped around the rock and they were not about to let me out. I had to wait a long time before the tide rose and allowed me an alternate route of escape over some sharp, shallow rocks that cut me up a little bit.

Gliding Over Africa

My worst close call with death was flying over Botswana on the way to a safari, along with my wife, Jackie, her sister Tania and our good friends Joe and Elizabeth "Lister" Bradley. Our pilot was a 21-year-old fellow named Ethyl! It turned out to be a prophetic name.

Ethyl had flown out to see his girlfriend the night before and had come back early in the morning with only about 15 or 20 pounds of fuel left. He figured he could make it to the safari base, for it was only a few miles away. He had no access to any more fuel, so he was living on the edge at our expense and we did not know it.

As soon as we took off, it was pretty clear that the plane had very little fuel, because it started jumping up and down with the air currents, bouncing like a feather. It should have had a few hundred pounds of fuel, but the tank was almost empty. When the engine went off, to my amazement the pilot became totally crazed with fear. He picked up the radio and dropped it, he was shaking so hard; so I picked up the mike and asked him what I should say. The pilot was frozen with fear, so I just pushed the button and said "Mayday" a few times, then waited for a response. There was no response, the engines were dead and we went into a steep free-fall.

I was certain we were all going to die. The first thing that entered my mind was the sight, earlier that morning, of the crumpled wreck of another small-engine plane, which had virtually disintegrated on impact. I remembered looking at that plane and commenting to the others, "There's nothing but a thin sheet of metal to protect us. Crashing in one of these would crush us instantly." I am sure everyone else was remembering that wrecked plane and thinking the same thing.

Oddly enough, I felt no fear, feeling that I had lived a good life up to then and I was ready to die. The only way I can describe it is as a religious experience. I have gotten into so many adventures like this, feeling I had some sort of "guardian angel" and that I had already died once so death held no more fear for me. I looked over at Joe Bradley and touched his hand, then held Jackie's hand, tight, and then I looked at each of the other passengers, one at a time. A couple of the women were quietly sobbing, but nobody was out of control.

All of a sudden, the pilot got control of himself and started using the clutch and choke to spurt a little more fuel into the engine, trying to turn a spiral circle back to the airport and hoping to land safely. The engine was popping, the plane was out of control. Then as we approached the airport the engine totally died, and we dropped very fast toward the trees in front of the airstrip. We just escaped the trees and hit the runway at a fairly level angle. It was a painful, jarring hit, but nobody was hurt.

After we had landed, my sense of calm disappeared. It seemed like everything hit me when we landed. I started shaking uncontrollably with the delayed effect of shock and fear and was very upset at the pilot for burning up all his fuel the night before and risking our lives just so that he could go up and see his girlfriend.

Ethyl siphoned gas off all the other planes at the airstrip and proved to us all he had sufficient fuel to get to the safari base camp. We were stuck with Ethyl and the same plane to fly south across the Kalahari Desert to home base in Johannesburg! I spent my next few hours looking out the window for places to land in an emergency.

Of course the recreations or adventures I mention above are not going to be for everyone. But I know that, old and young, people have their own favorite adventures. There is Howard Segermark, former aide to Senator Jesse Helms and now head of Free The Eagle and The Industry Council for Tangible Assets (ICTA). Howard enjoys his spare time by roaring around the back roads of America on the fastest motorcycle made. I have an 80-year-old client who spends his weekends soaring in a glider. There is the New Orleans businessman Al Copeland, president of the noted fried chicken chain Popeye's. He is worth several hundred million dollars, but he holds the world championship in powerboat racing. The list is endless but far shorter than it should be. You need to reach out and grab a big bite of life.

Visiting China Before the Revolution

When I visited Beijing, China, about a year before the crackdown of June 1989, my guide wanted to show me all the usual buildings and tourist sites. I would have nothing to do with that kind of propaganda. As in other places I have visited, I got off the beaten path and told him I just wanted to mix with the people and use him as translator.

It was great to get away from the government-approved travel plan and especially the mushy food in the government-approved restaurants. The private restaurants and hotels in China are much better, in terms of both food and hospitality, than the government tours. We were able to loosen up our guide and get him to talk more freely, sometimes under the influence of a few Chinese beers. He was a university student, about 20, working part time as a tourist guide and translator.

Once I got our guide far away from government watchdogs, I asked him what was really going on in China. How was the free-market revolution, compared with the Cultural Revolution? He told me that he was too young to remember the Cultural Revolution, but thought that today's regime was too repressive.

I said, "You have a Sony Walkman, a camera, a nice place to live, and you're only 20. How can you not be happy and hopeful for the future?" He said he and his friends were unhappy and restless because the old line was still in charge and the young people had no say in their government. They wanted the freedom to choose their professions, where they could live, and so forth.

At the time, I was shocked to hear him say these things, but it certainly rang true a year later when millions of young people like him staged a sit-down hunger strike, waving their signs for democracy and a Chinese version of the Statue of Liberty, demonstrating for democracy to the point of death.

A year earlier I could sense that the same kind of turmoil was brewing in China that resulted in our American Revolution over 200 years ago. These young people wanted a voice in their government—the same as our Founding Fathers did—and were willing to die to get it.

Throughout my tour I was able to meet dozens of Chinese, and they were all extremely open and positive about the developing freedom in their country, in public. Maybe they shared the same fears as my guide, in private. Knowing some of these people so well saddened me when the butchery took place a year later.

In 1988 everything in China felt free. There were a number of free, open markets in operation. Our tour guide explained the nature of the free markets and their level of support from the ruling structure. In fact China was almost shockingly free in 1988. I spent a lot of time right in the middle of free markets in China—with everyone circling my wheelchair curiously, because they had never seen anyone in a wheelchair—sharing my ideas of liberty with people who were hungry for any news from the West.

Smuggling in Books on Freedom

As I usually do on all my trips to totalitarian countries, I smuggled in a box of free-market literature to spread around, like a Johnny Appleseed of the mind. I brought works by Milton Friedman, Ludwig von Mises, Henry Hazlitt, Friedrich Hayek and others, in English, because most of the students can read English (and I did not yet know of any books on freedom written in Chinese).

The reason I keep spreading the word on freedom wherever I go is that, once planted, freedom is a very strong flower. It can grow through concrete, if necessary, once the seed is well planted. In China today, for instance, I sense that the seed of freedom is pretty firmly planted in the youth; and I do not see the old Communist thugs having the strength to keep that freedom down, in the long run. Once Mao's old gangsters die out, I think the new generation will not allow any more hard-core Communism to continue.

Pandora's box was opened when the Chinese turned on their own people and murdered hundreds of young students. World public opinion will never support those butchers again, and it is only a matter of time before freedom is victorious.

Another thing to bear in mind is that almost all the big publicity about the crackdown on freedom in China centers on Beijing. There are other parts of China in which capitalism is still tolerated and even encouraged. It is a big nation of 1.2 billion people spread over three million square miles, and some of the outlying areas (as in the Soviet Union) are much more free and independent than in the heart of Beijing.

When China becomes free, it will be a treat to see how fast they begin to excel in world markets. Throughout the Far East and in America, Chinese are excellent businessmen. They are an extremely productive people by nature, as shown by the great Chinese success stories in Hong Kong and Taiwan. Once freedom breaks through the Communist power structure in China, I am convinced that they will be among the most productive groups of people in the world.

According to reliable estimates, 14.5 million private businesses were launched in China in the decade ending in 1989. Even under the yoke of Communism, the growth rate of the Chinese economy led the entire world in the five years from 1984 through 1988, with over 10 percent per year growth in real terms. Think what they can do when they become truly free.

To show you how free markets can transform a nation, immediately after visiting China, I visited Bangkok, Thailand, which has a purely capitalist economy. This dramatized to me the difference in energy that is evident between a land that encourages freedom, next door to a nation that stifles it. Open-air markets in Bangkok operate through pure capitalism. Everyone was vying for your money in a free, open market. Thailand is supposedly a very poor nation, but its wealth is rapidly growing, as is the case in several other free-market Oriental nations.

Before going on with my travels, I would like you to meet my friend and business associate, Jack Wheeler, who first got me involved with serious adventure travel.

Meet Dr. Jack Wheeler

Jack Wheeler and I are almost like philosophical twins. We were born within hours of each other on November 9 and 10, 1943. In our youth, we read the same books, although quite independently of each other; we met many of the same people, although Jack and I never officially met until we were in our 40s and I had an idea for starting an adventure travel club.

Because of the list I had drawn up in 1982, I already knew what kind of adventures I wanted to go on, but I also wanted to go along with other like-minded people. So this "adventure club" needed a special kind of leader: a strong and virile man who was also philosophically aligned with our people and willing to risk adventuresome settings, with a persevering type of personality that could override foreign bureaucrats. In short, I was looking for a person who could inspire and attract adventure-oriented travelers and investors and go into business with me.

I sat down with my dictating machine one Sunday afternoon and dictated five pages of ideas about the travel club—where they would go, what type of person should head it up, and so on. By coincidence, that same weekend I was reading a series of *Reason* magazine articles by Dr. Jack Wheeler, who covered the eight wars of resistance against Communism. He had actually smuggled himself behind the lines of several conflicts, several times. That interested me deeply, not only philosophically, but also because of the adventure angle.

Quickly I found out that Jack was not just a writer but was a life-long adventurer who had climbed the Matterhorn at age 14, lived with the headhunting Jivaro Indians at age 16, and swam the Hellespont at 17 (over Christmas break in college). Jack was on Ralph Edwards' *This is Your Life* show when he was only 17, the youngest person ever to be profiled on that show. He was not only a great adventurer, but also a deep philosopher with a strongly conservative background. He earned a master's degree in anthropology from UCLA and a doctorate in philosophy from the University of Southern California.

Since graduating from college, he has not slowed down his adventurous spirit at all. He has been to the North Pole 20 times, more than anyone else; and he is the only person to have sky-dived right on the mark at 90 degrees north. Talk about being on top of the world! He also went over the Alps on elephants, following Hannibal's path, and so on. (All his youthful exploits are covered in his book *The Adventurer's Guide*, so I shall not try to repeat that book in this one.)

Wheeler-Blanchard Adventures

One day I invited Jack to New Orleans to tell him about my plan for an adventure travel club. We had a late lunch at 2:00 one Sunday afternoon. For about 10 hours, we sat reminiscing together, eating both lunch and dinner at the same table in the same restaurant and closing it down after midnight. We talked about everything—from reading Ayn Rand at about the same time to knowing certain people at the same time, to working on Youth for Goldwater in 1964 and having several of the same interests.

From 1983 to 1985, Jack had turned to the freedom fighter movement for his inspiration and adventure. He went behind the lines to report on those wars of liberation, and he has since been credited with giving rise to the Reagan Doctrine of official support for freedom fighters worldwide and especially in this hemisphere. As an important side benefit of my association with Jack Wheeler in the adventure tour business, we began to work on the freedom fighter cause too. (I shall discuss that more in the next chapter.)

I wrote up my notes of that meeting the next day, March 4, 1985. My concluding paragraph says, "Jack's dream is to refit an amphibious plane to handle up to ten passengers. It could then go anywhere in the world. We would even be in a position to inherit the Cousteau legacy."

In retrospect, however, we bit off a lot more than we could chew with Wheeler-Blanchard Adventures, which never made any money; but we certainly had some good times. One of our trips was behind the lines in liberated Angola, where our group of about eight or nine people met with leaders of the resistance movement. The first tourists in liberated Angola! Talk about adventure tours! Jack had to pull some strings to get air clearance in that war-torn region.

One of the most fascinating Wheeler-Blanchard Adventures was to the North Pole, which Jack had already visited 18 times by then.

Conning the Soviets Into
Flying Us to the North Pole

We planned a trip to the North Pole in the spring of 1988. The timing of any such trip must be exactly accurate between the coldness of winter and the spring thaw, so that you and your plane do not float off on some ice island that melts away from the main block of polar ice. Still, the weather is not guaranteed to be favorable; and both Jack Wheeler and I went into the trip with the understanding that it might have to be aborted at the last minute, due to the weather.

Besides Jack and me, our group included my son, Anthem; my friend, Lesia Hnatiw; John Perrott, a retired engineer who had worked in dozens of countries around the world and now resides in Texas; William De Fee, a doctor from central Louisiana; and a retired Broadway actress from New York, Joan Arliss.

As it happened, the weather did indeed turn bad on us; and we had to land short of the North Pole at a Soviet weather station. The airstrip was about a mile from the station, so we had a long walk through the bitter cold from the plane to the station to inquire whether we could hitch a helicopter ride to the North Pole. When we entered the weather station, I was immediately struck with the primitive nature of the Soviet buildings, like something you might expect from Byrd's first expedition to the Pole in 1909 or a Yukon gold rush camp of the 1890s. Soviet architecture is uniformly shoddy, even at the North Pole.

We could not get a straight answer right away, because the

Soviet helicopter pilots were tired from flying all the way from Moscow in the last few days and were sleeping in a canteen-style building in the middle of the day. As we sat there the tension was pretty thick between us, and it was frightfully cold outside. The wind was blowing harder, and I was not sure how soon we would be able to take off again even if we abandoned our plans to see the Pole.

What finally cut through the tension was the presence of my son, Anthem (8 at the time), and Lesia Hnatiw, who is Ukrainian by birth. One of the Soviet officials spoke Ukrainian, so she could converse with him and he would translate into Russian. One of the Soviet troops really took a liking to little Anthem, lifting him up and carrying him around, giving him a ride on a snowmobile and even giving him an official Soviet badge to wear.

Jack Wheeler is probably the world's greatest anti-Soviet activist. The Kremlin has called him an "international gangster," and I am sure there was a price on his head as a spy. Therefore it was convenient for Jack that these Soviets did not ask for our passports, but they did ask what each of us did for a living. When it came to me, I said I was a "capitalist." They laughed at that. No American had ever used that word in front of them in a positive context before.

We figured the best way to get to the North Pole was to keep loosening them up with humor and to play their game. Finally, we were almost begging for help, saying that we flew all the way from America, lost our luggage, could not land anywhere else. Still the answers to our entreaties were all "Nyet." Then the pilots started to wake up; and we were warming up, literally with some hot tea, and figuratively by praising the Soviet pilots and telling them how much our visit was "promoting world peace."

We told them it cost us $5,000 each to make it this far, so we would be delighted to pay them another $500 to fly us to the Pole, as a "monetary contribution to the Soviet effort for world peace." That must have hit a resonant chord, because they finally agreed.

As we were ready to take off, a tremendous number of people landed on the airstrip to celebrate a special occasion we knew nothing about.

A Crowd Converges at the Pole

In the whole history of North Pole expeditions, only 400 people had set foot on exactly 90 degrees north. But it so happened that on the very day we arrived in the neighborhood, the entire Canadian Olympic ski team and an elite Soviet ski team were making a symbolic gesture of world peace by skiing together from the edge of their respective countries to meet at the North Pole. The two ski teams were going to meet on the same day we arrived there. That is why the helicopter pilots had flown up from Moscow. Without such a coincidence, we never would have been able to hitch a ride to the Pole.

So the deal was done, and we got into the Soviet military helicopter to visit the Pole. They put Anthem and me in first and then the others followed. It took about 15 minutes to reach the Pole, and we were in the middle of all kinds of turbulence the whole way. The inside of the copter itself was in shambles, with loose wires and paneling hanging out here and there, typical of Soviet craftsmanship. It was so shaky that it scared a few of us, but we had to figure these top Soviet pilots knew what they were doing.

At the Pole there were Soviet flags flying. In fact, the copter pilots told us the North Pole Soviet Ice Station was Soviet territory. Whether that is true or not, it cannot be a very official border, because nobody asked for our passports throughout this whole episode. As we were about ready to leave, I volunteered my passport and asked them to stamp it, "Soviet North Pole."

When we finally landed at the Pole, we drank a glass of champagne at the top of the world. It was so cold that if you did not drink it right away, the champagne would freeze. If you spilled a drop, it would freeze before it hit your parka.

We spent about two hours at the top of the world, taking video films and still pictures of the event. Then we got into the helicopter and headed back toward the Soviet ice station. The head officer who accepted my $500 offer was not there any more, and the only fellows we saw were strangers, so we did not want to try to explain why a helicopter took us to the Pole. Instead of paying them the $500 cash I had agreed to give them, I made a mental note to send Gorbachev a check when I got back home; and I did, along with a letter of explanation and thanking him very much for helping my son be the youngest person ever to reach the Pole—soon to be in the *Guinness Book of World Records*.

I never got a letter back from Gorbachev, but I did get the canceled check back, stamped by some functionary office. I was hoping Gorbachev would autograph the back of the check, since I made it out to him, personally. Although I hate the fact I helped fund the Soviet empire in any small way, it must have really confused them and kept 50 Soviet bureaucrats busy. It took three months for them to process the check.

More Trips on My List

There are many other adventure outings on my list that are very special to me, but I have not found time to spend the several months necessary to plan and execute them. For instance, I want to rent a big sailing craft and sail off to some of the most beautiful uninhabited (and some inhabited) islands of the South Pacific and the Indian Ocean.

I want to go to Antarctica, completing a pair of polar journeys. I also want to go on a serious treasure ship hunt. In time, when China mellows a bit, I want to go on an overland wilderness trek through China; I want to spend some serious time in isolated parts of South America; I want to go to New Guinea and live with some of the tribes there; and I want to live with the bushmen in the Kalahari Desert before they become extinct.

Next year I plan to go on a lion hunt in Africa while living in a Masai mud-dung house, located around the area where the movie *Out of Africa* was filmed. I plan to go with eight or ten native Masai as my guides. (If we don't kill a lion, we'll settle for a warthog.)

Discover the Planet Earth

Who can forget the sight of the first full-color photographs of the beautiful blue and white isolated planet Earth from the first moon mission. I think it struck home to all of us; I know it did to me, how very lucky we are to be on Earth.

Wild, green jungles, blue and white-capped mountains, the fascination of the oceans, the abundance of the Western economies, the ease of transportation and communication, all these things and thousands more make Earth a unique and wonderful place to live.

Our best scientists can only imagine how many millions of light years it is to the next inhabited island in the endless sea of space. One can dream, as I do in my fascination with science fiction, about what it will be like in coming centuries to visit and develop the other planets...But for now we are limited in our explorations and our adventures to Earth.

But think about it in another way: Think about the endless places there are to visit and the wonderful cultures and people there are to discover on Earth. As we develop more leisure time and the youth of the West become monetarily successful enough to both enjoy a productive work style and a challenging lifestyle, the discovery of planet Earth will be experiencing a new renaissance.

Just one example of this is the extremely high popularity of

the nature and adventure channels and programs on both network and cable television. Adventure books and adventure
travel clubs have experienced a boom in the last several years.

Many people are discovering how silly the advertisements
are that talk about the "adventure" cruises from one Caribbean
island to another; cruises that concentrate on food, dance con-
tests and relaxing in the sauna. Hey, there is nothing wrong with
this; but it certainly is not very adventurous or challenging, and
there is *so* much more to do in life.

Consider the following. Most individuals will not be lucky
enough to do a lot of traveling to visit other cultures (because of
monetary limitation) until they are well into their 20s (say 25).
Most people cannot (because of health limitations) or will not
travel extensively past their 70th birthday. At maximum, that
leaves a precious few 45 years, most of which will be spent
working (hopefully, enjoying it). The typical American takes off
in vacation time approximately two weeks a year, and that means
an entire lifetime (with monetary and health limitations) of 90
weeks of travel.

Now do this exercise. List 20 really big trips you would like
to take, say to Australia, China, the South Pacific, or for the more
adventurous, exploring the Amazon, the Arctic, the wilder back
roads of South America, Asia and Africa.

Those who travel internationally know that the absolute
minimum for a big trip is two weeks, and you really need three
weeks. But even if you limit it to two weeks, in an entire lifetime
you would really have to make up your mind and dedicate
yourself to building up the resources to take those favorite 20 big
trips, or 40 weeks, to see the parts of the world that you most
wanted to see. That leaves 50 weeks for most people, almost by
definition, to spend in "non-adventure" semibusiness travel, and
the like.

If as you read this book you are 60 years old, even if you have
the money, you will not feel really comfortable doing an adven-

ture sort of travel much after age 70.

I am not trying to be melodramatic or pessimistic. I am trying to drive home the point that if you really want to invest in life, see the world and discover new cultures, then just as with making a big monetary investment or switching funds from your money market fund into some more speculative investment, you have to make the decision now and you have to begin to immediately implement it. You have to take action.

So many people say, "One of these days, I would really like to charter a sailboat and sail the lower Caribbean with some friends," or "Wasn't that movie *Out of Africa* beautiful? I'd love to go on safari. We must do it one day." In the meantime, the years tick by and those dream trips become just that, dreams.

As the philosopher Johann Wolfgang von Goethe said, "Whatever you can do, or dream you can do, begin it. Boldness has genius, power, and magic in it." And as Benjamin Disraeli said, "Action may not always bring happiness; but there is no happiness without action." Finally, as Helen Keller said, "Life is either a daring adventure or nothing."

The Big Payoff

What is the use of any investment unless you eventually receive the payoff-earnings or the capital gains? It is the same way in the philosophy of investing in your own life. The rewards can be simple things such as I have experienced—the unforgettable sound of beautiful music as you sail out into the Indian Ocean off the shores of the ancient African island city of Lamu into a sunset which is indescribable; the thrill of catching a massive barricuda in the blue-green waters of the Exuma Islands; the heart-pounding thrill of sliding down a snowy Colorado mountainside in a racing sled, here and there airborne as the sled flies over the mogels; the delight of driving a Honda Odyssey (a four-wheel-drive off-road vehicle) on the steep mountain trails of northern Georgia; or the shear joy of swimming slowly along, just inches from several giant manta rays as they gracefully arch their wings and swim over a world of beautiful coral reefs.

These are simple things, but all of us in relatively good health can experience them, and our life can be better for it. The payoff can be the simple thrill of doing it; but also, it is healthy, exciting and exhilarating. In my experience, these and other simple pleasures are among the highest dividends in life.

Friendships in Other Lands

We all know the rewards of true friendship. It is often said that you are lucky if you have only five really good, true friends in life. It is true with some people but not true with others, depending on personality. But far fewer people have ever commented on the thrill, the excitement and the rewards of developing friendships in different lands and totally different cultures.

In recent years, this is something I have tried to do. It is not easy, but the rewards are great. Let me give you two examples from the dozens available.

James, the Masai Warrior

Years ago, I met a young Masai "warrior." I met him when my friend David Galland and I made a business/political trip to Africa and decided to go on safari in the Masai area of Kenya, which is the beginning of the Serengeti Plain that flows into Tanzania. James, a Masai, was our game tracker and driver. It was slow at first, but we struck up a friendly relationship with James and eventually learned that he was famous in that region. Before he was 21 he killed two lions single-handedly, using the traditional Masai spear. James is the best game spotter and tracker I have ever met. He can spot a lion in high grass at hundreds of yards, and one day he spotted a cheetah curled up in high grass in the bush a half hour before we reached her and her cubs in our Land Rover.

I have been back to visit James four times now. As a wild coincidence, his personal tribal land contains the famous site in the movie *Out of Africa* where the famous white hunter, played by Robert Redford, was buried. It is one of the most beautiful sites on earth, hundreds of feet above the Masai Mara. (Mara means "spotted" in the Masai language, and the Masai Mara means "the spotted plain.") During the migration season, the Masai Mara is spotted with tens of thousands of wild animals. It also contains thousands of the beautiful African acacia trees, seeming lonely against the yellow grass of the plain.

Each year I go back to visit the Masai Mara, and James and I have become quite friendly. After visiting his family at his beautiful mountain compound, I learned that it was against informal tribal law to bring white tourists off the game preserve to Masai home sites. When I asked James about this, he gave me one of his great smiles, touched his heart and said, "Jim, on the inside, you don't know it, but you're more black than white."

Mohammed, the Dhow Captain

On my trips to Africa, I have stopped on a wonderful, little island off the coast of Kenya called Lamu. There are only a few hotels on the island, and you can get to the island only by ancient sailing dhow. There is a legend that the ancient town site was the home base for Sinbad the Sailor. There are no cars or trucks; travel on the island is by foot or donkey.

At any rate, the port of Lamu is an incredible little town on a beautiful white sand island. The winding streets of the town give you the feeling of an Indian Ocean African/Arab trading post of 500 years ago.

There is a very nice little hotel, the Peponi, at the end of the island where a beautiful white sand beach begins. There I met Mohammed. Mohammed and my friends and I have taken many a dinner sail into the Indian Ocean to watch the incredible sunset and moonrise. We have laughed until we cried and have talked for long hours about many things, including our different cultures.

On one of my trips to Lamu, I bought an ancient Arab trading trunk. The shopkeeper refused to have it shipped and told me that no one had ever bought one of these massive trunks and had it shipped. I asked the innovative Mohammed if he would find a way to have it shipped to New Orleans. I entrusted him with an advance payment for his travels to Mombasa, the main port of Kenya, north of Lamu. Over a period of many months Mohammed traveled to Mombasa on four different occasions and finally broke through the bureaucracy to find a shipping firm to ship the trunk to New Orleans. Almost nine months later, it showed up at my office.

Each time I go back and land by private charter to catch the dhow to Lamu, in the distance I can see Mohammed in his Arabian wrapped skirt with his shiny white teeth against that black, laughing face.

This is a far cry from the people most travelers meet—the airline stewardesses, the cab drivers, the waiters in their hotels and the receptionist at the registration desk.

There is nothing like getting outside your familiar environment to see what the people of our unique world are all about. It does not need to be any more dangerous than driving on the interstate, and it is good for your soul!

As Theodore Roosevelt said, "Far better is it to dare mighty things, to win glorious triumphs, even though checkered by failure, than to take rank with those poor spirits who neither enjoy much nor suffer much, because they live in the great twilight that knows neither victory nor defeat."

Chapter 12

Filling the Void—With Freedom

"All eyes are opened, or opening, to the rights of man. The general spread of the light of science has already laid open to every view the palpable truth that the mass of mankind has not been born with saddles on their backs, nor a favored few booted and spurred, ready to ride them."

—Thomas Jefferson, in his last letter (June 24, 1826)

Some of my business associates sometimes wish I would not talk about freedom fighters. They want me to stick with hard-money investing business and stay away from controversial political subjects like this. But freedom is, and always has been, the major prerequisite for building wealth. It does you no good to be the richest man in a Gulag.

The spread of Communism, or any totalitarian regime, is clearly a pocketbook issue of enormous proportions, especially when the threats to freedom are located in our own back yard.

Defending Our Back Door

I first visited Mexico when I was 18, as part of my recovery process. I lived there for a year and really grew to love the country, its beautiful land and its people. I guess I have been there 20 or 25 times since 1962 and have seen a continuous siege of inflation and bad government ravage that nation over the years. How well I remember buying a hamburger for a peso back in the early 1960s. Today the same hamburger would cost about a thousand pesos—100,000 percent inflation in the last 25 years.

As elsewhere in Latin America, the one-party system and near-total government control of industry is a major cause of the inflation and social unrest. In Mexico there is widespread popular and governmental support of the Communist Sandinistas, showing how attractive the socialist solution to their problems has become in the last generation.

I have also been to most of the Central American nations, including several visits to Costa Rica. I have talked with most of the leaders of the Contras, both those living in exile in America and those in hiding in Honduras and Nicaragua, on a trip I made to those two nations in 1987. The tension in Central America is so thick you can cut it. There is great suspicion of America by the average man on the street, and great frustration with America among the Contras, who are tired of our nation's "on-again, off-again" support.

In the last few years, I have visited most of the Caribbean islands and have seen the corruption of government there as well. In Jamaica I have seen how much their fling with communism cost their economy, in both tourist dollars and lost production. They are recovering now, but only under a more free market system.

The point of this quick tour of our nation's back yard is that, in all my extensive travels in Latin America, I have found that the situation is overripe for a communist revolution. Everywhere you travel in that region, the government has strong, often brutal, control; there is massive drug smuggling (often with a wink from the police), little or no efficiency in business, a surly service sector, graft, bribery, runaway inflation and near-total economic stagnation. These are prime breeding grounds for communism.

To fight Latin American communism effectively, we need do only two things: (1) Throw the Soviets out; make a firm stand against Eastern bloc aid. (2) Fill the void; help bring about free markets and free elections in both the right-wing and left-wing dictatorships that abound there. If we do not act to help solve these problems today, we will eventually be forced to solve them at our southern borders with millions of refugees pouring across the Rio Grande River.

As retired Navy Admiral Elmo Zumwalt told us at an NCMR conference a few years back, if we must defend our southern borders for the first time in over 70 years, we will literally need to pull our soldiers back home from around the world and leave Europe defenseless. Then, the Soviet Union could literally take over Europe without a fight.

Freedom is a financial and investment issue of the most important rank. If the communists come to dominate Central America through their enclave in Nicaragua, the refugee problem could literally overwhelm our welfare state, our military posture in the world, and our national security.

The Cost of Carter's Folly

If you doubt that freedom is a pocketbook issue, consider the tragic foreign policy result of voting Carter into the White House in 1976. His presidency was the greatest blow to freedom in the world since World War II. Over 30 years of postwar containment of communism was wiped out in the four years of the Carter administration in the late 1970s.

While Carter was in office, more than a dozen nations were overthrown or infiltrated by communism and other totalitarian systems. I can only imagine how many more nations will fall if we have the bad fortune to elect another liberal Democrat!

Under Carter we practically invited the Soviet Union to take over the Sandinista revolution in Nicaragua in 1979. Carter's men also hounded the Shah of Iran out of office, only to see him replaced by a far worse leader. Carter also let the communists roll through Southeast Asia, killing millions of Cambodians and enslaving Laos and all of Vietnam.

At least half a dozen African nations fell to communism during the late 1970s. I do not know whether the free world could survive another wishy-washy Carter-style Democrat in the White House! It really is frightening to consider what a repeat of the Carter years could bring to the world.

The Destruction of the Soviet Empire

In the years of President Carter, when communism seemed invincible and on the march in Southeast Asia and half a dozen African countries, who could have predicted that by 1989 the empire of the Soviet Union would be self-destructing? Make no mistake about it, there is a true revolution taking place in the Soviet Eastern European bloc. No one can precisely say what the result of this revolution will be; but one thing is absolutely clear: The political system in every communist country will eventually crumble, either in the 1990s or as we enter the new century.

For the past 20 years, I have talked about collectivism as the megatrend of the 20th century. I now firmly believe that the megatrend of the 21st century will be freedom. But before we get too optimistic, remember that the various revolutions that will take place within the Soviet Union, the Eastern European bloc, and other communist countries across the world will take many forms; and it is obvious that the immediate result will not be a traditional Western capitalist system.

Even in the West, the best we have is a mixed economy, where our economies are predominantly free, but still hindered by mass government regulations. The decline and decay of communism may first result in social democracies dominated by a mixed economy that allows some free markets, but with basic socialist control. I believe that Ayn Rand would have predicted that the movements within Eastern Europe, the Soviet Union, and other communist countries are more likely to end up, at least in the first stage, with a period of fascism. After all, fascism is a system that encourages big business and allows a mixed economy of free markets and socialism. But there are encouraging signs of hope for the longer term.

In October of 1989, the world was shocked to see the Communist party in Hungary renounce traditional communism and even change its name to the Socialist Party. At that time, the Communist Party in Hungary had 720,000 members. But when the renamed Socialist Party encouraged registering anew, the party literally almost ceased to exist. Of 720,000 former members, only 30,000 joined the new party.

Throughout the universities of Eastern Europe, there is a small, but growing, movement that advocates capitalism and a free society. In Poland, where I helped distribute free-market literature (in the Polish language), the Peace and Freedom party is purely libertarian. It even makes the conservative wing of the Young Republicans look wishy-washy in comparison.

My former wife, Jackie, and my closest friend and executive assistant, Lesia Hnatiw, are Ukrainian. For years I have had a special interest in the Ukraine. I even considered writing a book about Stalin's policy of genocide in the Ukraine, where the death toll was even greater than the number of Jews who died in the Holocaust in Nazi Germany.

It encourages me that the official government of the Ukraine has launched an autonomy movement, similar to the growing nationalist political parties of the Baltic states. As in Lithuania, Latvia and Estonia, activists in the Ukraine are calling for more freedom from the Soviet Union, for more autonomy.

On September 8, 1989, the Ukrainian Communist Party allowed a historic event to take place. It was called the First Congress of the Ukrainian Popular Movement for Perestroika. There were 1,105 delegates, who called not only for greater freedom in the Ukraine, but for the Soviet Union to be transformed into a confederation of sovereign republics.

One of the guests at the Congress was Polish Solidarity senior adviser Adam Michnik, who told the delegates, "Totalitarian communism is crumbling" all over the region.

The November 5, 1989, edition of *The New York Times* showed a photograph of 500,000 people rallying for change in East Germany. One week after this huge demonstration, the unheard-of happened. The entire East German government resigned, and the borders of Eastern Europe were thrown open. On the night of November 9, 1989, tremendous celebrations were held on the Berlin Wall. I will never forget watching the live video as young students hacked away at the Wall with pickaxes, and the Berlin Wall came crumbling down. Thus, the final confirmation that communism, as a system, has failed. In a matter of weeks, over a million people, voting with their feet, abandoned living under a Marxist/Leninist system.

I could go on and write an entire book about the developments that took place within the Soviet sphere in just 1989 alone. It is exciting. It is encouraging, and I think the eventual outcome will be extremely positive.

Few have failed to point out, however, that there are also dark clouds on the horizon. Out of revolution there could come chaos. At some point there probably will be a whiplash by the Soviet hard-line military leaders. Although the Ukrainians may desperately want their independence from the Soviet Union, it is highly unlikely that this would happen without war. The Ukraine is the breadbasket of the Soviet union. If the Ukraine fell, it would spell the doom of the Soviet Union, not in a matter of decades, but perhaps in a number of years. The Soviet military establishment would simply not allow that to happen.

We must continue to ask ourselves, Even if the anti-communist movements throughout the world are successful, what political system will replace the old, failed Marxist/Leninist system? That is why I called this chapter "Filling the Void—With Freedom."

The worst possible thing we can do is to allow ourselves to intervene and be drawn into massive military support in the coming years as the Soviet system falls apart. Yes, there may be special situations where military action could be called for, but the policy we should follow is the one suggested by our first president, George Washington: Let the light of freedom shine and spread the word of freedom throughout the world. Let the United States once again become the leader of a revolutionary new freedom and independence movement in the 1990s and 21st century.

I recently heard a pro-freedom Ukrainian leader say, "Our problem is no longer how to get the literature into the country; it is how to get all the literature we need and get it into the country at a faster pace." That should be our signal to begin a massive educational campaign for capitalism and the benefits of the free-market system to fill the void left by the collapse of the Marxist/Leninist system throughout the world. If the government is going to spend the money anyway, I would rather see the military budget cut by 20 percent and the money used for this kind of education.

This is the time for persons, organizations and businesses to join their resources in a movement for freedom throughout the world. In my own small way, that is what I have been trying to do, and you will read about some of my ideas in this chapter. But what we really need is an organized international movement for freedom. I believe that the young people of the communist world, provided with the proper "intellectual ammunition" on capitalism and free markets, eventually will win. I have no doubt that they would call for systems that are radically free-market and that would, ironically, make the present system in the United States appear left-wing in comparison.

Throughout the communist world, there is a rebellion against communism and even a fundamental mistrust of any collectivist kind of system. *It is our challenge to fill the void with freedom.*

Bringing Freedom to Africa—
One of My Greatest Goals

I have visited Africa about seven times since my first visit in 1977. At first I visited South Africa to study the gold mining industry there, and later we held a number of conferences in South Africa. The 1980 and 1984 editions lured from 300 to 400 people each. But South Africa is not the heart of Africa, and I quickly became more interested in other central and southern African nations. Soon I started visiting the front-line countries, places like Botswana, Malawi, Zimbabwe, and others. That is how I first got interested in the freedom fighters of Mozambique and Angola.

Africa is at once a land of incredible vistas and a continent slowly developing economically, overrun by man-made and natural plagues seemingly unmatched anywhere on earth, at least in the 1980s. It is not hard to come to the conclusion that the colonial occupation of the Eastern Soviet-bloc forces—including East Germans, Bulgarians and Russians—is ruining Africa. They are the last, and worst, colonial powers ever to dominate that continent; and I am doing all I can to get them out of Africa so that Africans can begin ruling themselves.

I first got involved with the freedom fighter issue through my contact with the RENAMO resistance in Mozambique. When a representative from the freedom fighter group approached me for a monetary contribution, I feared they wanted thousands of dollars a month; but when I found out how far something like $250 a month could go in Mozambique, I gladly started giving that reasonably small amount of money to their cause.

Because of the exchange rates over there and the low cost of living, my small contributions were able to buy a lot of non-lethal aid—spare parts for motorcycles, a radio system, an office with paper and typewriter—the kind of basics that we take for granted in America but that they could not hope to afford without some outside help.

Most of all, my relatively small contributions to RENAMO have been used to support the needy family members of key elements of RENAMO. I soon found out that RENAMO literally has no other friends in the world. The U.S. State Department supports the Communist FRELIMO Party in Mozambique and publishes reports specifically designed to discredit RENAMO. Our government not only fails to support freedom in Africa, but they also are actively working against many freedom fighters.

I have met most of the leaders of RENAMO over the years, and I find that they understand freedom far better than any other freedom fighter group I have ever met. When I first met the leaders of RENAMO, they were passing around a book about the formation of America and the Declaration of Independence. RENAMO's leader, President Afonso Dhlakama, has a pro-Western bias; he loves America and the freedoms America represents.

The Portuguese were some of the most brutal colonialists of the European colonial period, making the case for Mozambique and Angola as the people most in need of experiencing freedom in Africa today. That is why I am trying to spread the word for a free Mozambique and Angola.

Trying to Visit Mozambique

Formerly a jewel of a country with 1,500 miles of beautiful, clean white sand beaches, a booming tourist business, modern office buildings, tremendous resources, and immaculate plantations along the southeastern coast of Africa, Mozambique is currently one of the poorest nations in the world. Terror has replaced tranquility, and government food embargoes have replaced food surpluses of past years. This terrible transformation—mostly at the hands of the Marxist FRELIMO puppets in the capital city of Maputo—motivated me to do all I can to help free that nation from its bonds.

In 1986 I visited a neighboring country to Mozambique in order to meet a resistance official, whose code name is a very famous Libertarian phrase, NOTA (None Of The Above). With him and a few freedom activists who accompanied me there, we were scheduled to fly into Mozambique illegally, at treetop level to avoid radar identification, to deliver some gifts to the leaders. But the night before we were to enter the country, we heard secondhand that the BBC had found out that a major operation against RENAMO would be launched soon. As it turned out, our guide was identified as a spy of FRELIMO, who would use our plane as a signal to lead the FRELIMO forces to the RENAMO headquarters near Gorongoza.

In other words, we were the eye of the hurricane in this war and were becoming central figures of a major battle. That was not what I had in mind. Thankfully, we heard about this sting operation a few hours in advance, and so delayed our flight while considering what we might be able to do to help RENAMO. In the end we decided we would try to get a package in to the leaders.

In our package we had an engraved Bowie knife for President Afonso Dhlakama, "The George Washington of Mozambique," along with some financial contributions and the freedom papers we had drafted for Free Mozambique, with the provocative title "A Mandate For the Overthrow of FRELIMO." But before we could send these items over the border, one member of our group was put under house arrest and asked to leave the country the next day.

We were given very strong warnings that if we tried to smuggle anything into Mozambique, we would be in defiance of the internal affairs of both nations. I am sure our Bowie knife, letters to President Dhlakama, secret documents, and confirmation of radio and medicine on the way would have been extremely incriminating if officials had searched our rooms or briefcases.

After we agreed to leave the country, we still wanted to give our gifts to a representative of RENAMO before leaving. We tried a few amateur espionage techniques, and at one point, we were followed so closely by a small secret service car that we decided to "lose him." We punched our rented Mercedes Benz (the only car available for rent) up to 100 miles per hour in a James-Bond-style chase scene down one of those dirt/cement one-lane roads that serve foot traffic — the main form of transportation in Third World nations. With suitcases on top of the car and my wheelchair sticking out the trunk, we were quite a sight. It took a while to gain momentum with all that load, but we left our pursuers in the dust within just a few minutes.

We went by back roads to an English-style polo club, fairly cool under fire, but still nervous. We had one man look out the window while we held a strategy meeting, assuming that just about anybody outside our tight group could be a spy. It was a very tense moment. What could we do next? We were stymied, when our friend NOTA volunteered to take our package in to RENAMO even though it meant walking hundreds of miles through dangerous territory and he was already ticketed back to Kenya and safety.

As we sat in our typically 19th century colonial room in the polo club, we realized we could be arrested by a police sweep at any moment, so we secretly transferred the packages to NOTA. We then bade him good luck; he bade us goodbye and began his trip into Mozambique (which turned out to be successful).

Oddly enough the police never located us again. We no longer had incriminating evidence on our persons, so we stayed over another night, playing the role of tourist. The next morning we got on the plane and flew to Nairobi, Kenya, with nobody stopping to ask us any questions. Even though our mission "failed" on the surface, it was incredibly thrilling just to make the effort, to take the chance to step out of the rut of everyday life and get involved in helping to change the world. For every person willing to do that, you will hear a million people say, "You can't fight city hall;" but I would rather fight and fail than never fight at all.

Remember the Alamo!

Despite our ignominious early exit from southern Africa, the courageous NOTA did reach President Dhlakama with our gifts and returned to tell us about it. It gave me great pleasure to hear how much RENAMO appreciated our small gifts. The reason I gave President Dhlakama an engraved Bowie knife was to make a connection in his mind between American freedom and his struggle for freedom in Mozambique. I later found out that it meant a lot to him, but I think it meant even more to me.

The fight at the Alamo signifies what American independence is all about. I have visited the Alamo maybe five or six times and have read at least a dozen books about Texas independence and the Alamo. It is pretty amazing when you stop to think about what it was like for a former U.S. congressman named Davy Crockett to ride through the backwoods settlements of Tennessee drumming up support for Texans and saying something like, "Come on down to Texas. These boys need our help." For a congressman to round up a few dozen freedom fighters in a foreign land, as Texas was then, would be illegal today.

Then along came Jim Bowie from Louisiana, doing the same thing as Crockett. A successful businessman risked his life to help fight for freedom in Texas, for a neighboring colony that was declaring its independence from Mexico. Bowie was down sick when the Mexicans overrode the Alamo, but he still managed to kill a few of Santa Anna's troops with his Bowie knives before he was himself slain. That is why I gave RENAMO a special Bowie knife. I was trying to fulfill the role of a Bowie or a Crockett for their Alamo.

Today there are all kinds of laws prohibiting Americans from doing what Jim Bowie and Davy Crockett did for Texas at the Alamo, and I came under a great deal of criticism in the *New York Times* and other publications for helping RENAMO. Yet we Americans still visit the Alamo and honor those patriots in songs, movies and books while denying the need for similar stands against tyranny in the modern world.

In 1986 we failed in our attempt to visit Mozambique and meet with the president and commander of RENAMO, President Afonso Dhlakama, but it increased my curiosity and interest in RENAMO. In the years that followed, I increased my correspondence and meetings with members of RENAMO.

As I became more convinced that RENAMO could win and that it was not just anti-communist but pro-freedom, I increased my aid and support. I worked with other groups such as Free the Eagle and Freedom, Inc.

For two years I encouraged the idea of Radio Free Mozambique; and now, thanks to various individuals and groups in the United States and Europe, the first words of Radio Free Mozambique will be heard probably in early 1990.

But I was still unfulfilled in not having met personally and talked with President Dhlakama himself. Almost four years after my first attempt to meet with him, I finally succeeded. In mid-August of 1989, I received word via President Dhlakama's military headquarters in Gorongoza, Mozambique, that as part of a historic peace process, negotiations would begin between RENAMO and FRELIMO in Nairobi, Kenya. I was invited by President Dhlakama to be part of the RENAMO delegation. Within days I was in Nairobi under tight security, meeting and having long consultations with President Dhlakama and his aides.

It was truly a historic time for RENAMO and all of southern Africa. For the first time, a prominent African leader, President Daniel Moi of Kenya, had recognized President Dhlakama as a legitimate political force by inviting President Dhlakama and his delegation for the initial peace talks between the communist government of Maputo and RENAMO.

FRELIMO presented a 12-point peace plan, which was soon countered by RENAMO with a 16-point plan including demands for democracy, free markets, open elections, and so forth.

Almost daily for over two weeks, the southern African papers carried articles on the peace talks. These historic events were ignored in the Western press. At the time, the big news was Poland and Eastern Europe as well as the change of leadership in South Africa. But to those who have followed the situation in Mozambique, it was a clear victory for RENAMO.

A high Kenyan official told me that peace would come to Mozambique in 1990 or 1991. Obviously with RENAMO having the widespread support of most of the population of Mozambique, RENAMO will almost certainly one day be the governing party of Mozambique.

It was exciting and fulfilling to be a part of this process and to finally meet the guerrilla leader and commander in chief who had been fighting first the Portuguese colonialists and then the FRELIMO communists for 14 years in the bush.

I conducted an extensive five-hour interview with President Dhlakama; and at 37, with political and military control of over 85 percent of the vast country of Mozambique, he was an impressive figure. He never tried to dodge a question. His answers were well thought out, rational, with a true understanding of the social, political and military situation in southern Africa.

I believe that one day President Afonso Dhlakama will be one of the most important leaders in Africa and will be president of one of the most strategic nations in Africa—a free Mozambique.

Reforming South Africa

Besides Soviet colonialism, the other major social problem in Africa is apartheid in the Republic of South Africa. I have visited South Africa four times. I have taken time to interview the top government officials and private businessmen in the mining and finance sectors, and I can clearly see the problems faced by both sides. More importantly, I see the best solution, and I have helped publicize it to thousands of Americans who would not otherwise have considered it.

There has been a lot of misinformation coming out of South Africa regarding apartheid. The situation there is better for blacks than almost anywhere else on the continent. However, I find the current white government indefensible in its stubborn refusal to allow a black middle class to develop.

South Africa is obviously an oppressive climate for blacks, and I think the only solution is found in Frances Kendall's and Leon Louw's book *After Apartheid: The Solution for South Africa*. In essence, the authors (husband and wife) say, let each nationality or tribe rule its own independent state, on a one-man, one-vote basis, and then dismantle much of the central government, following the Swiss canton model of decentralized government power.

We publicized this solution as early as 1983 in *Gold Newsletter*, before any other major publication was able to cover it. Eventually their book became the number one best seller in South Africa; their solution has become popular with both the blacks and the whites and has a real chance of working if the radicals on both sides can agree to sit down and make it work.

The basic problem in South Africa, I believe, is that the South African government waited far too long before beginning to give blacks a measure of economic, if not political, freedom. If only they had allowed a black middle class to thrive earlier, the political situation would not have developed into the bombshell it is today.

Contributing to World Freedom

There is far more to life than making money. Part of the goal of earning money is to spend it on worthy causes, to invest a part of your wealth to support the continuation of the precious and fragile flower of freedom around the world. Freedom is being continually crushed by militarism and totalitarianism, particularly under the brutal Communist regime. If we want freedom to survive into the next century, I believe we must act now to protect it.

There is a great hunger all around the world for freedom. People I have met literally grab any book or pamphlet I have on freedom and they devour it, hungrily yearning for the freedom Americans, and others, take so much for granted. There is a strong gut-level feeling against communism in most of the nations occupied by Moscow, including all the ethnic Soviet republics, such as Latvia, Lithuania, Estonia, the Ukraine, Azerbaijan, as well as the Eastern European nations of Poland, Hungary, Czechoslovakia and others.

Many of these nations hunger for the intellectual ammunition to spread freedom. Their people risk imprisonment, even death, to smuggle in the works of freedom. Although I have never traveled in the Soviet Union (except for the North Pole!), I have talked with many expatriates over the years. When I visited the Soviet Embassy in Washington, D.C., in 1987, I got a feeling for how depressing life must be there. There were two-way mirrors everywhere. You knew the place was bugged. Their propaganda was all over the reception area. Even the photos of Gorbachev had the birthmark airbrushed out of the picture.

When I asked these Soviet officials if there would ever be any reforms in the Soviet Union, they would immediately answer "Nyet" to all my questions. They even said "Nyet" before I finished my question in English. There was no way they could have anticipated the trend toward *Glasnost* and *Perestroika* as recently as 1987, when I visited the embassy.

Translating Free-Market Literature

When most Latin American nations were freed from Spanish control in the 1820s and 1830s, there was precious little literature of freedom on which to build a more enlightened system. That is the key reason, I believe, why North America grew in freedom while South America did not.

I am trying to do my small part to remedy that situation. In 1987, I visited Honduras and Nicaragua along with my aides Lesia Hnatiw and Gary Alexander, smuggling in a box of free-market books written in Spanish. Working with Libertarian International and Laissez-Faire Books, I assembled some of the best Spanish-language books on freedom; and I donated these books to the library at COSEP, which is a Managua-based group of free-market businessmen trying to survive in that hard-core Communist nation.

Through my contacts with the Peace and Freedom underground organization in Poland and with the permission of Milton and Rose Friedman, I paid to have a Polish-language version of *Free to Choose* translated and circulated clandestinely. It soon became the underground best seller of the pro-freedom movement there, with our 5,000 copies being read so much that each copy of the book is now beginning to fall apart.

I have also paid to have other literature on freedom translated into Portuguese, the language of Mozambique, then had them printed to circulate through RENAMO. A young economist friend of mine, Lawrence Reed, wrote a kind of Declaration of Independence for RENAMO and we had it translated into Portuguese. That was one of the documents we presented to President Dhlakama, who was so moved by it that he agreed to use the document in peace negotiations as well as to make it a part of his constitution once RENAMO prevails.

We must get the information on freedom to the people who hunger for it, translated into their own language if possible. There is an awesome void out there. In America, books on freedom gather dust in our libraries. Very few people care to read them. It is the opposite in the rest of the world. They cannot get enough books; and when they find a book, it is passed around to so many people that it literally begins to fall apart in their hands.

What I am starting to assemble is a whole series of bound documents for the benefit of the future of free Africa and Latin America. These bound documents will contain an indictment of colonialism from the very beginning up through Soviet colonialism, and they will provide a practical outline of how to structure free markets for the rapid growth of wealth to overcome centuries of deprivation.

This packet of "intellectual ammunition" is what I want to circulate to tomorrow's leaders of poor Third World nations, to the students in the universities and the revolutionaries in the field. Too often the next generation comes to power with no blueprint for freedom, so they just install a new kind of dictatorship. I want to break that cycle, to make the next society totally different: a free society with as little government interference as is possible.

Building a Business Plan and a Bill of Rights

A Declaration of Independence is good, but it is not enough. We also prepared a Bill of Rights and a Business Plan for developing a new country for the benefit of that country's citizens, not outside colonialists. I firmly believe that with a wave of true freedom—unlike the dictatorships under the Uhuru movement of 1960—Africa can become like the Far East, with several enclaves of free-market capitalism, such as Hong Kong, Bangkok, Taiwan, South Korea and other areas.

Africa is huge—50 percent larger than the United States and Canada combined. Bigger than California, Mozambique has

1,500 miles of beach, much longer and more beautiful than California's beaches. It has tremendous reserves of gemstones, gold, lumber and other treasures. Tourism was once their number one industry, before the Communists took over. At one time South Africans flocked to Mozambique's beaches. Those beaches could soon be developed for tourists from around the world, with all revenues benefiting private entrepreneurs in Mozambique, not a colonial power.

Many African nations have the natural resources and the willing people who want and need the kind of development that North Americans have been able to accomplish over the last 200 years. We just need to show them the way and to get the Soviet colonialists off the continent.

Why Am I Doing This?

When I tell people how excited I am about the prospects for freedom in Africa, or Central America, or Eastern Europe, I am usually met with boredom; but often I hear a form of what I call an "unconscious racism." People think, usually without saying it, that black people, Latin Americans, or even Eastern Europeans cannot understand the finer points of freedom.

I think that is a terrible form of racism, in that it is basically paternalistic. What they are saying—without saying it—is that the Third World is the White Man's Burden: Only through more genteel colonialism, or the opposite extreme of socialism, can these nations hope to have a modicum of living standards, but never true wealth. Such people are really saying there is no way the Third World can ever avoid centuries of continuing poverty and squalor.

If such people put their feelings into words, they generally say something like this, "Why are you wasting time with those people?" Or, "You know they're all lazy and don't care to work hard enough to become good businessmen." Or, "They're a bunch of farmers who can't read or write. There's no hope."

That kind of thinking is what helps keep most of the world in poverty. If we could move beyond the unconscious racism of thinking these people cannot understand or appreciate freedom—and that they need some form of collectivism or continuous charity shipments to keep them alive—only then can we arrive at the "glorious truth" as Thomas Jefferson described it in his last letter, that no peoples are "born with saddles on their backs" while others are born with spurs "to ride them."

One of the most important goals of the second half of my life is to see the liberation of Africa, Latin America and the Soviet satellite states of Eastern Europe. Nothing would make me happier than to lie on a golden beach on the Indian Ocean in Free Mozambique. For that matter, I understand Cuba has some nice beaches, too. Wherever freedom breaks out next, you can expect me to be there, with some boxes of pro-freedom books to spread the word...and fill the void.

Book III

The Gold Bug's Handbook

Chapter 13

America's Original Gold Bugs

The Constitutional Money of
"Gold and Silver Coins" Solved the
"Pestilential Paper" Problem

"The Congress shall have power...To coin Money, regulate the Value thereof, and of foreign Coin, and fix the Standard of Weights and Measures....No State shall...make anything but gold and silver Coin a Tender in Payment of Debts."

—The Constitution of the United States of America, Art. I, Secs. 8 and 10

There are a number of men in the hard-money movement who have a legitimate claim to being the "original gold bug" of the 20th century—men such as Jim Dines, Harry Schultz, Richard Russell, Vern Myers, Colonel Harwood, Henry Hazlitt and, of course, Ludwig von Mises. But the original American gold bugs assembled over 200 years ago, in the summer of 1787 in Philadelphia, for the Constitutional Convention.

What these men wrote and said over 200 years ago was very important for defining our greatness as a nation; but—for the purposes of this book—the most important passage in that storied document has to do with monetary economics. It is quoted above and has to do with gold and silver coins.

Paper Money "Not Worth a Continental"

The delegates who came to Philadelphia in 1787 used many kinds of paper and metallic money, including the Pennsylvania system of British-based pounds and shillings. The paper money issued by at least seven of the Thirteen Colonies was not uniform in value and was not widely accepted outside each colony's borders. Fiat currency was in force in at least seven states, and three other states were contemplating the use of the well-worn paper path to riches.

Most delegates were therefore required to pay for their room, board and other expenses in various forms of "specie" (metal-weighted coins) of English, Spanish, French or Portuguese gold or silver coinage—because no strictly American gold or silver coin was in wide circulation at the time, and the paper money was not acceptable in most places.

Not many people realize that the currency problem these men faced was a 20-year headache that began with the British tax acts of 1765 and 1767 and was one of the main causes of the American Revolution. Benjamin Franklin said, "The refusal of King George to operate an honest colonial money system which freed the ordinary man from the clutches of the manipulators was probably the prime cause of the Revolution."

America's first unified paper currency was the "continental," a paper currency that became a laughingstock to the world during the Revolution when America could not pay its war bills and so began printing more and more paper. These continentals became so worthless that by the time the war was over they ceased to circulate. As one exceptional legal scholar of that era put it, the continentals "quietly died in the hands of the persons compelled to take them." (Edwin Vierra, *Pieces of Eight*)

The aggregate loss from the debasement of Continental currency was calculated at almost $200 million, a small figure today, but one which represented nearly three times the cost of fighting the entire Revolutionary War.

Between 1775 and 1779, the Continental Congress issued $241.5 million of non-interest-bearing obligations, and the states issued bills of credit totaling another $209.5 million. This massive $451 million infusion of nearly worthless paper money was still in the pockets and on the minds of the delegates to the Constitutional Convention in 1787. The Constitutional delegates were suffering from an "inflationary hangover" from the flood of paper money released in the late 1770s.

According to monetary historian Carol Schwalberg, a single Spanish milled dollar in 1781 "could buy from one hundred to one thousand Continental dollars. A bushel of corn sold for 150 Continental dollars; butter was twelve dollars a pound; tea, ninety dollars. Flour sold for $1,575 a barrel. Traders shut up shops, refusing any payment but gold and silver. The phrase 'Not worth a Continental' became a sad but permanent part of the American language." (*From Cattle to Credit Cards*)

A Famine of Gold in the Land

The lack of gold and silver specie in the colonial period was a main cause of the American Revolution, historians conclude. "A combination of the lack of circulating medium and the threat of high taxes helped create the conditions from which the radical spirit in America sprang." (John C. Miller, *Origins of the American Revolution*)

According to Constitutional historian Clinton Rossiter, "The critical problem was the alarming dearth of specie with which to pay for everything from taxes levied on the land to goods imported and still wanted from abroad. The drain of specie kept the back country in a state of political and social tension, while the balance of trade seemed to tip so drastically against the U.S. that even the most solid merchants wondered how long their credit would hold up in London and Amsterdam. At the same time, the absence of uniform currency in the 13 States made every dealing across a state line a small exercise in financial wizardry." (Clinton Rossiter, *1787: The Grand Convention*)

This proliferation of currency in the colonies lends special significance to the phrase eventually selected for our first U.S. coinage, E PLURIBUS UNUM ("Out of many, one"). The standard interpretation is "out of many colonies, one nation;" but on coinage, it definitely connotes "out of many currencies comes one gold and silver standard."

"A Pestilence of Paper Money"

The records of the Constitutional Convention show several references to impassioned speeches against the "pestilent effects of paper money" (a phrase James Madison later used in *The Federalist Papers*). On August 16, 1787, for instance, Oliver Ellsworth of Connecticut—later to be a senator, then chief justice of the Supreme Court—told the assembled delegates, "This is a favorable moment to shut and bar the door against paper money....Paper money can in no case be necessary....The power may do harm, never good."

Although he did not attend much of the convention, Alexander Hamilton of New York—later to be our first secretary of the treasury—wrote a strong anti-paper letter to the convention: "To emit an unfunded paper as the sign of value ought not to continue...being, in its nature, pregnant with abuses, and liable to be made the engine of imposition and fraud; holding out temptations equally pernicious to the integrity of government and to the morals of the people."

James Madison added that paper money could be used as a "form of aggression" by one state against the other, as, indeed, foreign paper currencies are a powerful weapon in the arsenal of trade warriors today. In arguing for gold and silver coinage in "Federalist Paper No. 44," James Madison wrote, "The loss which America has sustained since the peace, from the pestilent effects of paper money on the necessary confidence between man and man, on the necessary confidence in the public councils, on the industry and morals of the people, and on the character of republican government, constitutes an enormous debt against the states."

It is clearer the more you read about the era, that the Declaration of Independence in 1776 and the Constitutional Convention of 1787 brought together some of the finest philosopher-statesmen the world has ever seen or is likely to see at the birth of any future nation. It was probably the finest assemblage of minds ever convened toward the birth and design of a new nation.

In a period of one long summer of four months—a time of arduous work, scintillating oratory, heated debate, and magnanimous compromise—a document was signed by all in attendance. By June 21, 1788, the required nine states had ratified the Constitution of the United States. The 55 men who had gathered in Philadelphia had successfully united politics and a reservoir of practical experience in life to frame an entirely new charter of government .

Among their timeless words were the ones quoted at the top of this chapter: Congress shall have the power, "To coin Money, regulate the Value thereof, and of foreign Coin, and fix the Standard of Weights and Measures." (Article I, Section 8) Notice that it does not say "print money," as that would be a contradiction in terms. A short while later, in Article I, Section 10, the Constitution adds that states may make nothing but "gold and silver Coin a Tender in Payment of Debts."

Two years after these words were drafted, Secretary of the Treasury Alexander Hamilton was charged with developing a coinage system. In the end, he proposed gold denominations of

$10—with the "eagle" as the standard monetary unit, containing 247.5 grains of fine gold—then half-eagles and quarter-eagles at $5 and $2.50. (Hamilton introduced the $2.50 because it was between the highest silver coinage of $1 and the half-eagle.) The .917 fineness standard for gold coins was 11 parts gold to one part alloy.

After several more months of debate, the Coinage Act of April 2, 1792, brought Hamilton's proposal into law, and by 1795, the first gold coins rolled out of the mint on Seventh Street in Philadelphia. Over the years, I have been proud that our coin company has been able to sell several gold coins—including these first golden eagles from the 1790s—to our customers. An especially fine selection graced the cover of an edition of our coin magazine, *Blanchard's American Rarities*.

Whatever Happened to Constitutional Gold and Silver Coins?

For nearly 150 years, until 1933, the new constitutional U.S. currency was defined as a dollar's worth of gold. For a century— from 1834 to 1933, except for a brief time during the Civil War— gold was worth a consistent $20.67 per ounce. A $20 gold piece weighed about an ounce and contained .9675 ounces pure gold. The Gold Standard Act of 1834 made the constitutional mandate official and practical; every form of U.S. currency was to be maintained at full parity with gold and to be fully convertible into gold coin or bullion.

That period, except for the Civil War, is with great justification called America's "Golden Age," the time of America's greatest industrial growth, including most of the great inventions of the modern age—from the reaper to airplanes, from electric lights to automobiles, from primitive photography to moving pictures, from telegraphs to telephones—not to mention the leisure-time inventions of jazz, baseball, and radio. The great industries were born—railroads, mining, manufacturing, shipping and retailing.

All that progress came about without a Federal Reserve or income taxes—until 1913. It was all accomplished under a strong gold standard, with the natural accompaniments of low interest rates and zero inflation, even spells of deflation. It was a time of honest money—gold and silver coins.

There were some problems with the gold standard, but only because gold was artificially married to silver in what came to be known as the bimetallic standard. Because the western interests favored silver as a monetary standard, they used government as a tool to favor one particular special interest, the silver miners. It worked no better then than it does today. It caused silver to be priced artificially high, at a 15-to-1 or 16-to-1 ratio to gold (usually $1.29 per ounce).

By 1896 this bimetallic problem came to a head in William Jennings Bryan's eloquent but opportunistic "Cross of Gold" speech (in favor of silver), opposing William McKinley and his eastern "gold bugs." But the gold bugs won the popular vote in both 1896 and 1900.

The term *gold bug*, by the way, is a venerable old term which applied to William McKinley's supporters in 1896. At the convention of 1896, they wore tiny gold bugs on their lapels to identify their support of McKinley. *Gold bug* also appeared in an Edgar Allen Poe short story written 50 years before McKinley's supporters borrowed the term. But the term *gold bug* comes from a much earlier time and a different part of the world. Quite by accident in 1989 I enjoyed a private visit to the New Orleans Museum of Art. Because of my support for the museum and also because of a special exhibit of African art, I was looking forward to a leisurely visit to the museum in the "off hour." One display particularly caught my attention. There was a collection from West Africa (circa 1700) of gold counterweights used by local banker/goldsmiths to weigh gold nuggets and dust. The "advertising logo" of the African gold dealer was the shape of the small brass weights which ranged from reproductions of animals to interesting designs. However, I was struck with the fact that 75 percent of the brass weights were in the form of bugs. Gold bugs. With time and study and luck perhaps we will find earlier, "gold bugs" associated with monetary transactions.

I have never objected to being labeled a gold bug. Not only does the term have a fascinating history, but far more important, it represents a century-old principle—a moral monetary standard.

The Golden Age Ends

For 125-150 years America grew powerful as a nation without much help or hindrance from the federal government. Then out of the blue came the two scourges of 1913—the Federal Reserve System and the income tax amendment (16). For a long while the two curses traveled hand in hand, inflating our money and taxing it in the higher brackets created by the Federal Reserve's inflation.

America long resisted the imposition of a central bank. President Andrew Jackson squashed two early attempts to create a Bank of the United States in the 1830s. The idea died until the Panic of 1907, when bankers wanted to have an agency to prevent "Panics." By creating the Federal Reserve for that purpose, Congress forfeited its constitutional power to be responsible for the function of money.

The Federal Reserve—which is neither federal nor much of a reserve—is a private corporation owned by the power-elite bankers to function as a central bank. Since the Federal Reserve has taken the constitutional role of "regulating the value" of our money, they have been regulating it steadily downward.

The price of gold has grown twentyfold in those 75 years because that is the growth in the amount of new credit poured out by the Fed since its inception. The inflation rate has averaged over 4 percent a year since 1913, after being virtually flat for the 125 years preceding that date.

Once the door of federal power was unlocked in 1913, the rest of our rights became fair game to the politicians. In 1933 and 1934 Franklin Roosevelt progressively took away more of our liberties, including our right to own gold; then he devalued the dollar and revalued gold. That was probably unconstitutional, but nobody seriously challenged his actions, due to his popularity at the time.

America's Golden Age finally ended, for all practical purposes, on March 5, 1933, when Roosevelt took office and immediately proclaimed a national emergency, suspended all banking operations, ended the minting of gold coins, prohibited all further transactions in gold coins, and forced the surrender of most privately held gold and bullion in the Federal Reserve banking system.

Chapter 14

The Gold Bug's Handbook

A Compendium of Golden Rules
for the Modern Midas

"[In] *Havilah,...there is gold; and the gold of that land is good.*"

—Genesis 2:11-12

Gold was present from the Creation of the world—as this passage from the Bible strongly indicates. As far back as geologists can count their strata, up to 4.5 billion years ago, gold was there. Most of the gold in the earth's crust is found in what geologists call the Precambrian layer, the oldest-known sedimentary layer. From the evidence of the rocks beneath us, gold came to earth before all life—even the one-cell ooze, the trilobites, crustaceans, dinosaurs—and before cavemen, and before the Bank of England and the Federal Reserve Banking System.

Created As the Ideal Form of Money

Gold was designed from the beginning to be man's ideal physical representation of wealth. This is clear from the earliest writings of the Babylonian and Egyptian societies as well as from the Bible. Gold is woven very lightly into the texture and fabric of creation in a way that perfectly qualifies gold for its role as money. Gold never rusts or decays; it is malleable, ductile, divisible, compact and virtually indestructible. Besides, it is very beautiful.

Gold is a heavy metal with a light touch. It is not exactly play-dough, but its physical contortions are legendary. Hard enough to last forever, a single ounce of gold is soft enough to beat into a string 50 miles long, or a sheet covering 100 square feet, just 1/200,000 of an inch thick. Gold is often used in dental fillings because it is soft enough to bend with your bicuspids, but solid enough that you will not break off a golden chaw by accident.

Gold has several physical qualities money cannot buy. It is such an excellent conductor of electricity that an invisibly small amount of gold printed on a ceramic microchip saves miles of wiring in a computer. Gold plating of connectors and switches on undersea cables or overhead satellites insures long-lasting relia-bility.

Nothing is as good as gold for resistance to corrosion and reflection of heat. That is how our astronauts protected them-selves from a lunar sunburn, and that is how many glass and steel skyscrapers keep their air-conditioning bills low.

All these exceptional molecular gymnastics are just icing on the cake, however. Gold's primary role is as money, and that is how the lion's share of gold will always be used.

Gold—A Natural Rarity

There are several geological signposts of gold's rarity in the earth's crust, making it ideal for use as money. The formation of the earth left our planet with far less gold per cubic mile than the rest of the solar system. Most of the earth's gold is locked up in the ultimate safe-deposit box: deep in the core of the earth, more than 2,000 miles deep, and more than 2,000 degrees of molten heat.

The gold that remains near the surface of the earth is confined to Precambrian upthrusts. Roughly half the world's surface amount of gold is Archaen, i.e., formed from 2.5 billion to 4.5 billion years ago. Most of this Archaen gold was formed in greenstone belts, where the ancient ocean crust was cooked in the hotter depths of the earth and emerged, cooling as it rose, into surface intrusions along fault lines, which trained geologists can locate and old prospectors can "smell out."

The largest known deposits of gold in the world are in the Witwatersrand region of South Africa, as much as three miles below the surface; in northern Nevada, along the Carlin Trend; and in the greenstone belt of Canada, along the "Golden Highway" from Ontario to Quebec. The latest big gold rush may be taking place around the Ring of Fire, especially in Papua New Guinea, where gold is found in the form of epithermal intrusions.

The *placer* or surface deposits were pretty much fully mined in California and the Yukon in the last century. These deposits still provide both the lure and the lore of our 19th century history. They provide the stuff of Jack London's legends and old movies about treasures of the Sierra Madre, riverboat gambling and stage coach robberies.

In short, gold has been ingeniously and effectively buried in both land and sea and in molten rocks near volcanoes. Gold is found at the rate of one part per billion in ocean water and one part per million in our Western "heap leach" mining operations. So much of the "easy" gold has already been mined that finding any gold now is a cleverly designed scavenger hunt, requiring a geology degree, decades of experience, and the instincts of a Sherlock Holmes.

We are centuries away from mining the gold in the rest of the solar system—or in our own oceans—on any commercially viable basis. When that happens, gold production will likely continue to grow just as it has in the past—in a nearly perfect correlation to population and economic growth.

From the cold Canadian bush to the hellishly hot South African tunnels, men are still digging through the earth's crust in search of the chemical element No. 79—Au—for both mystical and practical reasons, which governments can neither understand nor prevent. It is as if the creator of the earth pinched off one part per billion of gold on land and sea—just enough to add a dash of lust and greed to find more—and then created man and said, "Dig for your supper."

Billions of years later, we're still digging.

In the next few pages, I have assembled a series of light-hearted essays I have written over the years in *Gold Newsletter* as my own "Gold Bug's Handbook:"

(1) Trial-and-Error Money

"In the history of the world, we find the record of savings really saved through buying gold, hoarding precious stones and other forms of 'hard wealth' privately secreted. In the future history of America, most of us will, in my opinion, learn this lesson too late."

—Investment adviser Gerald M. Loeb, 1935

Jim: *"Far from being a 'barbarous relic' (as Keynes called it), gold mirrors the barbarity of all systems which rival it."*

Gold has been used throughout recorded history as money, but it was by no means the only form of money ever to undergo the experimentation of man's governments and tribal customs. Gold is a constantly recurring result of rigorous trial-and-error testing, through many centuries of experimentation with different forms of money.

The Spartans used iron for money. The Romans used copper, after they clipped all the gold and silver coins down to nothing. Other empires used bronze. Africans used cowrie shells. Polynesians from the Isle of Yap used stone money sitting in a clear pool of water. (More on them later.) American Indians used wampum. During the world wars of this century, cigarettes became currency. Even dead rats have been used as money—for a very short time, I am sure.

Each of these monetary media would develop glaring weaknesses over time. Like paper, base metals can be easily mined in great quantity and can have higher denominations stamped on them, far out of relation to their weight. Stones, cigarettes, beads, and paper can all obviously be inflated beyond any objective value.

No other substance—not even ultra-expensive diamonds—can combine all the unique characteristics of gold. If gold did not exist, somebody would have to invent something just like it. Governments dislike gold because they cannot print any more of it. Thankfully, its role is not dependent on government support or opposition. It is beyond the power of government to control, as von Mises always said.

Money was invented by the market, not by governments. Gold best fulfills the three classic functions of money:

Monetary Function	How Gold Measures Up
1. A unit of account	Measured in troy ounces
2. A store of value	Compact and portable
3. A medium of exchange	Easily divisible

Only gold is capable of easy division into units, compact in size, and capable of storage for centuries without erosion of its weight and value. If any other form of wealth can fulfill the role of money better than gold, it would have been invented by now. The experiments have all been performed by now, and time has shown that gold works best.

(2) Paper Gold...Does Not Wash

"Government is the only agency that can take a valuable commodity like paper, slap some ink on it, and make it totally worthless."

—Ludwig von Mises

Jim: *"In a world run by angels, paper money could work. In a world run by fallible men, however, paper money will always lose its value, then perish."*

The majority of investors over the course of history have been forced, or have chosen, to put all their eggs in the government's paper-money basket. They have presumed a super-human level of integrity and responsibility and restraint by those running the central bank printing presses.

Nearly all world currencies have lost their value in this century, and many of them totally disappeared. Even the German mark—which is a major currency today—was totally destroyed in 1923 and had to be rebuilt from scratch.

The majority of historical money systems—probably all of them—have failed to preserve the wealth of the citizens. Not one has retained its buying power over the last 50 years. Even the mightiest currency of all—the U.S. dollar, the reserve currency of the world from 1944 onward—has lost 90 percent of its purchasing power in the last 50 years.

About 90 percent of American investors and savers rely solely on the long-term stability of the paper currency the government prints for them. They have no gold or silver, or even Swiss francs and German marks, for monetary "insurance." Most investments are based entirely on the value of the currency which underlies them. Stocks, bonds, money market funds, Treasury bills—all are based on the health of the dollar.

History shows that paper money does not wash. It loses its value, generally within the span of a single lifetime. So why trust all of your eggs—in one form or another—to the same paper-money basket?

(3) How Hyper-Inflation
Destroys Paper Wealth

"Gold is not dependent for its value upon the state and therefore confers upon its possessor wealth which makes him in that respect independent of the state."

—Lord William Rees-Mogg

Jim: *"Once the printing presses roll, and the decimal points drift to the right, you're done for. It only takes a moment to wipe out a lifetime of careful savings."*

Consider the frightening power of hyper-inflation. Like a tornado, hurricane or earthquake, it can destroy lives in no time at all. In the space of a few months in Germany in 1923, whole life savings of millions of middle-class Germans were destroyed, laying the philosophical groundwork for the rise of the Nazi Party and the destruction of all Europe.

Those few Germans of the 1920s who held gold were protected from the debauchery of the Imperial German currency. Today that currency is still virtually worthless, worth a few pennies as a curiosity item, but the gold coins of Imperial Germany are worth more now than when they were minted.

By comparison, consider another famous event of 1923. That is when an archaeologist named Howard Carter stumbled upon Tutankhamen's tomb in Egypt. He unlocked the door to hundreds of gold artifacts, which still looked as brilliant as the day King Tut's tomb was sealed more than 3,250 years previously. Gold simply does not lose its luster over time.

Every year some nation shows us the ravages of hyper-inflation all over again. In the 1980s, several Latin American nations experienced 10,000 percent or more in annual rates of inflation. One year, Bolivia had 10,000 percent inflation, and the next year Argentina had 13,000 percent inflation. Nicaragua had a few consecutive years of 10,000 percent inflation; then it was Mexico, Peru, and back to Bolivia again.

In recurring cycles the hyper-inflation of money in Latin America threatens to wipe out a generation of savings, making hard assets the only assets that consistently retain their value: not only gold, but real estate, fruit trees, base metals (like tin in Bolivia) and, sadly, drugs like cocaine. Without such continual hyper-inflation and exchange controls, I wonder if there would be such a market for earning hard currencies and gold through the medium of drug trafficking.

(4) How the Paper Money Idea Reached Europe

"Experience shows that neither a State nor a Bank ever had the unrestricted power of issuing paper money without abusing that power."

—Economist David Ricardo, 1817

Jim: *"When Marco Polo witnessed Kublai Khan's pleasure palace, financed with mulberry bark as money, Marco brought the idea back to Europe, where it destroyed more lives than the Black Plague."*

The first recorded use of paper money was from the writings of Marco Polo in 13th century China. The powerful ruler Kublai Khan (1216-1294) manufactured paper money from the bark of the Chinese mulberry tree. The result of this paper-money experiment was no different then than now.

In the words of Marco Polo, "All these pieces of paper are issued with as much solemnity and authority as if they were of pure gold or silver...Anyone forging it would be punished with death. And the Khan causes every year to be made such a vast quantity of this money, which costs him nothing, that it must equal in amount all the treasures of the world."

From this mulberry bark, the great Khan built his pleasure palace, Xanadu. At first he backed his mulberry bark 50 percent with gold and 50 percent other hard assets, but the Khan soon found that paper money was so easy to manufacture that he saw no reason to match any new paper money with gold backing.

The reaction to the Khan's printing of fiat mulberry bark was predictable. More people began to turn their paper money in for gold until, as Marco Polo put it, "It was ordered by law that what in the future should be stipulated for in iron and copper money, should be paid partly in bills." Finally, there was no convertibility at all, not even in copper.

European heads of state were more enamored of the luxuries of Xanadu than the results of the experiment with mulberry money, so they started printing paper bank notes. The rest, as they say, is history—a history of broken promises, poverty, war and inflation, a more persistent and damaging plague than the Black Death itself.

(5) Newton's Golden Rule

"You have a choice between trusting to the natural stability of gold and the honesty and intelligence of the members of government. And, with all due respect for these gentlemen, I advise you, as long as the capitalist system lasts, vote for gold."

—George Bernard Shaw

Jim: *"By making the pound sterling as good as gold, Sir Isaac Newton suspended gravity's pull on the pound for almost 200 years, financing the world's greatest empire and bringing peace to Europe."*

Newton defined gravity, inertia, entropy, and a variety of other physical principles; but his greatest contribution to his country may have been a simple stroke of his pen in 1717, when he declared the British pound sterling would equal a specific weight of gold (about a quarter of a troy ounce), making the sovereign the most commonly traded gold coin in the world from that day forward for about 200 years.

The England of 1717 was not very strong yet. The nation was bubbling over with inflationary paper money schemes, including John Law's South Sea Bubble and Tulip Mania. Newton's gold standard effectively put the end to such foolishness and allowed for stable growth in Britain.

The British currency was not devalued from Newton's weight standard for 197 years, until 1914, when Chancellor of the Exchequer Winston Churchill took Britain off the gold standard. During those two centuries, Britain gained the highest power and influence known in the world to that time. But as soon as gold was abandoned as a currency discipline, in order to fight World War I, British power began crumbling.

Now, the British pound is subject to gravity, inertia and entropy once again. The only solution is another Newtonian decree and the gold to back it up.

(6) The Christmas Currency Caper of 1913

"If Congress has the right to issue paper money, it was given them to be used by themselves, and not to be delegated to individuals or corporations."

—President Andrew Jackson, 1836

Jim: *"On December 23, 1913, at 6:02 p.m., Woodrow Wilson signed a bad check with a golden pen. History calls it the Federal*

Reserve Act of 1913. I call it the beginning of the end for the dollar."

For 125 years America survived without a Federal Reserve System. President Jackson effectively killed the idea of a central bank during his two terms in office (1829-1837), and the idea never seriously resurfaced until after the Panic of 1907. The bankers got together to try to "prevent panics" in the future, but in truth they wanted to forge a monopoly of monetary powers into their consortium of private banks.

There were plenty of opponents to this idea, but the bill was rushed through Congress in a hectic Christmas week. It was introduced on Monday, December 15, 1913, and was signed into law by Woodrow Wilson, using four gold pens, eight days later—at 6:02 p.m. on December 23, 1913.

Were those pesky "panics" wiped out? No, there was another panic in 1920-1921, and a decade-long depression in the 1930s. How about the dollar, was it stabilized by the Federal Reserve? When the 1913 bill was signed there were only 3.4 billion U.S. dollars in circulation, or $35 per American citizen.

After more than 75 years of Fed money mismanagement, there are now over 240 billion Federal Reserve notes in the United States—about 1,000 FRNs per person—for a 2,757 percent rate of inflation per capita, and over 7,000 percent inflation overall.

After 75 years the dollar is now worth 1/28 of its 1913 value, in terms of gold. At $360 gold in late 1989, that is 1,700 percent inflation in terms of the dollar to gold in 75 years.

The annual rate of dollar devaluation (vs. gold) for the last 75 years is 4 percent per year, compounded. While some analysts say that 4 percent per year is pretty low, over the 75-year life expectancy of the average American baby born this year, that rate would turn their birthright of dollars into a deathbed inheritance of nickels—a 95 percent devaluation over a lifetime.

(7) The Mood of the Souks

"Gold is still the bastion...a social symbol...it is the only way a villager in this country can get instant liquidity. He doesn't have a bank in his village and he doesn't buy government bonds, because they cannot be cashed instantly. Gold can."

—A senior economist at the Reserve Bank of India.

Jim: *"Once the Mideast was called the Golden Crescent, but for its waves of grain. It still is a Golden Crescent, but more in terms of metallic gold, trading in bazaars all the way from Casablanca to the golden department stores in Tokyo."*

The "souks" are those steamy, open-air markets in the Mideast, where gold is bought and sold "on the spot." It looks extremely primitive but is highly sophisticated in terms of accurate market information. The mood of the souks is the key to the price of gold, according to *World of Gold* author Timothy Green. These primitive-looking gold traders are often at least tenth-generation traders, with the gold trading sense seemingly churning through their veins. While they do not have the air conditioning and electronics of New York or London, they usually buy low and sell high, unlike most first-generation hotshot commodity traders in America.

In a new Golden Crescent stretching from Casablanca in the west to Tokyo in the east, the majority of the world's gold reaches its final destination each year. More than 30 percent of each year's supply is traded in the Third World souks, and another 30 percent in the highly sophisticated markets of Hong Kong, Bangkok, Tokyo, Taiwan and other Far Eastern gold havens.

In the souks, gold jewelry is the coin of the realm. High-karat jewelry, priced narrowly above its melt value, is the investment of choice. It is a tangible savings account for those who have no bank, no safety-deposit box, no telephone switch funds. They wear their wealth and protect it.

If you want to know the direction gold is going, then take a trip through the streets of Dubai, or Bangkok, or Bombay, or Tangier. You may not speak the language; but if the din is overwhelming and the lines are long, that is the first clue that a bull market is brewing. When gold was cheap at $300 in 1985, the souks were buying. When it hit $500 in late 1987, sales were slow. When the souk takes a siesta, so too does the price of gold, in more cases than not.

(8) A Life Belt for All Seasons

"What gold still has going for it, even in the era of the electronic marketplace, is that it remains the only universally accepted medium of exchange. It is the life belt for all seasons."

—Timothy Green, *The Prospects For Gold*

Jim: *"When you absolutely, positively, have to get out of a country, gold is your only internationally recognized underground passport. Don't leave home without it."*

Gold has always served the world's refugees as the wealth of last resort. The boat people of Southeast Asia bought their freedom with gold. The others, in many cases, not only lost their freedom, but their lives.

In World War II, a number of people from different nations used gold to save their lives. Thousands of Jews escaped Nazi Germany through their hoard of gold, some of it stored in Switzerland with a few spare gold coins to buy their way out of Germany and into Switzerland. The French sewed gold into their mattresses, or buried it in their fields, to escape Nazi occupation in 1940, or to use on the underground market after the war.

American pilots in World War II and every war since then have carried emergency supplies of gold coins in case they were downed in enemy territory and needed to buy their way out. By the same token, several American embassies overseas carry vast quantities of gold coins to make a quick escape in case of war or terrorism.

(9) Lenin's Law at Work

"If you want to destroy capitalism and the society that goes with it, you must begin by debauching the currency."

—V.I. Lenin, 1917

Jim: *"Lenin was right. Since the world abandoned all gold standards in 1971, the forbidden fruit has soared, while paper money has lost value."*

Between March 1968, when the London Gold Pool collapsed, and August 1971, when Nixon devalued the dollar, the world progressively shed all the last remnants of the gold standard which built the capitalistic system to its peak of productivity over the previous 250 years. Consider now the fruits of the last 20 years of currency debauchery, in terms of a $10,000 investment from 1969 to the present.

• $10,000 invested in an interest-bearing bank account in U.S. dollars at the prevailing interest rates since then, would be worth $65,000 today. After subtracting for the effects of inflation, you would have $19,100, for a 91 percent gain in 20 years. That works out to +3.3 percent per year.

• $10,000 invested in the Dow Jones Industrials in 1969 would now be worth $54,000, including dividends reinvested. The real return after inflation is $15,900, +2.3 percent per year.

• $10,000 invested in gold at $35 per ounce would now be worth $105,715, at $370 gold. Without bearing a penny of interest in the meantime, gold is worth $31,090, after accounting for inflation and using real 1968 dollars. That gives you a real annual return of 6.5 percent—double the rate of cash and triple the rate of stocks.

Despite this high level of performance, gold is often called a "non-income-producing" investment or a "wasting asset" or a "speculation" by Wall Street professionals. Far from speculative, however, gold is stable, and paper money is a speculation, a risky bet on government responsibility.

Gold is seldom anyone's first investment, but—like insurance—it belongs as one of a young person's first and most important investments. Given human nature, most people wait to buy insurance until they are in trouble. It is the same with gold. Most people put all their money into cash and stocks until they lose their value, then consider gold, like this anonymous fellow, whose gravestone tells the story...

> He held his wealth in paper.
> Then came the dollar's doom.
> His casket's lined with greenbacks,
> And T-bills mark his tomb.

(10) The Parable of the Stones of Yap and York

"Yap people lose lives mining stone money. Canoes sink. Stone money valued on how many lives lost getting it. Each stone has history. Yap people know who owns each stone. Stone money always good."

—Chief Pitmag of Yap

Jim adds: *"Besides gold, the most stable currency ever devised by man was the stones of Yap. Their fascinating tale shows how gold could still serve the same monetary role in the 1990s for our more civilized (?) world."*

What is money? Perhaps the most stable currency, next to gold, has been discovered in the Caroline Islands of the South

Pacific, on an island called Yap. Although worthless in any other nation, these stones have all the qualities of gold to the 4,000 island people who own them.

On the tropical island of Yap are 30,000 huge, limestone doughnut-shaped stones that have survived several centuries, despite innumerable foreign occupations, without a trace of inflation or devaluation. How did they do it?

An anthropologist interviewed one of the island's richest chieftains, named Pitmag, who explained in his pidgin English the stone secrets of Yap: "When Spanish were here, they had Spanish money. Then the Germans came, and Spanish money no good. When Japanese came, German money no good. When Americans came, Japanese money no good. Maybe somebody else come, and American money no good. Stone money always good."

Pitmag explained why "stone money always good." He said, "Yap people go across big water for many days to find stone money. Many moons go by. Cut stone out of mountain, put hole in middle, pull money down mountain to canoe. Very hard work. Yap people lose lives mining stone money. Some canoes sink. Stone money valued on how many lives lost getting here. Each stone has history. Yap people know who owns each stone. Cannot hide money. Cannot put money in pockets—if we had pockets."

So far the story sounds a lot like the dangers of mining and refining gold, valued on how difficult it is to find. The story continues, with another similarity to gold.

"One day, big storm hit Yap," said Pitmag. "Many stones fall from homes into lagoon. Didn't matter. Each person knew what stones were his." Trade continued as usual, he said, because the owner would point to his stone in the crystal-clear, emerald lagoon as collateral for his trade.

Like Yap limestone rocks, gold is scarce and endangers the lives of those who mine it. Until 1968 anyway, this gold was shipped under great security through various intricate channels from South Africa to the coffers of the Federal Reserve Bank of New York City, where it was stored 85 feet below the street level. When other nations claimed U.S. gold in exchange for dollars, the caretakers of the Stones of York would shift that amount of gold from one room to another, from the room marked "United States" to the room marked "France" or "West Germany."

This way, the central bankers in their gray business suits could "peer into the emerald lagoon" to determine whether they had the collateral to engage in world trade. But between 1968—when the "London Gold Pool" (an apt name) was closed down and 1971—when Nixon closed the "Gold Window" (another apt image of the Isle of Yap), there was no such reference to gold to finance world trade.

However, Yap money was never devalued. The "emerald lagoon window" never closed and the "stone pool" remained open for trading. It makes you wonder...have we really advanced very far beyond the monetary principles of the Island of Yap?

Chapter 15

The Crises of the 1990s

"Continued inflation must finally end in the crack-up boom, the complete breakdown of the currency system. Deflationary policy is costly for the treasury and unpopular with the masses. But inflationary policy is a boon for the treasury and very popular with the ignorant. Practically, the danger of deflation is but slight and the danger of inflation tremendous."

—Ludwig von Mises, *Human Action*

Now that the dollar has been progressively devalued ever since 1913, how much longer can the U.S. economy and money be held together with government-manufactured bailing wire, gum and mirrors? More importantly, what can you and I do to continue to protect our wealth? Before I tell you my specific investment strategy for the 1990s, I need to lay the groundwork for what I see as the fundamental crises of the 1990s.

I wrote an earlier book on this subject—*How to Profit From the Panic of 1989*—in which, among other things, I predicted a rapid and massive 1,000-point drop in the Dow Jones industrial average. That book was written early in 1987. As it turns out, we witnessed a crash just like that on Bloody Monday, October 19,

1987, when the Dow Jones industrial average skidded 508 points in one day, 800 points in four days, and about 1,000 points from its August peaks.

As I wrote in my 1987 book, prophetically as it turned out, "It could happen even before this book is printed." It actually happened after only a few thousand books had been circulated. After that crash, many people asked if my "Crash of 1989" came two years early. I said at the time that 1987 was not the final crash, but something like a "preview" of an even bigger crash ahead.

Back then I wrote, "I think the stock market will recover to a certain extent, test those highs and maybe enter the 3,000-point range before entering a super-bearish 'double top' formation some time in 1989 or the early 1990s." I still think that is likely. I may be wrong on timing, but it seems certain that something big is brewing in all of the markets, to strike sometime in the early 1990s.

After so many books have been written on the "crisis to come"—including my own 1987 book—you might think I am just crying wolf again. But the fundamental factors, such as those cited by Ludwig von Mises at the beginning of this chapter, are certain. Only the timing is difficult. Some of the problems inherent in our mixed economy (socialism plus capitalism) came to a boil back in 1979-1980. Others (like the banking crisis) began simmering in 1982-1983. But soon, for the first time in my lifetime, we will be seeing an alarming number of threats approaching us all at once.

Several Cycles Are Peaking

Under a centrally controlled economy, where the govern-ment lurches from bouts of easy money to a sobering hangover cure of tight money and back to easy money—usually for political reasons, the economy has moved in cycles of panic to prosperity and back to panic again. That is the business cycle, and we are all familiar with it by now, but it is not something that happens without an assist from government.

In fact Ludwig von Mises and Friedrich A. Hayek showed how the business cycle itself is a natural outgrowth of unnatural money—too much money and credit—seducing businesses into an expansionary mode—followed by an abrupt contraction, which causes many of those businesses to become overextended and then to fail to meet their obligations, resulting in bankruptcy.

We have now been fortunate enough to have an economic expansion without recession for seven years, the longest peacetime expansion in this century, perhaps since the 1830s, depending on how you define recessions. It is my feeling that the problems our economy has developed in the debt-ridden expansion of the 1980s make the coming recession more dangerous than any of the recessions of the last 40 years—far more serious than any threat since the 1930s.

In my earlier book, I defined this coming crisis as the "convergence" of many seemingly unrelated forces, cycles and trends happening at once. In that book, I identified no fewer than 10 cycles and 10 other non-cyclical trends which were pointing toward a single window of time in 1989 or the early 1990s as a release point for a buildup of debt in the economy.

For the moment, I will ignore the convergence of several long-term technical cycles, such as the 200-year Supercycle of the Elliott Wave and the 57-year Kondratieff Wave. In case you do not believe in these technical economic cycles—and I still remain somewhat skeptical of them myself—I will not rely on any of these cycles as my main body of evidence for pointing to the convergence of forces in the 1990s. Instead, I will expand on some more fundamental factors.

A Dozen Debt-Based Trends Are Peaking

A partial list of trends reaching a crisis stage in the next few years includes the following trends, as reflected in some of the chapter titles of my 1987 book: (1) The Oil Crisis, (2) The Farm Crisis, (3) The Federal Debt Crisis, (4) The Banking and S&L Crisis, (5) The Third World Loan Crisis, (6) Chronic Inflation, (7) Corporate and Personal Debt, (8) The Dying Dollar, (9) The Coming Trade War, (10) Terrorism in Our Hemisphere, (11) The AIDS Epidemic, and (12) A Political Change, from conservatism to liberalism, due in the 1990s.

If you put these all together you may get a migraine headache, but you will have a clear but potent picture of our debt-based house of cards and the resulting economic trends you hear about in the news each day. I think no investor can possibly ignore the danger of so many strong trends converging at one time.

I will not try to summarize all the information in my 1987 book; but I would like to summarize some of the facts on inflation and debt, two interacting crises which feed on each other. As I wrote, the national debt is nearing $3 trillion—and 90 percent of it has been rolled up in just the last 25 years. Incredibly, 70 percent of it has been spent in peacetime during the "conservative" Reagan years!

Now consider the deficit's twin brother, price inflation. Irresponsible spending has created a substantial inflationary bias in our economy since the last year with a balanced budget, 1969. Prices have risen 250 percent since then. Prices today are double those of 1977, triple those of 1970, five times the price levels of 1950, and 12 times the price levels of 1940! Today's dollar is worth less than a 1940 silver dime from my parents' pockets three years before I was born! The connection between inflation and federal debt is inseparable.

Price Inflation Comes
From Monetary Inflation

Our current level of price inflation—up twelvefold since 1940—reflects nothing more than the inflation of money supply since then. As Austrian economists have taught us, the true definition of *inflation* is an increase in the supply of credit and monetary instruments.

Since 1982 the M-1 money supply has almost doubled. Much of that money has flowed into the stock market; but when the stock market finally declined in 1987, we began to see price inflation throughout the rest of the economy, with 4.4 percent inflation in both 1987 and 1988 and a much higher level in 1989. It takes just 16 years for prices to double at only 4.4 percent inflation per year.

Because of the other major economic problems facing this world—the current S&L crisis, for instance, I think you can expect to see the government's printing presses called upon to bail out the banking system, the farming system and several other troubled economic sectors. The current bailout bill for the "thrifts" (an ironic name for the savings and loan outlets) totals $164 billion, and that assumes an economic paradise of (1) No recession in the 1990s, (2) Zero inflation and 4 percent interest rates, (3) A gain in depositors at the thrifts of 7 percent per year, and (4) An ability to finance the bailout off-budget, due to Gramm-Rudman restrictions on the 1990 deficit.

Maybe now you can see why I believe that when the next recession finally hits, probably in 1990, federal deficits will multiply and a larger portion of the debt will have to be monetized, turned into paper money instead of debt instruments like T-bills and Treasury bonds. With tax payments declining and more revenue spent on transfer payments or welfare for the unemployed, the deficits will likely top $300 billion in the early 1990s.

No less a figure than my previous gold-phobe enemy, the

former Federal Reserve Chairman Paul Volcker, said, "When we are living on this much borrowed money, we are also living on borrowed time.....We don't generate enough savings at home to finance our deficit. We are relying on capital inflow from foreign investors to finance our deficit."

What is most amazing to me is that this massive increase in federal spending, federal debt, and money supply has occurred under the direction of the most allegedly conservative president (Ronald Reagan) and the supposedly tightest money-supply czar (Paul Volcker) in recent memory. But now Paul Volcker and Ronald Reagan are gone; and our new liberal Congress and President Bush will likely raise both spending and taxes, unleashing powerful inflationary forces on the economy.

Banks in Trouble— S&Ls at Death's Door

Over 650 banks failed under the Reagan presidency—that is nearly four times as many banks as failed in the 30 years before he took office! Over 200 banks failed in 1988, according to the chairman of the FDIC, the agency which supposedly backs up all your bank deposits.

If some of the bank failures in the next few years are big banks, they could single-handedly wipe out all of the $15 billion FDIC fund, leaving the agency with its first net loss in 52 years, and leaving you—the depositor—in the lurch. Of course the FDIC will eventually pay you back, but it will probably be in newly printed dollars or even a new kind of currency—something I have been hearing about just recently—called "FDIC Notes."

If the FDIC is in danger, the Federal Savings and Loan Insurance Corporation (FSLIC) is already insolvent. In 1989 Congress voted to pour $164 billion into the rescue plan. Over 1,300 savings and loans are now described as "weak"—even by the Government Accounting Office. At least 782 of them are in the "red alert" category.

It is my feeling that your bank CD, if you still have one, may be one of your riskiest investments of the late 1980s. The bottom line is that the government is pledged to bail out these failed banking institutions; but as the situation grows worse, the bailout will have to come at the cost of higher inflation and larger federal deficits.

I believe several of these crises will converge because they are all interrelated at some level. I think two other crises—the Farm Crisis and the Third World Loan Crisis—are tied very closely to the banking problem. It is as if we were dealing with one huge financial monster that happens to have a dozen heads. You really cannot attack one problem at a time. Instead, you must find the heart of the beast. And the "heart of the beast" is debt, but debt which comes out in many different ways.

Debt—The Heart of the Beast

Debt is the heart of the beast. Most debt is at the federal government level; but as bad as the official federal deficits are, they pale in comparison with the off-budget deficit items, including unfunded retirement programs.

Let me put these debt figures to you in terms of our national net worth. If you add up the value of all of the assets in the United States—all of the money, the homes, the factories, the automobiles...everything we own—the total value would be around $10 trillion. However, the total debt in this country is now estimated to be between $10 trillion and $20 trillion—as much as double the total value of all the property in the United States!

Taking the middle range of that estimate, $15 trillion in debt represents a debt load of about $65,000 for every man, woman and child in the United States—about a quarter of a million dollars for a family of four. Obviously, not very many families have a quarter of a million dollars in net worth to offset their share of the debt load.

Even now, every nickel of the personal income taxes collected west of the Mississippi River goes only to pay the *interest* on the national debt. But that is only the beginning. Several valid debt projections—including those by the president's Grace Commission—indicate that by the year 2000, the annual budget of the federal government will exceed $13 trillion a year, the deficit will be $2 trillion a year, and interest on the debt will exceed $1.5 trillion per year. Obviously, such debt levels cannot be sustained long.

Private debt is just as dangerous to the economy in the long run. Servicing consumer debt now requires one-third of all take-home pay in the average paycheck! Corporate debt is also at record highs. The number of corporations with triple-A credit ratings is now less than half of what it was 10 years ago. New "junk bond" issues jumped from just $1 billion in 1977 to $20 billion in 1985, and losses resulting from junk bond defaults grew by 121.3 percent in the last two years. That is all in the midst of a record-long business recovery. Defaults of junk bonds will get dramatically worse in times of a recession.

The Third World debt problem is one head that just refuses to be chopped off. The Third World nations have borrowed over a *trillion* dollars, which they simply cannot repay. It is a political crisis of immense international proportions. Third World debtors, one by one, have refused to pay their debts. Brazil called a moratorium on February 20, 1987...Ecuador limited its payments to 10 percent of export income and canceled payments altogether for 1987...Bolivia stopped making interest payments in late 1986. Taken together, hardly a dime on the dollar of principal has been paid by any of these nations in the last five years. Instead, the major Latin American debtor nations are demanding more money—they want U.S. banks to throw good money after bad—before even discussing a repayment schedule.

Several major U.S. banks, beginning with Citicorp, have set aside loan loss reserves of up to $3 billion each, but even those high reserves will prove inadequate to meet their Latin losses. It looks like the only solution to this crisis is to forgive the debts and have the U.S. government then bail out the banking system with massive money creation. This may occur soon—perhaps in the next 18 to 24 months. That is how the banking crisis, inflation, deficit spending and other crises are so closely related with an underlying theme of uncontrollable debt.

The Farm and Weather Crisis

Since the early 1980s, the farming industry has been in dire trouble. U.S. farm exports have declined 40 percent in the last five years. Since 1979, more than 250,000 farms have been lost...and 550,000 farm-related jobs have disappeared with them. Another 50,000 farms will likely fold this year. Farm debt is now at an all-time high—higher than Mexican and Brazilian debt combined—and the Farm Credit system is on the verge of bankruptcy, asking Congress for federal bailouts.

I feel the worsening farm situation is closely related to the federal budget deficit and to a totally "unexpected" new crisis on the horizon—something Dr. Iben Browning has been saying at our investment conferences for years, but which only now is reaching national attention. In essence, Browning says that tidal cycles cause increased volcanic action, which throws more sulphur dioxide into the air, restricting the sun's warmth reaching the earth, and causing a long-term cooling trend. Put simply, Canada's weather of the 1930s will be Mississippi's weather in the 1990s, and that is *cold*.

Dr. Browning sees a "convergence of events"—a sunspot low in 1989 and a tidal high in 1990. He says, "The sun's rays will be one degree Celsius cooler than in the 1930s. These things in combination will produce a very cold climate." Needless to say, this cooling trend will have a profound effect on the economy. It will produce a lower-than-average yield of farm crops, increase demand for energy to heat our homes and businesses, and re-create the "Dust Bowl Days." Weather changes also bring political changes, according to Browning: "To be a great leader, you need followers, and followers only arise when they're hungry or cold."

These can be scary predictions, but I point them out only to help investors foresee the problems and ride out the storm. America is still the best country in the world for riding out a depression, but I would add that it could be smart right now to invest in some long commodity futures, such as soybean con-tracts on the Chicago Board of Trade. As prices plummet during a depression, I think it would be smart to invest in some Sun Belt real estate as a first or second home, and I would also buy the long contracts on inflation barometers, such as gold, silver and crude oil.

The Energy Shortage Is Not Over

The long-term oil shortage is another crisis situation that just will not go away. America controls just 3.8 percent of total world oil reserves. We are rich in many natural resources, but oil is not one of them. In 1985 the United States imported 5 million barrels of oil a day. Today that is up to 7 million, and by 1995 experts predict we will be importing 10 million barrels a day. Former Energy Secretary Donald P. Hodel warned, "We will be sitting in gas lines...anytime within the next two to five years." Charles DiBona, president of the American Petroleum Institute, agrees: "Overdependence on costly and insecure foreign sources of oil could well be the major national problem of the 1990s."

Meanwhile Saudi Arabia, Iran, Iraq, Kuwait, Oman and the United Arab Emirates own over 50 percent of the world's known reserves of oil—and these nations are constantly torn by wars, threats of revolution, and terrorism. Violence in the Middle East and the economic desperation of the oil-rich countries virtually guarantee rapidly rising oil prices throughout the end of the decade. You can expect to pay well over $1 per gallon from now on and maybe up to $2 in the NEXT "Oil Crisis" of the 1990s.

New Social Crises: Terrorism, AIDS

As I showed in a previous chapter, Latin America is already ripe for revolution. Several nations are the targets of both Soviet and Cuban terrorists operating out of the new Marxist haven in Nicaragua. I think we could have a real crisis on our hands if Marxism reaches our border and millions of Mexicans flee across the Rio Grande. Since Mexico is so big and our border is so long, the refugee problem would be numbered in the tens of millions! That would be another welfare problem and potential military drain.

As if all these financial and political crises were not enough, we now have a major health care crisis on our hands as well. AIDS is a financial disaster waiting to happen. It costs about $150,000 to care for an AIDS victim from first diagnosis to the person's inevitable and painful death. The cost of treating the 270,000 victims expected by the year 1990 will be $40.5 billion that year, $80 billion the next year, and so forth. We already have seen that most insurance companies refuse to issue health plans to anyone who tests positive for AIDS, or who is in the high-risk groups.

This means you and I, the taxpayers, will eventually pick up the tab. Ted Kennedy is already asking taxpayers to underwrite an additional $40 billion per year in budget deficits to fund AIDS treatment. In addition to the cost in tax dollars and inflation, AIDS will also extract a huge cost in lost productivity and consumption among our peak wage-earning age group, which is most subject to the disease. The demand for products will decline, the tax base will decline, and the deficits will be increased by an order of magnitude.

A Leftist Backlash in the 1990s?

Even after the Reagan years added such debt while allegedly cutting back social programs (I have seen no evidence of this myself), there have been several news specials talking about the case for new social spending. I am convinced average Americans support a more socially activist government if the action affects their own region or profession, or if their own "ox" is being gored by proposed budget cuts.

I believe there will be much more social spending in the 1990s, whether or not Bush remains president after the 1992 election. There is no question that the electorate is ripe for a big spender in the White House and huge, new social programs coming out of Congress: new billions spent to fight real and imaginary ecological crises; and a renewed war (equally as ineffective as the old wars) on poverty, drugs, crime, unemployment, the homeless and illiteracy, among many other social ills that were largely caused by the government in the first place.

Even the Republicans are selling out to the new, liberal national mood. George Bush recently said that under his new leadership there will be "a reordering of priorities...more emphasis on government's role." The political pendulum has come full circle. The liberal congressmen who survived the Reagan revolution—meaning the guys who for seven years had to hang their heads in shame—are now boldly promising to outspend each other in their efforts to buy votes.

Who will pay the bills? You and I. The taxpayers.

Not a Gloom-and-Doomer

Gold bugs are often considered to be gloom-and-doomers, and this chapter probably confirmed your suspicions that I am just another one of those gloomy, old gold bugs, but I don't feel that way at all, and I never have. I see a time of crises ahead, but I think our children will inherit a wonderful century in the year 2000 and beyond. But there will have to be a time of painful transition first, a cleansing of the financial order.

I know that being a gloom-and-doomer is out of style. As an example of how times have changed, I just got rid of a whole cache of "survival food" I bought in 1979. I had stored several gallons of incredibly bad stuff like "powdered peanut butter" and other unspeakable materials. They were finally going sour. I could not bear trying to mix some of that stuff up, much less to eat it, so I gave it away.

The point of this final note is that I think it is symbolic of the end of the "survivalist" era that a bunch of us are now throwing away our ten-year-old canned food.

I figure gold will buy me some survival food, if it comes to that. Gold serves as insurance against the bad times ahead; but more positively, I think gold will also be valuable in a world of more relative peace. Ironically, I think the price of gold will continue to rise in such a positive world because of the need for more gold to finance a more gold-based financial order in the new century. In the early 1970s many people thought the world would come to an end if the price of gold were $300 and average houses in some cities cost $300,000, but this is happening today, and the world still goes on.

I have seen the leading cities within Brazil and Argentina continue to flourish after suffering through millions of percent inflation over the years. I have seen Japan and Germany thrive after being wiped out in a world war. I have seen Third World nations turned into textbook free markets on the Asian rim. And I have seen America emerge from a Great Depression and Great War which only a great nation could have endured. I simply do not think big financial problems are the end of the world. They can be stepping-stones to greatness.

Investment Implications of the
Crises of the 1990s

The world's three most precious metals—gold, platinum and palladium—are produced primarily in the Soviet Union and in South Africa. Those two nations are the number one and number two producers of each of those three metals. Between the two nations, they control 93 percent of the world's platinum, 90 percent of the world's palladium, and 75 percent of the world's gold. Think what would happen if that supply could be disrupted by any one of several scenarios presented by the financial crises of the United States in the 1990s. Precious metals prices could skyrocket as a result.

In the next few years, I feel that we are in for a time of unprecedented investment opportunities. We have learned in the stock market of 1987, as in the gold market of 1980, that trees do not grow to the sky. They rise and fall. The metals have been sluggish for about a decade now, and the stock market rose for five years in a straight line, dropped nearly 15 percent, and then rose straight up for another two years. Within the next one or two years, that could change overnight, as a result of the problems we have been discussing.

The crises of the 1990s may not happen today, tomorrow or next month; but certainly in the early to mid-1990s, there will probably be the kind of dramatic change that could wipe out billions of dollars of investment equities, causing a wave of government and private bankruptcies that could result in the investment opportunities of a lifetime.

I think we are entering a period of time when the world will seem to have been turned upside down, when economic survival will be threatened by crises on every side. As we have seen in several similar crisis situations, gold and the other precious metals will be the only safe havens for capital preservation. I think those who hold tangible assets will profit no matter what occurs in the economy.

Besides facing double-digit inflation, we will also have several other crises to contend with. Our economy and the world's are literally operating in uncharted waters. No matter what the mainstream economists may tell you, nobody knows what effect a $2 trillion or $3 trillion debt load could have, or a stream of $200 billion deficits each year, or a doubling of money supply each five years. Our government is taking tremendous risks with our lives and our fortunes, and it is up to each investor to be informed and act to protect their hard-earned wealth.

In the last few chapters, I want to give you the groundwork for surviving the 1990s, for applying my success principles of the past to the next decade and beyond.

Chapter 16

How to Invest in Coins and Precious Metals

"When two coins are equal in debt-paying value, but unequal in intrinsic value, the one having the lesser intrinsic value tends to remain in circulation and the other to be hoarded."

—Sir Thomas Gresham

Precious metals and investment rare coins deserve a prominent place in everyone's portfolio. That simple statement is clear enough, following the background we have covered in this book; but it is not so widely practiced as you might imagine. The latest polls show that only 8 percent of U.S. adults own gold as an investment, and fewer still, rare U.S. coins.

The bullion and rare coin markets are so thin—compared with stock, bond, and money markets—that the slightest amount of switching from those media into gold could have a dramatic effect on the market. The total volume of gold investments over the last decade was only 0.5 percent of the capital now invested in world stock markets, and 0.3 percent of bond markets.

Timothy Green, in his excellent book *Gold: The Prospects for the Year 2000,* believes that sometime in the 1990s "a tidal wave of investors' money switching momentarily out of bonds, equities or currencies can engulf the relatively small gold market...in an afternoon. Given such a switch from time to time, one cannot rule out prices of $1,000-$2,000 or even beyond."

There is no telling when the next big shift from securities to gold and other hard assets will take place, but history shows that the rise is sudden and can be very profitable. The trouble with gold bullion alone is that it is so cyclical. Over the long term you could make money, but in these troubled times it can be a bumpy road to riches. It pays to be fully invested in your core portion of gold during "quiet times," and then just forget about it until the crisis comes.

How much gold should you own? That would be like asking, "How much insurance should the average family buy?" The answer varies on each family's particular needs; but on a general basis, the correct answer is somewhere from 10 percent to 20 percent of one's assets, with the 10 percent being a permanent core holding, and the second 10 percent being a trading portion, in and out of the bull and bear market cycles.

The Best Investment for the 1990s

The stock market has proved to be an excellent investment for the 1980s, but trees do not grow to the sky. I feel the bull market in stocks and, in fact, in most paper assets, is near a decade-long peak.

As we enter the 1990s there will be many of the traditional investments, such as stocks, bonds, certain forms of real estate, some businesses, government currencies and other investments, that will have massive bear markets. Billions of dollars of individual and institutional wealth will disappear.

I believe the big investment in the 1990s, as in the 1970s, will once again be hard assets. These include gold mining shares, both the large firms and the young start-up producers. Even penny gold mining shares will be big winners, but make sure to spread out your investment and use a good adviser. (I recommend Jerry Pogue, National Securities Corporation, 1001 Fourth Avenue, Suite 2200, Seattle, WA 98154.) If you are more conservative, pick out a balanced precious metals fund that is professionally managed. (I am biased, but would recommend the Blanchard Precious Metals Fund, 41 Madison Avenue, 24th Floor, New York, NY 10010.)

Certain commodities, such as grains, should do very well. But by far, I see the most powerful investment being within the collectibles area. Yes, antique stamps, antique furniture, antique weapons have all been and will be good investments in the future.

The best investment, an investment that can outperform gold by three to five times, is certified, graded and sealed U.S. rare coins, and secondarily, other investment-grade coins, such as modern proof issues and foreign high-grade gold coins.

The Case for Coins

Rare coins are both a collectible (like art and antiques) and an investment. People choose coins either as a hobby or strictly as an investment. The optimum way to invest in coins is from both angles at once. The best investments in coins, over the years, have been the intelligently assembled collections by wealthy "hobbyists," such as the Norweb family, Louis Eliasberg, Buddy Ebsen, the Garrett family, King Farouk, Elias Lilly, and the du Pont family.

You are probably familiar with the fact that the Salomon Brothers survey of the last several years has rated rare U.S. coins as the number one investment of the last 20 years, and also of the last 10, five and one years, in many cases. What you may not know is that these Salomon survey coins are the exceptional rarities of the 19th century and early 20th century, in BU (brilliant uncirculated) condition. These are the kinds of rarities you should learn to collect in sets for the second 5 percent of your precious metals portfolio, as described above.

Here are 16 reasons why I like these rare coins, with the first half covering the investment angle and the last eight concerning the collectible angle.

The Investment Angle

(1) Diminishing Supply. The most fundamental law of economics is supply and demand. Low supply with high demand means that price increases are more likely. Compared with the growing supply of bullion on earth, the supply of rare coins is constantly shrinking—through loss, theft, mishandling, damage, and various historic mass meltdowns. No government agency or private entrepreneur can increase the supply of historical, high-grade, investment-quality coins, any more than a man can create a new work of art by a Rembrandt or a Renoir. The supply can only go down, not up.

(2) Increasing Demand. On the demand side, the army of coin collectors and investors is increasing dramatically. There were only two million coin collectors and investors in 1960, but 10 million more were added by 1978. The gold and silver boom of 1980 swelled their ranks to 15 million by 1982 and approximately 20 million today. Still, the number of coin "demanders" is increasing geometrically with the rising market, making further price rises in the future more likely.

(3) Bullion Double Play. Some few coin series—such as the BU Morgan and Peace Dollars and the $20 Saint-Gaudens and Liberty gold pieces—are also tied to the price of bullion. When gold and silver start going up, these coins will go up on the basis of their bullion value alone, plus whatever numismatic premium is attached to them. Other rare coins often go up in sympathy with the price of bullion as well.

(4) Lower Downside Risk. The track record of rare coin performance is impressive on the upside, but is even more so on the downside. When silver bullion dropped from $50 down to $5 (a 90 percent drop), many silver dollars actually went up in price. In the worst case, silver coins dropped only 30 percent to 50 percent, while silver lost 90 percent. Part of the reason for the high upside performance over the long term (since the 1950s) is that there were lower drops on the downside.

(5) Gresham's Law. This law is stated at the beginning of this chapter: "When two coins are equal in debt-paying value, but unequal in intrinsic value, the one having the lesser intrinsic value tends to remain in circulation and the other to be hoarded." Named after the financial adviser to Queen Elizabeth I, Sir Thomas Gresham, who spoke in reaction to the debasement of currency under King Henry VIII, this law is usually shortened to say, "Bad money drives good money out of circulation." Applying this principle to rare coins, we can say: The higher grades are generally hoarded more than the lower grades, and any older rare coin will be hoarded more than today's base metal coins.

(6) Instant Liquidity. Unlike almost any other collectible market, rare coins enjoy liquidity similar to the stock and bond markets. A major Teletype system, The American Numismatic Exchange, circulates real-time bid and ask prices on thousands of issues sight-unseen. Like works of art, rare coins are also auctioned in several major sites each year. However, works of art are not traded by Teletype, giving rare coins a unique advantage.

(7) Wall Street Money. A new demand factor is the involvement of major Wall Street firms in the rare coin business. Merrill Lynch started the trend with their Athena II fund, even though it was composed of ancient (non-U.S.) coins. Then Kidder Peabody launched a major U.S. rare coin fund, which is still accumulating millions of dollars of rarities as this book goes to press. Also, Shearson Lehman Hutton is planning to support the certified coin market in their brokerage operations. This new infusion of Wall Street money has already sent the rare coin

market skyrocketing in 1988 and 1989, with promise of more millions of dollars in buying power in the 1990s.

(8) Certified Quality. Since early 1986, rare coins have been certified by two highly qualified groups of rare coin experts, the Professional Coin Grading Service (PCGS) and the Numismatic Guaranty Corporation (NGC). They not only have graded and assured the quality and authenticity of the coins they package, but they also have developed the two-way, buy-sell market for all rare coins (well over a million) that are encased in their tamper-proof containers. This gives rare coins the same kind of sight-unseen market as those of stocks or commodities.

The Collectible Angle

(9) Set Building Potential. Perhaps no other collectible lends itself to building complete sets better than coins. There are short sets, such as the 7-coin silver proof sets minted from 1936 to 1942. There are medium-length sets, such as the 14 gold $2.50 Indians or the 24 silver Peace Dollars (1921-1935). And there are the ultimate challenges of 100 different Morgan dollars (1878-1921) or the 150 varieties of silver Commemorative dates, designs and mint marks, minted from 1892 to 1954. The investment angle on these sets is that they often sell for significantly more as a set than the sum of their parts; but to collectors, they also provide the ultimate challenge and fun of their hobby.

(10) Strong Hands. Collectors hold for the long term, often for life, and smart investors are beginning to do the same. This means that rare coins are now being taken off the market for decades at a time, reducing the "float" of available supply. We call these holders the "strong hands" in the market. In other words, they will neither make a panic sell when the market drops, nor take profits at the first big rise.

(11) History Lessons. As a former U.S. history teacher, I can attest to the great enjoyment I have received from learning U.S.

history through coins. The time of our nation's greatest growth is reflected in the major series of gold, silver, copper and nickel coins. My own personal favorite of the series is the $20 Liberty gold coins, minted from 1849 to 1907—spanning the time from the California Gold Rush to such revolutionary inventions as the automobile and the airplane. However, you can pick any period of U.S. history you like, from the 1790s to the 1960s, and build a collection around it.

(12) Aesthetic Value. Early on, I discovered that owning a well-crafted coin is a far more rewarding way to hold gold and silver than just owning a cold bar of metal. Not only is there history in the coin, but you can also capture the growth of what I call "vintage coloring," which makes each coin a unique work of art. (Numismatists call this the patina, or toning, on a coin.) There is also the beauty of mint luster, the sharpness of the strike (especially on certain old nickels), the special look of a deeply mirrored, prooflike (DMPL) surface, and the eye appeal which makes each coin special. Even though many coins are minted from the same die, each coin can become as unique as one of a series of Picasso sketches of the same subject.

(13) The Grading Multiplier. Due to the advent of certified grading by PCGS and NGC, the higher grades of rare coins are taking on the nature of a market unto themselves. MS-65 coins can trade at 25 times the level of MS-63 coins because of their great rarity and desirability. With only a few known examples of some issues in higher grades, their prices tend to rise much faster in a bull market. One thing I have noticed over many years, however, is that the lesser grades tend to catch up, one by one, once the higher grades disappear into strong hands. Once MS-65 prices have gone out of sight, I always like to buy MS-64 and MS-63, since they are usually next in line for the big price moves.

(14) Privacy. Rare coins are one of the last remaining privately held investments in America not subject to excessive government reporting requirements. I suppose that is poetic justice, because the government took away all our gold rare coins

in 1934. By the same token, to prevent any future confiscation, I constantly fight for the right of privacy for rare-coin investors. Currently, any coin with more than a 15 percent premium over the bullion melt value does not carry the reporting requirement when customers sell back their coins to a broker or dealer, and there are no reporting requirements at all—regardless of the premium—on dealer sales of coins.

(15) Collectibles Fever. There's no fever like "gold fever," unless it is collectibles fever. In recent years, we have seen record sales for Van Gogh paintings set at $39 million, then $54 million. We have seen vintage cars sell for over $1 million and baseball cards for several thousands of dollars. I collect all forms of Americana—from guns, to autographs, to furniture—and I can tell you the prices are skyrocketing all across the board. It is only a matter of time until we see the first $2 million-dollar rare coin, then $3 million and up.

(16) The Wave of the Future. The biggest demographic fact of life in America today is the financial impact of the "Baby Boomers" as their generation moves through life. The 80+ million Americans (one third of us) who were born between 1946 and 1964 are now between 25 and 43 years old and so are just beginning to earn the disposable income to get involved in the lifelong hobby-investment of coins. These young people are already involved in preserving the artifacts of their youth— Barbie dolls in mint condition cost several thousands of dollars already; and one of the major artifacts of their youth was 90-percent-silver coinage, circulated through 1964. Many of these youth of the "Baby Boom" generation remember, as I do, going through their pocket change in the late 1960s looking for silver. That habit should resurface in their later years in the form of an interest in 20th century rare coins in the 21st century. This is why I believe rare coins are going to increase in popularity and value well into the next century.

Above I have listed 16 bullish points for the future of rare coins in general. Here are some specific recommendations for rare-coin portfolios for the 1990s. During the relatively slow markets of the 1980s, many investment advisers, including me, have recommended positions of only 10 percent to 15 percent in hard assets. As we enter the 1990s, I am increasing the investment position as high as 30 percent, depending on your own comfort level. In general, I would diversify the portfolio as follows:

(1) 5 percent in bullion gold coins; for example, American one-ounce gold eagles.

(2) 2.5 percent in high-grade 18th and 19th century European gold coins.

(3) 10 percent in common-date "generic" Morgan and Peace dollars in MS-63 and higher grades. I would strongly include in this category the common-date U.S. gold double eagles, both of the Liberty and the Saint-Gaudens types, in MS-60 and higher.

(Note: I personally try to get as many different dates in MS-60 and higher grades as possible in the Liberty and Saint-Gaudens double eagles...It is profitable and fun to build sets.)

(4) 10 percent in rare U.S. coins, defined as those that are $2,500 and up in price and MS-60 to MS-65 in grade. These include type coins of the 19th and 20th centuries. (Note: I also recommend the extreme U.S. rarities, coins of which there might be only two to twenty known in a certain type and condition. These coins are recommended only for wealthy investors. Such coins should generally be purchased with the expert guidance of a firm with highly rated and recommended numismatists. These coins will sell for from $10,000 to $100,000 and higher.)

In this category, as in the other categories, I put my money where my mouth is. Through Blanchard & Company I purchased, along with The American Rare Coin Fund, a 50 percent interest in the highest-priced U.S. rare coin ever sold at auction, the "most important coin in American history," the one-of-a-kind 1804 Dexter dollar, for $990,000. One day my partners and I expect to sell this coin for $2 million or more.

(5) Finally, I would recommend a modest position of 2.5 percent of your hard- asset portfolio in modern proof coins of the major nations, such as Australia and Great Britain. This category can also include platinum and palladium proof coins.

Simply put, the idea is to have a very balanced portfolio in rare coins, the highest percentage being in U.S. rare coins (the biggest and most liquid market in the world) with some foreign coins as well. This will represent an incredible upside potential, but it also will provide security and safety.

An Example of a Specific Recommendation

Within the above portfolio, I could give you dozens of specific recommendations that I think will go up in value. Let me give you the reasoning for one particular type of coin that I highly recommend. I think this coin could be three to five times more profitable than the price of gold, even if gold goes to $1,000 or higher. I am talking about common-date Saint-Gaudens uncirculated double eagles minted from 1907 to 1933, in MS-63 grades, purchased because of their gold content, their scarcity, and their relatively high MS-63 grade.

Here are some examples of just how good a buy these coins really are:

(1) How well have $20 Saints done in the past? Just go back to 1926. An investment of $1,000 in U.S. T-bills in 1926 would be worth $9,000 today. That same $1,000 invested in T-bonds would be worth $22,000. However if you had gone to the bank and taken your $1,000 in paper currency in 1926, and converted it to fifty $20 Saint-Gaudens and put them in a safe-deposit box, on the basis of a predominance of MS-63 coins and some MS-65 coins and a gold price of approximately $360, the coins would now be worth over $55,000.

(2) Now I want to compare the relative scarcity of Saint-Gaudens $20 double eagles in MS-63 condition with that of the

favorite hard-asset investment of all—gold bullion.

By far, the number one U.S. coin-grading service is the Professional Coin Grading Service (PCGS). According to their August 1, 1989, population report, which lists the amount of all coins graded in a specific condition, only 31,000 Saint-Gaudens double eagles in MS-63 condition have been processed. Remember that as many as 20 percent of those coins probably have been broken out of their holders, so the actual number of PCGS coins (the most liquid) would be perhaps only 24,800 by the end of 1989. In that same time period the wholesale value of these coins would be approximately $600 each, or only $14,880,000 total. Anyone who is familiar with the regular bullion markets knows that this is a tiny fraction of the volume of the bullion markets.

One simple example is that the size of the U.S. gold reserve, made up mostly of melted gold coins, amounts to approximately 264 million ounces. At $360 gold, this is $95 *billion* dollars.

So there you have it, a comparison in scarcity of a tiny $14.8 million with the $95 *billion* value of the world's largest gold reserve of 264 million ounces.

In dollar terms this makes MS-63 Saint-Gaudens gold double eagles 6,418 times more valuable than the gold in the U.S. gold reserve. (In other words, these coins are super rare relative to bullion.)

Now we come to a comparison of the staggering numbers of government debt plus the interest that must be paid on it each year with the total value of approximately $14.8 million of certified PCGS MS-63 Saints.

If this sounds like a silly comparison, it really is not. What we are trying to establish is the relative scarcity of these Saints in comparison with the vast amount of capital available in the most "Establishment" investments of all (for example, financing the U.S. debt via T-bills or T-bonds).

Our present U.S. debt, approximately $500 billion in 1975, is now well over $2 trillion. By early 1990, the interest on the national debt will be over *$200 billion per year*! As mentioned elsewhere in this book, every nickel of personal income taxes collected west of the Mississippi goes only to pay the interest on the national debt. Soon this will not be enough.

Actually, new money invested by both U.S. and foreign investors to finance the U.S. debt is far greater than $200 billion, but let us use just the interest on the national debt to show how massive the monetary numbers become in comparison with such excellent investments as the MS-63 Saint-Gaudens.

Although $14.8 million seems like a lot of money to most of us, it is really a drop in the bucket when we start talking about the world's monetary system. If we take $14.8 million and divide it by the interest on the national debt ($200 billion), we see that just the payment of $200 billion of interest on the national debt is 13,513 times more in monetary value than that of the certified MS-63 Saints. And remember, they are not minting any more MS-63 Saints. Yet the debt and the interest from the debt grows daily.

That, in a nutshell, is one of the best arguments for rare coins. Every year rare coins get more scarce because of damage, loss, increased population, and the growth of investor interest, including institutional interest. There is a finite supply of U.S. rare coins.

In contrast, world monetary instruments are now increasing at a rate approaching 20 percent annually, and from a more massive base. In the world of investments, comparing rare coins with monetary instruments is equivalent to comparing the finest one-carat diamonds with grains of sand.

For these and many other reasons, I believe that rare coins—particularly U.S. certified rare coins, but also certain special categories, such as high-grade European gold coins—will far outperform other investments, with gains of 25 percent to 30 percent annually. In a more inflationary period of the 1990s, gains of 100 percent and higher are not only possible, but probable.

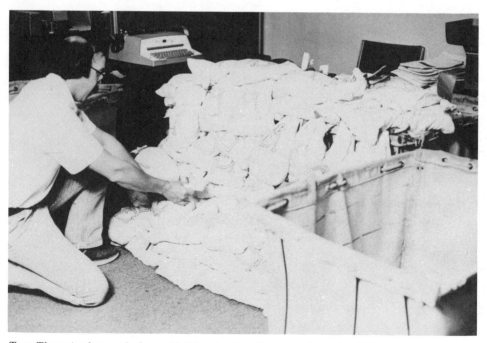

Top: The coin that made James U. Blanchard & Company, Inc. what it is today—the Morgan silver dollar. Bottom: Bob Jané, one of Blanchard & Company's numismatists, stocks hundreds of bags of silver coins in the vault, 1985.

In the early days before we had our own vaults, we rented storage space from the Security Center, formerly the original Federal Reserve Bank in New Orleans. Top: Here I am pictured inspecting vault security. Bottom left: The vault inside the Security Center. Right: The old Federal Reserve once held millions of silver dollars in the late 1800s.

Clockwise from top: John Muery, executive vice president, James U. Blanchard & Company, Inc., and I discussing grading problems, 1987. The Saint-Gaudens double eagle, called the world's most beautiful coin. An example of a rare-coin portfolio.

Top: Mary Anne Aden (left) and Pam Aden in the mid-1980s. Those were the good old days: At one point, The Aden Analysis *generated over 20,000 subscribers at $195—nearly $4 million in revenue from subscribers in 45 countries. Bottom: Photo of me holding a bag of coins amidst my collection of American art and antiques.*

A group of gold bugs picketing against gold sales from the U.S. Treasury in the early 1970s.

Top: Entering Nicaraguan refugee camp near Danli, Honduras, 1988. Bottom: Having a discussion with injured members of the Nicaraguan resistance at Contra camp in Honduras, near Nicaraguan border.

Top: Desperate Nicaraguans await the possibility of a visit from relatives at the Nicaraguan/Honduran border. Hours after we left, several hundred Nicaraguans broke through the border barrier and headed for Honduras and freedom. Bottom: Lesia Hnatiw, Gary Alexander (former editor of Gold Newsletter) *and I at the famous last Honduran/Nicaraguan border crossing, 1988.*

Top: Honduran soldiers maneuvering to keep the crowds under control. Bottom: Stan Patrick (a major Contra supporter) and I visit with Nicaraguan refugees and their children near Danli, Honduras, 1988.

Top: Honduran soldier, carrying automatic weapons, guards against a break from the border by Nicaraguans. Bottom left: A Nicaraguan mother pleads for the cause of freedom in Nicaragua from a pickup truck complete with a loudspeaker system. Bottom right: Shot taken from inside our van as we approach one of several military police check points north of the border. At that time, we were giving a ride to an illegal Nicaraguan refugee, who was looking for his relatives in Danli. While we were driving, he showed us a bullet hole in the back of his head. It was a wound he had received after being tortured by the Sandinistas.

Top: My good friend Lesia takes videos of a border crossing. Bottom (left to right): My good friend, adventurer, and freedom fighter, Jack Wheeler and I meet with Francisco Moises of Mozambique's anti-Marxist organization, RENAMO, Malawi, 1986.

Chapter 17

The Root Problem: Collectivism

"Despots and democratic majorities are drunk with power.... In fact, economic history is a long record of government policies that failed because they were designed with a bold disregard for the laws of economics. It is impossible to understand the history of economic thought if one does not pay attention to the fact that economics as such is a challenge to the conceit of those in power."

—Ludwig von Mises, *Human Action*

Megatrends have very long staying power, usually more than a century. Over 100 years ago, back in the 1880s, we saw the first moves toward a welfare state in modern times, in Bismarck's Germany and in the activities of the Fabian Society in Great Britain. Then, in the work of John Maynard Keynes and several socialist activists, the biggest body of "intellectual ammunition" for the collectivist movement became available in the 1930s.

Collectivism probably reached its full fruition by the 1960s, when Marxism was in vogue on the campuses and the Keynesian economists were in power in the White House. All in all, the collectivist movement that started over 100 years ago and peaked in the 1960s and 1970s is going downhill now, but it still has great strength.

Even though the intellectual peak in collectivist thought has already passed, the aftermath of these decisions is still being felt throughout the economy. One of these aftereffects is that the collectivist students of the 1960s are now entering their most productive years in government, large institutions and business. That means that collectivist *actions* in our society probably have not peaked yet and will continue to affect us through the 1990s. (Our various governments—state, local and federal—spend about 40 percent of our national income, and in Europe the average is over 50 percent.)

It will take a painful transition to change the strength of a megatrend that involves trillions of dollars of government transfer payments each year and the brute power of several million bureaucrats, police and soldiers; but as Victor Hugo said, "An idea whose time has come is stronger than a standing army." I believe that freedom is an idea whose time has come (and flourished, in 1776-1913), then it went away (1913-?), and it will come again.

The Last 30 Years of Monetary Depreciation

Just the other day, I calculated all the changes in the U.S. economy that have taken place since I was that young and idealistic 15-year-old boy you met on page one of this book, the little trouble-making fellow who early on discovered a philosophy from reading Emerson and Thoreau and dreaming about what he would do when he grew up.

Since 1960, when John Kennedy was elected and I was 17, only one balanced budget has been passed. The volume of money, debt and spending in the nation has grown at least tenfold in every imaginable category:

• Money supply—as measured by the broad M-2 index—has

grown from $298.2 billion in 1960 to $3.2 billion in 1989, a growth of 973 percent.

• The federal debt has grown from $234 billion in 1960 to $2.8 trillion today, up 1,097 percent.

• Federal spending has grown from just $90 billion per year in Kennedy's first year to $1.2 trillion today, a 1,233 percent growth.

• Federal non-defense spending has grown much more, from $45 billion per year to $850 billion, up 1,789 percent.

• Inflation is up over 350 percent, making today's dollars worth only about 22 cents in 1960 money.

If the next 30 years are anything like the last 30 years, the federal debt will be over $30 trillion in 2020. The rate of annual federal spending will be $16 trillion, almost all on non-defense programs, and everything will cost five or 10 times as much as it does today. Newspapers will cost five dollars, a McDonald's hamburger will cost $15, and an average home will cost $1.5 million.

However, long before we reach that level of price inflation and debt, I believe the system will come crashing down.

Reorganization of Debt Into Currency

Lyndon Johnson declared war on both poverty and Vietnam in 1965; he lost both wars. Vietnam was short-lived but the economic poverty wrought from his policies will have implications for decades and generations to come. After a generation of spending trillions on warring against poverty, we still have the same percentage of poor people.

It still astounds me that people think that all of this deficit spending and all of our other financial problems are going to be solved in some kind of soft landing. The only way this huge debt

the '95 buzz word

problem is going to be solved is by the slow but sure destruction of the currency.

A book which I read decades ago explained all this. *The Reorganization of Debt Into Currency* shows several examples of debt being paid off with new currency. This book points out that governments are so tempted to print more money that none has really resisted the temptation for very long. Printing money pays for wars and, historically, wars have been very popular ways to rally the populace behind the crown. And nothing kills a currency as rapidly as war.

You can see the effects of debt inflation in the Civil War, with the Confederate currency running aground and Lincoln's greenbacks becoming worthless. Gold traded much higher in that period, even though we were technically under a gold coin standard. The $10 gold eagles, minted from 1838 on, were trading for $15 to $20 in terms of Lincoln's greenbacks.

In the future there is no question that our politicians will use popular political terms like "saving jobs" or "giving our people a decent standard of living" as excuses to print more money and fuel more inflation in the process.

When inflation kills the bond market, recession floors the stock market, and money markets are yielding a guaranteed 5 percent real loss each year, I believe you will see billions of dollars a day flooding into gold. Now that gold and rare coins are institutionalized on Wall Street, I believe those institutions are finally able to diversify into gold on a moment's notice and to move some of their big institutional investors into the metal. That could have a tremendous effect on the price of gold, perhaps fulfilling all those "crazy" predictions of years ago about $3,000 gold and up.

Ten years ago a sudden big move into gold would have been impossible; but today's big firms all have gold-trading departments wired into Chicago, London, Hong Kong, Tokyo and Zurich, as well as to New York's COMEX market, the biggest public gold-trading market in America. At a moment's notice, the institutions can make the move to dump bonds and buy gold.

Philosophy Has the Answers

Ayn Rand used to talk about the fact that what is wrong with most people's thinking is their lack of a philosophy of life. She said that most people have no "center point" to wrap their life around. This is why she based her Objectivist philosophy upon Aristotle's simple phrase—"A is A"—and then she built an entire philosophy from that simple point.

One central point in my life's philosophy is the firm belief that governments have never been able to manage money or currency. Despite some economic good times—brief periods when the budget is balanced and inflation is low—I never gave up the firm belief that government's undisciplined fiscal and monetary policy will result in runaway inflation and the death of the dollar.

The current system is dominated from top to bottom by those who believe in collectivism—even including the young people who made millions in junk bonds and growth stocks back in the mid-1980s bull market. Our whole national socio-economic structure is based on collectivism—including central control of the money supply, which has always led to inflation and the destruction of currency.

The System Is Running on Fumes

The American miracle is running on fumes now, and I feel there will be a "gut check" in the decade ahead, that will make the 1930s look tame by comparison. The whole society will collapse and people will question basic values they have assumed were true since birth.

Today everyone looks to government to solve their problems, but this next time we will find that relying on government will be like throwing gasoline on a fire. The government's solutions will be window dressing, patchwork solutions and political mumbo jumbo. Our leaders may even talk the right talk, but they will not walk the right walk.

Even Ronald Reagan and George Bush are collectivists at heart; and even if they were pure libertarians, their whole band of bureaucrats in power would do an "end run" around any president who proposed a free-market solution. Bush has delegated all the important decisions to the hard core of collectivists on his staff.

Investing for the Coming Crisis and Beyond

Over the last few years, I have talked with several market experts and governmental insiders in the process of putting together my conferences and publications. I find that a shocking number of them are totally convinced that a number of strong forces are going to converge soon and cause the whole system to come apart.

Most investors have been lulled into complacency by the new stock bull market—once again setting new highs in 1989; but I feel that once the liberal Congress starts its spending programs and tax increases, it will no longer be a question of who is in charge at the Federal Reserve, or how careful and conservative he may be. Whoever is there will be obliged to bail out the system or become the "Herbert Hoover" of our generation.

In other words, it does not matter how conservative Alan Greenspan really is, or how much he still believes in Ayn Rand's philosophy; I believe he will have to become a political animal at the Fed. I feel that he will certainly compromise his purest values when called upon to do so in the future, as he did under

President Ford as the Chairman of the Council of Economic Advisors.

The Reagan Revolution—Fizzled

In 1980 Reagan's election was based almost entirely on rhetoric. As a communicator and spokesman for free enterprise, Reagan was excellent; and there was a strong pro-free-market group of people behind him and a large intellectual movement supporting what he was saying. But the vast majority of people who voted for him were still under the sway of collectivism, and Reagan himself was not thoroughgoing in his philosophical roots, or strong enough in his convictions to make the necessary changes in large transfer payment programs like Social Security, farm aid, foreign aid, and civil service pensions.

What was overlooked in those heady days of 1980-1981 was the collectivist nature of the core of the power structure of the mainstream political coalition. Centrist Republicans were still in the highest positions—career politicians who rose to the top of the political ladder, such as Senate Majority Leader Robert Dole and President George Bush. The very fact that these two men are our leading Republicans shows how far the party has forgotten its basic philosophical ideals as expressed by Goldwater in 1964. Today's Republican leaders—not to mention the lost-cause Democrats—are basically collectivists who are temporarily "riding with the tide" of the conservative wave until the "fad" blows over.

My 1980 prediction that Reagan would go down in history as the biggest spender (with the record buildup in debt, etc.) was not an attack on him as a person. He seemed to sincerely believe what he said. He became our worst debtor while dealing with conditions that were mostly beyond his control—spending was based mostly on what Congress would do despite him; benefits, people vote for. All of that would have taken place even if President

Reagan were more firmly committed to free-market principles than he has turned out to be.

As you look back now, after Reagan's eight years in office, it would seem that back in 1980 we had elected the biggest-spending Democrat in the history of the nation. Debt tripled in just eight years; federal spending is now well over a trillion dollars a year. Think how much worse it would get under any other conceivable combination of factors: a Democrat president, a recession, or any of a dozen crises.

Even though I know the long-term fundamentals have not changed, I made one mistake in 1980. I should have realized that the public would be fooled by Reagan's rhetoric in the short term. In retrospect, I can see that the public's misconception is the reason why gold went down from $850 in 1980 to $297 in 1982.

Reagan's actions in his first two years were remarkable; he made powerful progress in his policies while Congress was still in its "honeymoon" period with him. He passed a major tax-reform law, sliced inflation to the bone, brought interest rates down, cut some domestic spending (but only the "window dressing"), and so forth. All this added up to a major bear market in gold during Reagan's first term!

Even though the public was fooled by this short-term success, I knew this wave of conservative action would backfire on Reagan when people realized that they would have to sacrifice some of their middle-class entitlements in order to make the Revolution work. When political reality finally dawned on America, gold started to go back up again, gradually at first, at the beginning of Reagan's second term.

I knew all this would happen, but what I did not realize was how long it would take the public to wake up to the facts. If I had thought they would be so completely duped by his charisma, I would have told everybody to sell half of their gold holdings in 1980 and buy it back in 1985 when the dream was over and the inflationary hangover started to return.

Several newsletter editors, myself included, made the mistake in 1980 of making predictions based on timing instead of logic. Sure, we could see what was going to happen, but that did not give us the knowledge of when it was going to happen. In 1979 and 1980 we thought we were witnessing the end of the monetary system as we knew it, so we got carried away in our hopes for gold. But now we can see that it was just one of many peaks, perhaps leading up to a blow-off to much higher prices at some future date we do not know yet.

In 1980 a lot of economic newsletters celebrated the end of liberalism prematurely, saying that this was the end of an era of collectivism and that Ronald Reagan would be the messiah of a new conservative age. I disagreed, and said so in the very week he was elected and repeatedly during his administration. But for the first two years of his administration, they appeared to be right and I to be wrong. In the end, though, it is clear that we have a lot more lessons to learn as a nation before we can assume that a single spokesman—even a Great Communicator—can change the underlying root of collectivism in our society.

Cruising Toward a Crash

Three, four and five years from now, even the most avid hard-money people will say that they never would have believed that the stock market collapse could be this bad. The majority of today's investors are so young, or so new in the market, that they do not even remember the bear market crash of 1973-1974, much less the Great Depression in the 1930s. How well I remember that back in 1973 the OTC stocks virtually disappeared and the AMEX was down 80 percent, and then in 1975-1976 gold stocks went down even further. Those were truly scary bear markets that make even "Black Monday" of 1987 look tame by comparison.

Today's investors have only superficial investment knowledge, based on a few articles in the *Wall Street Journal* or one or two newsletters. They lack the philosophical background to understand why they are investing the way they are. Many of them are heavily invested on margin, which is debt financing, and that is the same kind of house of cards that fell in 1929. I am not sure today's investors have the intestinal fortitude to weather another Great Depression, but they need to find the guts somewhere, because a testing time is coming.

Hope for the Future

Because of the impact of Ayn Rand, Ludwig von Mises, Friedrich Hayek, and other great 20th century thinkers and writers, we now have a strong intellectual community that supports freedom in America. It is still only a small group of people, compared with the collectivist community, but right-thinking people are now in key places in the universities and think tanks of America—even in the media, that great bastion of collectivism. Almost all the think tanks today are freedom-oriented. (Collectivism is a tired, old idea that has not generated a fresh thought in 25 years.)

Because of this predominance of avant-garde freedom-thinkers in academia, today's young people can take part in that intellectual revolution and get a jump on their contemporaries, as I did back in the 1960s.

The second positive thing going for Americans in the coming panic and depression is the fact that most American people still think in terms of solid conservative values: patriotism, heroism, rugged individualism, faith and determination (even though their daily actions are usually collectivist in nature). I think these values will find expression in the future in a more freedom-oriented society. The vast majority of Americans will come to see large government as the "hideous strength" that C.S. Lewis once called it. I am hopeful that in the 21st century we will have leaders who will understand and practice the philosophy summarized in the following quotation:

> "You cannot bring about prosperity by discouraging thrift. You cannot strengthen the weak by weakening the strong. You cannot help the wage earner by pulling down the wage payer. You cannot further the brotherhood of man by encouraging class hatred. You cannot help the poor by destroying the rich. You cannot keep out of trouble by spending more than you earn. You cannot build character and courage by taking away man's initiative and independence. You cannot help men permanently by doing for them what they could and should do themselves."
>
> —Abraham Lincoln

In the initial stages of a coming inflationary depression, I think that far more than 50 percent of the American people will line up for the dole to gain handouts of one kind or another. At some point, though, when the system becomes overloaded with people wanting handouts, the government will try to take total control of our lives—freezing prices and wages, blocking all foreign trade, slapping on exchange controls, providing make-work jobs, taxing the successful investors into poverty; and people will be looking for a change. The ultra-liberal collectivists will be blamed for letting it get this bad, and the American public will want to throw the rascals out.

I remember Friedrich Hayek saying in the last recession (1979-1982) that if Americans were strong enough to take their medicine early in the game and if the politicians had the guts to let a deep recession just happen, it could cause blood in the streets; but capitalism and free markets would prevail. Strong businesses would survive and weak ones would fail. But if the government were to try to administer painkilling medicine instead, he said, they would only prolong the depression into a 12-year nightmare, like the Great Depression of the 1930s.

It looks like Reagan left office in the nick of time, just before all this happens. With today's smorgasbord of 25,000 or more registered lobbyists and special interest groups in Washington, the ruling coalition has retaken control of the beast on the Potomac; and they will continue to be in favor of strict, regimented collectivism and total intervention in the marketplace for the foreseeable future—including the first years of the panic/depression. But that is when we will see the invisible economic regulator—gold and the other precious metals—take off like a rocket. That's when there will be danger of gold confiscation once again.

Gold as the Ultimate Security Blanket

You need not anticipate total calamity to buy gold as a security blanket for the 1990s. People who buy gold today are "voting" in a way, they are making a socio-economic, political statement. They are casting a vote of no-confidence in their government's paper money and political actions. (A crisis of no-confidence is not as easily resolved as a more visible crisis.) This type of person is not as likely to turn his gold over to the federal agents as the more docile, desperate Americans did in the 1930s.

In any time of "extreme national emergency," there could be another gold call-in. I would just advise people to examine their premises and ask themselves if they would be willing to break the law, or at least bend it badly, in order to hold on to their gold for self-preservation. Those who surrender their gold are defenseless. Those who keep it can survive. (Look at the boat people of Southeast Asia in the 1970s, or the Jews escaping Europe in the 1930s. Gold was their only ticket to freedom, and to life.)

Perhaps a better alternative is to buy U.S. Gold Double Eagles, which are legally exempt from the U.S. gold confiscation powers. As I have said many times, U.S. gold coins, and to a lesser extent foreign gold coins in uncirculated condition, are excellent long-term buys.

In short, I feel that America's inherent patriotism and individualism, along with the free market values newly discovered in the think tanks and in the media, will combine to bring back the free-market by the late 1990s.

Nobody knows exactly what the future holds; but if you can look at the current economy and ask certain key questions, it is pretty likely you will agree that the future involves some form of debt collapse, inflation and social upheaval.

Chapter 18

A Vision for the 1990s and Beyond

"I have seen the future, and it works."

—R. Buckminster Fuller

In the 1990s I expect that millions of new people will come to gold from the mainstream markets—stocks, bonds and money markets. There will be a revival of interest in hard money when the next shoe drops, after the next stock market crash. Those who are currently enamored of their paper assets and think that trees grow to the sky will be severely decimated if they stick with the stock market in the coming crash or major correction. They will either lose half their wealth in short order—and learn a painful lesson—or they will learn from the last crash, get smart early, and bail out a little before the top. Either way, they will be impressed with the stability of precious metals, rare coins, and other hard assets as opposed to paper. The new group of gold bugs who will come to us in the 1990s will need a widely diversified portfolio of financial assets.

Investment Strategies for the 1990s

Most people are so petrified with fear of a possible deflation that they put their money into money-market funds—which is precisely the most dangerous thing to do in a time of inflation and debt default. (After inflation and taxes on your interest, your net yield in most money-market funds is below zero. Besides, a lot of the "top performing" money-market funds are only top-performing because they are tied to risky Eurodollars—the kind of cash that is riskiest to hold in times of crisis.)

You can bet on the short-term myopia of most investors—in fact you can make a lot of money going the opposite of what the leading indicators and analysts say you should do. But if you want to sleep better at night, I advise you just to buy and hold the most solid forms of non-reportable wealth.

One of the myths of owning gold is that it bears no interest and hence goes down in times of rising interest rates; but if you can remember as far back as 1979, you will remember that the government was selling off massive amounts of gold during a time of record-high interest rates—and yet gold had its biggest bull market of modern times.

I have been successful at investing because I have been involved with every kind of market at one time or another, and usually at every stage of the cycle. I have been in the most solid and most speculative markets at the same time—in the stock market, with some commodity trading, oil drilling partnerships, penny shares, and bullion.

The best investments I have ever made have been those maverick investments that I simply put away in a vault and forgot, just waiting for something to happen, like the penny stocks. There are some losers, but the winners can experience a growth of 10-to-1, 20-to-1 and even 50-to-1. They do not increase overnight, and they may break your heart somewhere along the line, but investing that is based on fundamentals eventually pays off.

The same is true of my own personal coin portfolio. I might have made a lot more money over the years by trading vigorously with the cycles, but instead I have just put away coins for the long term and have not worried about the short-term trend.

Speculation is one of the major reasons why people who retire or sell their business too early have to go back to work. They speculate too much for the short term and get fooled into thinking that they are brilliant investors. Then they retire early; the market turns against them; and they are suddenly without savings, with little or no income to offset their losses. Before, they invested a share of their income; but as full-time investors, they are gambling with their seed money.

A New Gold Standard by the Year 2000?

As crazy as it sounds, my lifelong wish for a return to the gold standard may be coming true already. Investors all over the world are getting so heavily involved in gold that several nations are giving their people the option of buying gold coins with their paper money. The world is gradually moving into a position where most people will instantaneously be able to choose between accepting paper money or the real thing.

Although I have long been an advocate of the Treasury holding onto its core supply of 264 million ounces of gold, I feel that the gradual selling off of Treasury gold could be a healthy trend if spread over a lengthy period of time. What would be destructive would be a rapid dumping of gold at market prices, which would hurt investors and not really reduce the budget by anywhere near the amount they could get later on. Since government has a long track record of buying precious metals at an irrationally high price and selling them at an irrationally low price, I am not too excited about the chances of government selling Treasury gold in a rational or gradual manner.

When this book reaches most of its readers, the 1990s will be just beginning. I remember when that date sounded mystic and far away. Well, the same is now true of the year 2000. It will be here before you know it. In the early 1990s, I feel we will have an explosion of negative economic forces, like a volcano, and the small corps of people who surfaced in the anomaly called the Reagan Revolution will come back into power in both houses of Congress and in the presidency, perhaps as early as 1992. If a big-taxing Democrat tries to keep spending us out of trouble, imitating FDR, I believe he eventually will run up against a tax revolt that will make 1979-1980 look like a dress rehearsal for the Boston Tea Party.

A View Toward the Year 2000

For the longer term, here is what I think is going to happen: The economy will soon fall under the weight of our government's economic sins of the last six or seven decades, and we will witness a rebirth of the system under a new, true free-market revolution that could be the most positive shock of the 21st century. This revival of freedom could launch private enterprise into space, bringing the benefits of modern technology to new planets, and bringing the correct understanding of free-market economics and individualism to a whole new world—to planet Earth—for the first time in recorded history.

The 21st century will be as revolutionary as the Industrial Revolution 200 years ago. The next century could make the accomplishments of the 20th century pale by comparison, and it could leave the pains of war and deprivation suffered in this century as a kind of lasting monument to the folly of the fruits of centralized government.

Long term, I am a super-optimist, because the longest megatrend in existence is the continued ascent of evolutionary man. I think man will continue to ascend toward greatness again in the next century. We are seeing only hints of that today. The big question is what to do between now and the beginning of the 21st century, and I think this is where we will need to see some culmination of the current order.

The trend toward collectivism has certain absolutes flowing from it: the decline of the dollar, the "biggest debtor nation" status, inflation, and taxes—but that is only the beginning. The whole shape of what one would consider a viable investment portfolio and strategic policy will be totally different in the future from what it is now. You need not be an economist with a Ph.D., or study every stock and bond from a microscopic, technical, computerized view, to know that something big is coming. You just have to look at the world with a certain amount of disciplined common sense.

Although anyone can see that socialism is an economic bad joke and a worldwide laughingstock, several key policy-makers will try to make it work, fighting against human nature in their misguided beliefs about what the world should be like. I think the battle between these two intellectual forces will culminate around the turn of the century with the defeat of collectivism and the victory for liberty.

Even if I am wrong and the United States sinks into the torpor of European-style socialism, I still feel that the 21st century will be a century of freedom, but with the center of power shifting westerly, from the United States to Japan and the free markets of the Asian rim, such as South Korea, Hong Kong, Taiwan, and Singapore.

In America, if it is not too late, we could also have a renaissance of individualism and freedom, with perhaps a Libertarian Party president (or a Libertarian Republican) sometime in the next century, and a last chance to beat the natural tide of history, which indicates we are a maturing democracy with roots of socialism pointing us toward the inevitable senility and death that all great nations and civilizations have gone through. The only way our society will cheat senility and death is to wake up to the vigorous strength of freedom, which fueled our growth for the first 200 years.

As an investor, you have the choice to do something more than just protect your wealth. You have the opportunity to be a part of a changing of the guard. Your vote for gold is a vote for individual freedom. Even if gold does not dazzle you with top quarterly performances year in and year out, what you are saying with your gold ownership is that you prefer to owe no man anything—you prefer to have the only form of money which is not someone else's promise of wealth, some government or corporation's promissory note or debt instrument. By owning gold, you not only protect your wealth, but you contribute toward the rebirth of freedom in the 21st century.

Wherever you find collectivism in control of a nation's money, the demand for confiscating gold in the "best interests of the public" is always a threat. In that regard, I think the reforms of the Reagan Revolution were very superficial. If you were to scratch the surface of people who voted for Reagan, you would find that most of them are really collectivists down deep. The majority of Republicans are collectivists, and the vast majority of Democrats always have been.

How Business People Can
Help to Further Freedom

Those who have some money and are interested in promoting freedom while possibly making some more money should consider producing films that glorify freedom in America, that take an adversarial role with respect to the IRS and government regulations, and that champion the individual against the collective. Good movies make a lot of money, and they also deeply affect the youth of America with their portrayal of ideals—for good or evil.

So few Hollywood films exhibit a respect for freedom. Most

movies about business portray corporate executives as greedy philanderers at best and murderous conspirators at worst. You can hardly find any movie that portrays small-business men in a positive light. There are very few movies that portray government in a negative light, just businessmen.

A few movies have carried this theme, such as Ayn Rand's two films, *We The Living* and *The Fountainhead*, the recent movie about the automobile innovator, *Tucker*, and an old underground classic against IRS terrorist tactics, called *Harry's War*. But these movies are so few and far between and so weakly promoted that very few people have seen any of these classic pro-business, pro-freedom films.

Another way to do this, on a much cheaper basis, is to finance a one-act, one-man screenplay that dramatizes the life and sayings of a freedom philosopher such as Thomas Jefferson, Ayn Rand or Ludwig von Mises. This has been done with the words of populist philosophers such as Will Rogers, Mark Twain and Harry Truman, but why not bring the ideas of the greatest Americans back to life on stage and have them comment on current issues. A group of writers, philosophers and businessmen recently put this idea together under the auspices of Knowledge Products, but they are just audio tapes. To reach today's youngsters, you need to tickle their eyes as well as their ears and brains.

Can you imagine the effect of the dramatized words of a brilliant writer like Tom Jefferson applied to today's current events? I cannot imagine his not having some strong comments to make about today's deficit spending, government regulations, and lack of interest in freedom issues.

While its true that there are few screenwriters or producers who have much interest in freedom issues, I have often recommended that the libertarian think tanks like Reason Foundation and CATO Institute produce some original literary works that dramatize freedom instead of all the wonderful, thorough (but sometimes boring) studies on how society "should" work under the freedom ideal. I feel the only way to reach young minds is to dramatize the facts for them. Don't preach, or even teach, but dramatize.

How Corporations Can Help

A few corporations, like Mobil Oil, have printed public service announcements on behalf of American capitalism, but I would love to see several other companies follow their example by using corporate funds to invest in the future of American capitalism. A smaller company in Richmond, Virginia—Figgie International—did a great job of dramatizing the national debt in a series of advertisements, because of the strong leadership of the owner, Harry Figgie, Jr.

The best example of a private businessman making a big contribution to freedom is J. Peter Grace, the chairman (since 1945) of W.R. Grace and Company. He devoted years of his time, along with more than 2,000 executives from corporations throughout the United States, to show how the federal government could cut waste, fraud and overspending. He showed over 2,000 ways to save $424 billion, and about one-third of those savings were actually realized, saving each taxpayer well over $1,000 in the last five years. That is a real contribution.

Ironically, Mr. Grace is only able to make these kinds of contributions because he is not the typical kind of businessman. His dad gave him the reins to the company in 1945, so he did not have to climb the corporate ladder over the years. He did not have to "play it safe" over a period of 30 or 40 years, as so many executives do.

A Vision for the Next Century

In the next century, I believe, the megatrend will be toward privatization, as part of a long-term trend toward freedom. I believe we will pay off our $10 trillion national debt (now it is "only" $3 trillion) by selling federal assets to the private sector; then we will build a workable libertarian, capitalistic society in America and probably around the world. There will be a growing realization that collectivism will not work; that governmental intervention will not work; and that the Communist empire will gradually, and then more suddenly, collapse of its own inefficiency and waste.

In fact, the way things look now—with the dramatic news coming out of the Soviet Union and the retreat of their empire—there may be no Communist state by the year 2000. In a world in which there is no Communist state and only a few scattered totalitarian states unable to support themselves, we could probably go back to a gold standard sometime in the next century, with a revaluation of all currencies to gold making its price go up despite the generally peaceful state of the world. Demand will be way up when most governments need to back their currency. More people will wear gold jewelry and hoard some gold, further adding to demand.

Already, we have massive new gold demand in Japan, Taiwan and many other nations in the Far East. They are playing catch-up to the rest of the world in terms of "central bank" gold holdings. When the world goes toward a gold standard in the next century, we will see all nations bidding up the price of gold so as to finance their external trade and their internal money supply. In other words, there is still tremendous potential for the price of gold, whether in a negative, inflationary or deflationary world or in the most positive scenario.

The *Real* New Frontier

There was a time in America when anyone could saddle up a horse and head west. Nothing was to hold you back. West was always "out there"—even back in 1607, when Jamestown, Virginia, was the farthest west the settlers could safely reach. Tomorrow's "West" is trying to discover a way to explore space. Maybe not in the next century, but eventually. Someday people will explore space in the non-structured entrepreneurial way in which our own West was settled. It will not all be a government-sponsored expansion, or if it is, you will find settlers on new planets rebelling against Earth's government, just as our colonies rebelled against the British Crown in 1776.

Just as it took almost three centuries to get from Columbus' discovery in 1492 to the constitutional government of 1789, I think it will take several centuries to get from the first manned flight to the moon to actually having large communities on the moon or other planets, with people beginning to break their political bonds to the planet Earth.

Continuing the intellectual revolution into the next century, we will throw off the shackles of the collectivist philosophers who dominated the 20th century college campuses. If the wave of the 1980s and the Reagan years has been the economics of Milton Friedman, the wave of the future is David Friedman, his son, a brilliant academic anarchist and libertarian, who has his father's ability for thorough analysis, along with a more radical way of looking at society in non-governmental terms.

Ideas *Still* Have Consequences

Just 20 years ago, the think tanks were almost all liberal but today the best think tanks are all freedom-oriented, like the CATO Institute, Reason Foundation, the Heritage Foundation and the Institute for Humane Studies at George Mason University. Old-time liberal newspapers and magazines are turning "moderate" or even "neo-conservative" in their outlook. In fact you would be hard put to name one liberal think tank that exists anymore. That is because the modern liberal point of view has never been intellectual; it has always been emotional, irrational and hysterical.

The typical modern liberal says, "We need to do something about saving the poor. It doesn't matter if our plan works or not. The poor may get poorer. We just have to do something." A liberal refuses to listen to logic, but keeps coming back with two basic statements: "We must do something" and "It probably won't work, but we've got to try." By contrast, a conservative or libertarian thinker would devise a specific, workable plan for helping the poor by allowing them access to free markets. If poverty is the problem, wealth is the solution; and Adam Smith showed that the wealth of nations grows only in a laissez-faire (let it alone) environment.

Education is still our best hope. As my son, Anthem, turned 10—in October 1989—one of my greatest pleasures was to replicate the opportunities of my own youth in his development, particularly in introducing to him the exciting books about the great American West that so inspired me as a youngster of his age. Our children are the future of America, our best investment in the growth of the great American ideals in the next century. I hope to be around long enough to read Anthem's own memoir, filled with as many exciting challenges, ideas and triumphs as I have been blessed to know in the last 45 years.

Epilogue

Events in the 1990s will move very rapidly, and the timing of events is beyond even our best-educated guesstimate. But I believe one thing is certain...the megatrend of 20th century collectivism will result in an international socio-political crisis unparalleled in the last 100 years.

Life, not just investment success, will be difficult for many of us during this period. The 1990s will see a difficult time for even the best-educated and rational investors. There will be wild swings in all the markets. Power and wealth will shift from one group to another, from one nation to another; and there may even be international war.

It will not be a time to invest a high percentage of your savings in government "guaranteed" paper. Governments, financial institutions and individuals will become increasingly skeptical of government money management. The ultimate crisis will be the failure of confidence in government-created fiat currency.

A massive international monetary crisis will hit us in the 1990s. The effect on investments will be catastrophic. The challenge will be to preserve your savings, your investments, your capital and your business. Because of the wide swings in the marketplace, there definitely will be chances to make huge profits; but these will be very speculative times.

Perhaps the safest investment hedges will be hard assets, especially gold, rare coins and semi-rare coins.

These hard-money assets will be a hedge against the inevitable socio-political and economic problems that we will see in the 1990s. If you work hard at it, and have a little luck, you should be able to protect your business and family and preserve your capital and investments. In doing this, you will be way ahead of the crowd.

The only real hope is not short-term investment success but a renaissance of freedom, individualism and an open market, which can bring us peace and prosperity after the crisis/chaos of the 1990s.

Society in the 21st century will learn from the mistakes of the 20th century, and we will experience a boom based on a new international understanding of the benefits of freedom and an open libertarian society.

As we enter the 1990s and see the hard problems which confront us, it may be difficult to be optimistic. Everything goes in cycles; but as Rose Wilder Lane pointed out, the mainspring of human progress is the liberty of each person to choose his own way.

But first we will have the bad times and the resulting necessary lessons.

In the 21st century, a thousand flowers will bloom. The following generations will experience the ultimate freedom: exploration and eventual settlement of space. But in the meantime, keep your powder dry. An incredible emergence of major political and economic problems faces us. Buy some gold and some rare coins, keep liquid, do not depend on government promises, and perhaps most of all, invest some of your time in enjoying your life and spreading the word about the golden benefits of freedom and individualism.

For More Information

Books

Rather than falling into the trap of most bibliographies—listing a hundred or more unrelated books in alphabetical order, by author—I would like to divide the key books by chronology, author and subject, to show a logical way to become educated in free markets.

You can order any and all of these books from three specialized sources of free-market information. Write or call for a free catalog to Laissez Faire Books, 942 Howard St., San Francisco, CA 94103 (800-326-0996, Monday-Friday, 9-6 PST), the Foundation for Economic Education (FEE), 30 South Broadway, Irvington-on-Hudson, NY 10533; 914-591-7230 or Liberty Tree Network, 134 98th Ave., Oakland, CA 94603; 415-981-1326.

First, let's go back 150 years to some small classics. Frederic Bastiat's *The Law* (1847), only 76 pages long, still contains one of the best arguments for limited government. Another short (125 pages) classic is Andrew Dixon Whites' *Fiat Money Inflation in France*, about the French assignat currency of the 1790s. Both of these classics are available from the Foundation for Economic Education at a very low price, especially in bulk purchase.

The next step is to go back to classic Austrian economics with Ludwig von Mises, whose major books were written during

285

the first half of this century. Start—like I did—with his shorter, easier-to-digest classic, *Planned Chaos* (90 pages) and then move up to his more difficult classic economic testbooks: *Human Action* (907 pages), *Socialism* (599 pages) and *The Theory of Money and Credit* (413 pages). If these books are too tough for you, read one of the von Mises "samplers" written by Murray Rothbard and Percy Greaves, two excellent writers who were disciples of von Mises.

Moving up, chronologically, to the time of World War II, there were many epochal essays on freedom published in the 1940s. The classic was Friedrich Hayek's *The Road to Serfdom* (1944), which was originally written to warn British bureaucrats away from their policies of creeping socialism.

Just after the war, economic journalist Henry Hazlitt (now 95) wrote his classic *Economics in One Lesson* (1946), the one book to read on economics, if you only want to read one book. Then comes Henry Grady Weaver's *The Mainspring of Human Progress* (1947). This book was written "in white heat" by an industrialist (at General Motors) who was tired of hearing capitalism blamed for society's problems when it was the system mankind uses for solving those problems. It is based largely on a small classic from 1942, *The Discovery of Freedom* by Rose Wilder Lane, daughter of Laura Ingalls Wilder of *Little House on the Prarie* fame.

Also in the 1940s, novelist Ayn Rand was reaching the peak of her powers with *The Fountainhead* (1943), having previously published two smaller novels in the 1930s, *Anthem* and *We the Living*. She worked for 12 years on her fiction classic, *Atlas Shrugged* (1957), and then branched off into non-fiction Objectivist philosophy with *Capitalism: The Unknown Ideal* and *The Virtue of Selfishness*, among other "collected writings" over the years.

Perhaps the most eloquent and wide-ranging Austrian economist of the last 25 years is Professor Murray Rothbard, author of a landmark historical treatise of the 1920s and 1930s, *America's*

Great Depression (1975, 351 pages), a two volume economic framework, *Man, Economy and State* (1962, 987 pages), and the Libertarian Party manifesto, *For a New Liberty*. In monetary economics, he wrote the short classic, *What Has Government Done To Our Money* (68 pages), the best short review of monetary economics I have ever read.

In parallel with Rothbard, Rand and von Mises, it is instructive to read the freedom philosophy of Rose and Milton Friedman, beginning with *Capitalism and Freedom* (1960), continuing with *Free to Choose* (1980) and *The Tyranny of the Status Quo* (1984). The most interesting Friedman work, I must admit, is *The Machinery of Freedom* (newly revised in 1989) by their son, David Friedman. It is a detailed defense of total freedom in the marketplace.

For a popular review of libertarianism for the Average American, I recommend Robert Ringer's *Restoring the American Dream* (1979). It is his best book, in my opinion; unfortunately, it sold far fewer copies than his big best-sellers of the 1970s about deal-making and *Looking Out For #1*.

Another excellent introduction, because of its wide range of authors and subjects, is *The Free Market Reader* (1988), edited by Lew Rockwell, published by The Ludwig von Mises Institute, 851 Burlway Road, Bulingame, CA 94010, and available in quality paperback for $11.95. This collection of free-market essays includes works by Ludwig von Mises and his leading modern disciples, such as Murray Rothbard, Mark Skousen, Lawrence Reed, Ron Paul, Walter Block and many more.

Magazines

The Economist (P.O. Box 2700, Woburn, MA 01888, $85 per year) is essential if you want to cover news from foreign lands, with an economic perspective on world political events. It is not particularly conservative or free-market oriented, but neither is it leftist, which is a welcome relief these days. The editors are also quite clever, with their dry British humor, in choice titles and caricatures of world leaders.

The Freeman (free), published by the Foundation for Economic Education, contains book reviews, issues in the news, letters, and long articles giving the "freedom angle" to particular social and economic issues.

Insight (weekly) and the *Washington Times* (daily, Monday through Friday), 3600 New York Ave. NE, Washinton, DC 20002, Arnald DeBorchigrave, editor. I am tempted to say that the *Washington Times* is the only newspaper in America with a pro-freedom bias, and *Insight* is the only weekly news magazine that presents both sides of many controversial issues. Yet neither of these publications would exist without the deficit financing provided by the Unification Church of Dr. Sun Myung Moon. That is a pretty sad commentary on our news media today: It takes money from an off-beat church cult to provide an alternative voice in America! To get this alternative view, you can subscribe by mail to either publication from anywhere in the United States.

Liberty, $19.50 per year (6 issues), P.O. Box 1167, Port Townsend, WA 98368. A purely libertarian journal, *Liberty* covers the "advanced level courses" in free markets, and the virtues of anarchy. A typical issue will cover someone's personal experiences with the "Ayn Rand cult," a philosophical examination of epistemology, a radical proposal to privatize roads (or police, or the courts), several long book reviews, comments on the news, and more. Very mind-opening reading, and highly recommended.

Reason, $24 per year (monthly), P.O. Box 3724, Escondido, CA 92025. Subtitled "Free Minds & Free Markets," *Reason* is the pioneer in popularized writing on the free markets since 1969. It is published by the Reason Foundation, 2716 Ocean Park Blvd., Suite 1062, Santa Monica, CA 90405.

Newsletters

The Aden Analysis, editors: Mary Anne Aden and Pamela Aden; P.O. Box 523, Bethel, CT 06801; 203-798-7967; one year (12 issues), $195. I originally published this newsletter form 1982 to 1988, but sold my interests in 1988 as part of the sale of Blanchard & Company. The Adens have been extremely conservative and accurate in their trend-following analysis over the years.

Analysis & Outlook, editor: R.W. Bradford; P.O. Box 1167, Port Townsend, WA 98368; $78 per year (monthly). Although published by one of my competitors in the coin business, I recommend Bradford for his excellent monthly four-page analysis of metals and coins, which he sandwiches between the editing of his six-times-a-year labor of love, *Liberty* magazine—a far better deal, at $19.50 per year (same address as above).

Daily News Digest, editor: W.A. "Johnny" Johnson; P.O. Box 84900, Phoenix, AZ 85071; 602-993-1910. Compiled weekly, with a conservative, free-market outlook on a wide variety of world news issues, *DND* is available for two years (104 issues!) for $177, or one year for $97, or six months for $57.

Deliberations, Ian McAvity, editor; P.O. Box 182, Adelaide Street Station, Toronto, Ontario, Canada, M5C 2J1; $215 for 24 issues (one year), or five issues for $49. Ian covers all markets, but with special expertise in gold and gold shares. Excellent charts, combined with Ian's unique analytical abilities.

Dines Letter, James Dines, editor; P.O. Box 22, Belvedere; CA 94920, $220 per year. Jim Dines is another one of the three or four original gold bugs, and often a voice-in-the-wilderness contrarian in the markets.

Dow Theory Letters, Richard Russell, editor; P.O. Box 1759, La Jolla, CA 92038; 26 letters a year for $225. Published since 1958 and a clear gold bug since 1961, Richard is one of the handful of men entitled to be called an original gold bug. His letter is still written with energy, clarity and personal flair.

Forcasts & Strategies, Mark Skousen, editor; 7811 Montrose Road, Potomac, MD 20811; $139 per year. Mark is dedicated to the hard-money, free-market economics cause. His newsletter is 90 percent specific investment strategies for making money, while some space each month is devoted to ways you can help promote freedom in the world.

Gold Newsletter, James U. Blanchard III, editor; 2400 Jefferson Highway, Jefferson, LA 70121; $95 per year (12 issues). You will forgive me for including my own letter amidst such stellar competition, but we are the longest-running investment newsletter dedicated solely to the precious metals, entering our 20th year in 1990.

Harry Browne's Special Reports, Harry Browne, editor, P.O. Box 5586, Austin, TX 78763; $225 for ten massive issues (averaging 24 to 32 pages, organized and collated by subject matter, for easy filing). Harry is one of the most responsive of editors, devoting several pages each issue to answering reader questions; and he has a puckish sense of humor as well.

Insider Report, Larry Abraham, editor; P.O. Box 39895, Phoenix, AZ 85069; two years for $175, one year for $95. Larry has a long history of activism on behalf of freedom and conservative causes in America. He co-founded (along with Harry Schultz) an important business enterprise, Freedom, Inc., to help spread the word and "fill the void" around the planet.

The International Harry Schultz Letter, Harry Schultz, editor; $258 per year from FERC, P.O. Box 622, CH-1001 Lausanne, Switzerland. Harry has been trading in gold since 1946 and writing about it in his brilliant, quirky newsletter since 1964. Living overseas most of the time, Harry has pioneered the Permanent Traveler, Part-time Taxpayer—or "P.T."—strategy. He has been one of my great mentors for over 20 years, truly one of a kind, and a great contributor to world freedom as well as investment riches and market knowledge.

International Living, Cathleen Pettiford, editor; $29 (12 issues); Agora, 824 E. Baltimore Ave., Baltimore, MD 21202,

Bill Bonner, publisher. This is a delightful, low-cost letter about living and investing abroad. Even if you do not travel much, it gives you a great feel for the globe and for planning your own list of places you want to visit "someday."

Investing in Crisis, Doug Casey, editor; Agora, 824 E. Baltimore Ave., Baltimore, MD 21202; 303-234-0515; $97.50 for first-time subscribers. Doug is one of the true characters of the hard-money movement. His writing will always entertain you, while his real estate, penny stock and commodity picks are truly 10:1 speculative possibilities, as a true contrarian.

Investment Analyst, Adrian Day, editor; Agora, 824 E. Baltimore Ave., Baltimore, MD 21202; $19 for five issues, $49 for one year, introductory offer only (301-234-0515). Adrian is best at picking foreign stocks that are not the big, overbought mainstream favorites. He also picks North American mining shares that have an exceptional competitive edge. He wrote the book on international investing and updates the book each month in this fine, low-priced newsletter.

Investor's Hotline, Joe Bradley, editor; 10616 Beaver Dam Road, Hunt Valley, MD 21030. One year (12 issues, and 12 cassettes), $195. Joe has been one of my best friends for 15 years, since he attended and recorded the first NCMR conference. He carved out the perfect niche for his unique talents in *Investor's Hotline*, tape-recording four market professionals each month, and transcribing the notes into-a four-page executive summary. Nobody brings out the experts half as well as Joe. This is an excellent service for busy investors who can only get deep into investing by using a tape recording during their drive time.

The McAlvany Intelligence Advisor, Don McAlvany, editor; P.O. Box 84904, Phoenix, AZ 85071. Two years, $165; 1 year, $95; six months, $57. Don is a hard-core advocate of liberty. He tells it as it is and doesn't worry if you label him a right-winger. A typical issue is 12 to 16 pages, not the normal eight pages; and spends 90 percent of his time on world geopolitics, with only a slight mention of gold and his coin business toward the end.

Myers' Finance & Energy, Vern Myers, editor; N. 7307 Division, Suite 204, Spokane, WA 99208; $200 for one year, $110 for six months. Vern is one of the three or four original gold bugs and he taught me a lot over the years, including how to use Thoreau's civil disobedience to help change government policies. He is a courageous freedom fighter. Whether or not you subscribe to his letter, send $18.95 to Falcon Press (P.O. Box 18586, Spokane, WA 99208) for a copy of his hardbound memoirs, *Fifty Years in the Furnace*. If you like his book, you will like Vern's newsletter as well, maybe even better, because he is such a character.

Remnant Review, Gary North, editor; P.O. Box 8704, Fort Worth, TX 76124; one year (22 issues), $95. Gary is able to write a book about as fast as most people read a newsletter. His newsletter is an amazing repository of new slants on the potential crises in the economy and how to protect yourself from them.

Ruff Times, Howard Ruff, editor; Target Inc., 4457 Willow Road, Pleasanton, CA 94566; 415-463-2200. One year, $149, or $5 per sample issue. Howard helped put the hard-money, alternative investment newsletter business on the map back in the mid-1970s. He offers one of the most popular and practical newsletters around, now on a weekly basis. (I don't know how he keeps coming up with good new ideas so often and for so long.)

Silver & Gold Report, Dan Rosenthal, editor; P.O. Box 510, Bethel, CT 06801; one year (22 issues), $144; two years, $58; single issue, $9. Dan rates the silver and gold dealers from time to time, but I think his most valuable information comes in the form of little-known supply and demand factors in the market. He is a super analyst of the precious metals markets.

Strategic Investments, edited by Jim Davidson and Lord Rees-Mogg, Agora, 824 E. Baltimore Ave., Baltimore, MD 21202; $59 for one year. My old friend Lord Rees-Mogg was editor of the London *Times* for several years. His American co-editor, Jim Davidson, is a Rhodes Scholar and head of the

National Taxpayer's Union. Together, their brain power is harnessed in one of the most interesting newsletters regarding profit potential from emerging world crises and geopolitical tension. Fascinating reading.

World Market Perspective, Eric Jones, executive editor; WMP Enterprises, P.O. Box 2289, Winter Park, FL 32790; $96 per year. Started by my silver mentor, Jerome Smith, this monthly journal still features a free-market editorial board composed of Doug Casey, Rick Maybury, Jim Moore, John Pugsley, Murray Rothbard and Diego J. Veitia, whose brother Roberto publishes WMP.

Young's International Gold Reports, Richard Young, editor; 7811 Montrose Road, Potomac, MD 20854 $149 per year (12 issues). Richard is an excellent gold share analyst who pours a lot of work into his unique trading strategies. He is not an ideological gold bug as such, but perhaps that helps him be more objective in rating the mining shares as pure investment plays.

Organizations

As I have said throughout this book, the intellectual tide has turned from collectivism to free markets. The most vigorous inquiry today comes from the conservative libertarian sources. The liberal ideas are old and stale; nobody buys their game anymore. Just 10 or 15 years ago, this was not ture. The light of freedom was a fragile candle in many areas of the globe in the 1960s, especially on American campuses.

As Friedrich Hayek said back then, "Unless we can make the philosophic foundations of a free society once more a living intellectual issue, and its implementation a task which challenges the ingenuity and imagination of our liveliest minds, the prospects for freedom are indeed dark." Hayek must be pleased to see the reversal of the fortunes of free-market think tanks in the last decades, particularly the emergence of these organizations:

The CATO Institute, 224 Second St. SE, Washington, DC 20003; Bill Niskanen, Chairman; Edward H. Crane III, president; 202-546-0200. CATO is based on classic (Jeffersonian) liberalism, with the intention of reducing the size and scope of government, especially the federal branch. I am proud to be a board member of CATO, which provides columns to several national newspapers and contributes material for business conferences. Your contribution gets you on the mailing list for several valuable brochures, position papers, and other publications. In 1989 alone, they published 10 books, 20 monographs, two scholarly journals, many position papers. They sponsored seven conferences, including two overseas. CATO is one of our best investments in the future.

The Center for the Study of Market Processes and The Institute for Humane Studies, George Mason University, 4400 University Drive, Fairfax, VA 22030. Although they are separate entities, both organizations are found on one campus. The George Mason economics department is one of the best in the nation, including libertarians Walter Williams, Leonard Liggio and Walter Grinder. Founded in 1961 by Liggio, the IHS now has over $1 million budgeted each year for promoting freedom issues. It has been instrumental in turning the tide toward freedom on college campuses. The Center (CSMP) is headed by economist Jack High to help train economists in the Austrian perspective. Our own Loyola University in New Orleans recently hired one of CSMP's star pupils, Deborah Walker, to head up the Austrian economics school, and she has had a great impact on economic studies in New Orleans.

Citizens for a Sound Economy (CSE) and its division, the Council for a Competitive Economy, 122 C Street NW, Suite 700, Washington, DC 20001; 202-638-1401 (CSE), or 638-1403 (CCE). This grass-roots organization has grown rapidly into one of the largest free-market organizations in America. It has grown, while its old-line liberal "consumer" counterpart, Ralph Nader, has dwindled into insignificance, because they have promoted the revolutionary, but obvious, idea that consumers are best served by an economy free of excessive regulation, trade barriers, bureaucracy, and taxation. The CSE has authored many significant studies on how government assets could be sold and their services "privatized."

The Conservative Caucus, Howard Phillips, founder and chairman; 450 Maple Ave. E, Vienna, VA 22180; 703-893-1550. Since his days of being probably the only outspoken teenage political conservative on the Harvard campus in the late 1950s, Howard Phillips has made a practice of keeping his principles focused and fighting for freedom long after the mass of conservatives have compromised away their intitial position on the subject. As I have tried to do for Mozambique, Howard has led the battle for a free Angola. The Conservative Caucus publishes a weekly "Issues and Strategy Bulletin" for members. Make a contribution and get on his mailing list.

The Foundation for Economic Education (FEE), 30 South Broadway, Irvington-on-Hudson, NY 10533. This organization was founded some four decades ago by Leonard Read and has been like "Old Man River" throughout those 40 years, constantly feeding the basic "intellectual ammunition" to generations of inquiring students. They refuse to get swept into a radical ditch on one side, or the ditch of "compromise" of freedom on the other. FEE has the kind of balanced approach you could show to your grandparents and it would make sense to them, no matter what their political background. Through contributions from others, FEE sends out free subscriptions to the monthly *Freeman*, plus several books and pamphlets at deep discount prices.

Freedom Research Foundation, 214 Massachusetts Avenue NE, Suite 450, Washington, DC 20002, Dr. Jack Wheeler, Director. Jack Wheeler has demonstrated his love for freedom in the world more than anyone I know, having risked his life literally dozens of times, behind the lines in socialist and Communist nations who brand him an "international gangster" to be shot on sight. Recently, Dr. Wheeler moved from his beautiful home in La Jolla, California, to fight in an even more frustrating arena—Washington, DC—for the future of freedom around the world. To get his newsletter and keep up with the fight for freedom around the world, be sure to contribute to the Freedom Research Foundation.

The Heritage Foundation, 214 Massachusetts Ave. NE, Washington, DC; 202-546-4400. Heritage is now the biggest private think tank in America, employing some 170 to 200 people at last count, churning out conservative and pro-free-market literature by the ton. More power to them. They also serve as an umbrella address for other freedom-related causes, such as the Freedom Research Foundation, listed above.

The Ludwig von Mises Institute, 851 Burlway Road, Burlingame, CA 94010; 415-579-2500; Lew Rockwell, executive director. The organization publishes a fine monthly newsletter called *The Free Market*, probably the best popular publication concerning Austrian economics available in America today. The Mises Institute also has offices at Thach Hall on the Auburn University campus and in Washington, DC (322 Massachusetts Ave. NE). The Institute sponsors several academic symposia around the country each year. Lew Rockwell has done a great service in furthering the ideas of von Mises in the popular press, appearing often on television and radio programs to defend the controversial viewpoint of no government intervention in the economy.

The Mackinac Center for the study of public policy, 119 Ashman Street, P.O. Box 568, Midland, MI 48640; 517-631-0900; Lawrence Reed, director. This free-market think tank is now home base for one of my favorite young (36) economists, Lawrence Reed, who has written more than 300 newspaper columns, 150 radio commentaries, and numerous magazine articles. He has visited some 30 countries since 1985, most of them socialist economies on the brink of callapse; and he has joined me in the freedom fight in several nations around the world, including Nicaragua, Poland, Mozambique, China and Cambodia.

The Reason Foundation, 2716 Ocean park Blvd., Suite 1062, Santa Monica, CA 90405; Robert W. Poole, Jr., president. Founded in the late 1960s as a free-market alternative to radical public policy, the Reason Foundation has gone a long way toward bringing free-market issues to the public eye. Their magazine, *Reason*, has the largest circulation of any free-market "idea" magazine in America; and the Reason Foundation sponsors many practical experiments and studies in real-life freedom issues. For example, they sponsored Dr. Jack Wheeler's coverage of the freedom fighter movements back in the early 1980s, thus giving birth to the Reagan Doctrine, which was instrumental in the partial (so far) liberation of nations such as Afghanistan and Angola.

United States Chamber of Commerce, 1615 H Street NW, Washington, DC 20062; Richard Rahn, chief economist. The Chamber publishes the *Journal of Economic Growth*, edited by Dr. Rahn, a free-market economist and head of the Chamber's economic section since February of 1980.